Liquid Gold

Liquid Gold

Energy Privatization in British Columbia

John Calvert

Fernwood Publishing • Halifax & Winnipeg

Editing: Scott Milsom
Cover Design: John van der Woude
Cover Photo: Jeremy Williams
Printed and bound in Canada by Hignell Book Printing

Published in Canada by Fernwood Publishing
Site 2A, Box 5, 32 Oceanvista Lane
Black Point, Nova Scotia, B0J 1B0
and 324 Clare Avenue, Winnipeg, Manitoba, R3L 1S3
www.fernwoodpublishing.ca

Fernwood Publishing Company Limited gratefully acknowledges the financial support of the Government of Canada through the Book Publishing Industry Development Program (BPDIP), the Canada Council for the Arts and the Nova Scotia Department of Tourism and Culture for our publishing program.

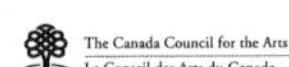

Library and Archives Canada Cataloguing in Publication

Calvert, John, 1947-
Liquid gold : privatization, power and water in British Columbia / John Calvert.

Includes bibliographical references and index.
ISBN 978-1-55266-244-1

1. Energy policy--British Columbia. 2. Power resources--Economic aspects--British Columbia. 3. Electric power--British Columbia. I. Title.

HD9685.C33B7 2007 333.79'09711 C2007-903407-1

Contents

Preface

By writing this book I hope to stimulate a wider debate about the provincial government's electricity policy agenda. This issue has, in my view, received far too little public scrutiny, despite its enormous implications for the future of BC Hydro and for the future ability of the public to control and manage its electricity system. I have no wish to minimize the significance of the considerable number of worthwhile and informative studies that have been published in recent years by environmentalists, community activists, advocacy groups, economists, and electricity policy analysts about specific aspects of the government's energy privatization policies. But I believe there is still a major gap in the current literature concerning the broader implications of what the government is now doing to both BC Hydro and our electricity system. Given the importance of electricity to the province's economy, and given the scope and depth of the changes that have been introduced over the past six years, it is extremely worrisome that there has been so little public debate on this issue. I hope this study will contribute to a more detailed examination of these developments.

In developing my own analysis, I have been mindful of the scope of the task and of the challenges associated with attempting to incorporate a range of seemingly disparate issues and different policy perspectives into a larger policy framework that will make sense of what the government is doing. Many of the areas touched upon in specific chapters themselves merit a full-scale study. I am acutely aware that there is much more to be said than I have been able to incorporate within the confines of this text, and I recognize that I have only been able to scratch the surface of some of these important issues. We need, for example, a comprehensive study of the economic implications of private wind-farm projects in B.C. We need a much more detailed account of the impact of small hydro developments on the environment and on local communities across the province. We need systematic and critical analyses of the probable consequences of fully integrating our electricity system into the larger, American-dominated Pacific Northwest grid. And, we need much more research on the consequences of private wind, hydro, and geothermal projects on First Nations' treaty rights, to cite only a few of the areas that merit much more detailed study. I hope others will be encouraged to pursue these various areas of research in the near future.

As well as identifying some of the key issues and challenges arising from recent government policy decisions, my intent is to question the basic direction of the government's energy strategy. Based on evidence I have reviewed, my conclusion is that we are rapidly losing public control of our electricity system, a development that will have enormous — and negative — repercussions for British Columbians. We will pay dearly for the government's rash decisions in terms of needless environmental damage, in terms of much higher energy prices, and in terms of the loss of the considerable revenue base provided by BC Hydro, which has historically been a major contributor to the province's finances. A clearer public understanding of the full implications of current policy will, I hope, lead to demands that it be reversed. And, I hope that future policies will focus on restoring public ownership, control, and management of B.C.'s electricity system.

This study would not have been possible without the help and support of a number of people to whom I am indebted, either directly from discussions about various issues covered in the book, or indirectly as a consequence of the work they have done in this area. During the eighteen months I served on BC Hydro's Integrated Electricity Planning Committee, I benefited enormously from the high quality of presentations by staff assigned to the Committee and from discussions with fellow Committee members. As a Board member of B.C. Citizens for Public Power, I have taken full advantage of the knowledge of my fellow board members and staff, including, in particular, Marjorie Griffin Cohen, Murray Dobbin, Mark Veerkamp, Jerri New, Michelle Laurie, Jim Sinclair, and Blair Redlin. Bill Tieleman kindly lent me his well-researched study on the establishment of BC Hydro by W.A.C. Bennett. I relied on the work of Ryan Durand and Patrick Yarnell for background on the Cascades Heritage Power Park. Stuart Smith, Tom Rankin, and Pina Belperino provided considerable information on the Ashlu dispute. Trafford Hall assisted me with the background to the Alcan issue. Marvin Shaffer's analyses in submissions to the British Columbia Utilities Commission and his public presentations proved very helpful in understanding the dynamics of energy trading and the way BC Hydro has benefited from its reservoir storage. Also, a number of people kindly reviewed sections of the text, including Ed Lavalle, Jim Quail, and Peter Dimitrov. Craig Williams has done invaluable work in mapping private power projects through his creative work on Google Earth, which I recommend readers to explore further. Special thanks should also go to my editor, Scott Milsom, who converted my somewhat awkward prose into text that I believe is far clearer and more accessible than my original scribbling.

Finally, I am deeply indebted to the ongoing support and encouragement of my partner, Colleen Fuller, who tolerated my obsession with this issue and kindly gave me much-needed support while I was researching and writing this book. She read and commented on much of the text, challenging me to clarify my views and tighten my arguments. This was of enormous help to me, as was the knowledge that she fully endorsed my decision to write the book in the first place.

I alone, of course, am responsible for any weaknesses or limitations in the following pages.

John Calvert
June 2007

INTRODUCTION
The Provincial Government's Energy Privatization Agenda

BRITISH COLUMBIA HAS ONE of the most reliable, secure, and low-cost electricity systems in the world. Based on public ownership of the province's electricity through BC Hydro, a provincially owned Crown corporation, the system has served the public well, providing affordable energy to the province's major industries, while giving commercial and residential customers the benefit of low, stable prices over the past three decades. BC Hydro has been a major contributor to provincial finances, paying almost three quarters of a billion dollars, annually, through dividends, water rentals, and taxes in lieu for local government. It has also supported B.C.'s economic development, particularly in the regions, by providing high-paying, secure employment to thousands of B.C. residents while acting as a major market for provincial suppliers. Cheap, reliable energy has been one of B.C.'s most important competitive advantages and a key contributor to the province's prosperity.

Yet, despite the advantages of an electricity system founded on public ownership and control of production, transmission, and distribution of B.C.'s energy, the current provincial government is jettisoning the public-ownership approach. It has embarked on a comprehensive restructuring of B.C.'s electricity system in order to eliminate the dominant role of the public sector as a supplier of energy to British Columbians. This is being done by dramatically expanding the role of private energy interests in supplying new energy, while simultaneously shifting control of the electricity system from BC Hydro to the international energy market through integration with the adjacent American electricity grid.

The government's policies are founded on the view that B.C.'s future energy supplies — and the prices paid by British Columbians — should no longer be based on the actual cost of producing publicly owned energy. Rather, they should be determined through the operation of an energy market in which new supplies of electricity will come almost entirely from private energy developers. B.C.'s future energy will not be generated by BC Hydro. Rather the Crown utility will purchase it from private power producers. In the short term, the price it pays to acquire this energy will reflect a politically constrained tendering process within B.C. designed to give investors the revenue and profits they need to build new power plants. In the longer term, energy prices will reflect supply and demand in the West Coast regional energy market — a market that will, eventually, result in B.C. customers paying rates for new energy similar to those prevailing in Washington, Oregon, and California — rates far higher than British Columbians currently pay.[1]

To implement this shift to private control of B.C.'s electrical energy system, the government has restructured BC Hydro. It has contracted out key administrative, computer, accounting, and customer services — almost one-third of the entire workforce — to the recently established Accenture Business Services for Utilities.[2] It has carved out the transmission system into a separate company, the B.C. Transmission Corporation (BCTC) to give private energy developers better access to the province's electricity grid. It has also given assurances to private energy interests that B.C.'s publicly owned transmission system will no longer "discriminate" in favour of BC Hydro when allocating transmission access. Instead, this new entity will manage B.C.'s transmission grid according to market-based principles based on a template advocated by the United States Federal Energy Regulatory Commission (normally referred to as FERC), regardless of the impact on the ability of BC Hydro to make the most efficient use of its own energy resources (U.S. Federal Energy Regulatory Commission 1997a, 1997b, 1999, 2005, 2006).

In its 2002 "Energy for Our Future: A Plan for B.C." (hereafter referred to as the province's "Energy Plan") the government established a new policy framework designed to eliminate the historical function of BC Hydro as an investor — and owner — of energy on behalf of the province. It arbitrarily banned the public utility from building new electricity generating facilities (except for upgrading turbines in existing dams and, possibly, building a new dam at "Site C" on the Peace River — but only with explicit Cabinet approval). Over time, this policy will transform BC Hydro's role from an owner and producer of public electricity to a purchaser and distributor of private energy (Cohen 2002b, 2003).

Through the use of Energy Purchase Agreements (EPAs), BC Hydro is now required to meet almost all the province's future energy needs from investor-owned generating plants. This policy directive has resulted in a highly restrictive tendering process that gives preference to private power projects. It does not distinguish between foreign or domestically owned suppliers, as long as the projects are located in the province. Nor does it impose any restrictions on the ability of their owners to export energy once their contracts with BC Hydro end.

Because BC Hydro is required to purchase energy from private power developers located within the province, it is now paying as much as double current energy-market rates under the terms of inflation-indexed, long-term contracts. The system effectively makes B.C. ratepayers, through EPAs, pay the capital costs of new power projects being built by private energy developers. Yet, at the end of the day, despite the very high prices it pays for private energy, the public gets no assets, no guarantee that the energy will not be exported in future, and no price protection once contracts have expired.

The government's restructuring of the electricity system is also placing major strains on BC Hydro's ability to oversee and manage that system. Rather than focussing primarily on ensuring that it can deliver the energy it owns to B.C. customers in a reliable, secure, and efficient manner, BC Hydro must now take into account the demands of numerous private energy developers, all of whom are interested in shifting as much of the cost of their projects as possible to the Crown utility by minimizing their payments for the use of public infrastructure and transferring their risks to BC Hydro. In the process, the government has also created a new — and highly influential — group of private-sector energy lobbyists who now expect that provincial energy policy will accommodate the need for B.C. and foreign investors to continue to reap a high rate of return from their energy developments, regardless of the impact on ratepayers.

In carrying out this restructuring, the B.C. government is embarking on a huge gamble — one with enormous risks for the public, both as citizens and as customers. It is deliberately abandoning policies that have given B.C. customers the second-lowest energy prices in North America — policies that have also provided British Columbians with enormous financial benefits, through BC Hydro's dividends, water rentals, and payments in lieu of local taxes. It is restructuring a system that has provided both security of supply and a gold standard of reliability to its customers — one that has sheltered them from the blackouts that have become so prevalent in recent years in American states that have embraced deregulation, as well as in Alberta and Ontario, where deregulation has also been implemented.

In sum, B.C.'s successful public energy legacy is now being supplanted by a policy designed to deregulate and privatize the province's electricity system — a policy that will effectively transfer control of the system from the public to local and foreign private interests. It will expose B.C. ratepayers to the risks and uncertainties associated with the volatile American energy market, as the provincial system is gradually incorporated into the much larger Pacific Northwest transmission grid — a grid largely controlled by American energy corporations. The policy will also result in integrating the electricity into a NAFTA-based continental energy market, where it will now join the oil and gas sectors, which have already been integrated on a continental basis.

In placing its faith in the ability of private energy developers to supply B.C.'s future energy needs, the government is gambling with future electricity prices and BC Hydro dividends, as well as with the security and reliability of the province's future electricity supply. Yet it is a gamble about which the public is largely unaware, despite the long-term — and arguably irreversible — policy decisions the province is now quietly making.

Given the profound changes to the province's electricity system, the question logically arises: why has there not been more public debate about the government's new approach? The answer is that British Columbians are largely unaware of the extent of these policy changes because the government has carefully crafted its description of them to downplay their scope and future implications. It has repeatedly reassured the public that its Energy Plan will provide the province with the best of all possible worlds. The new energy required to meet projected increases in demand will come from innovative private-sector investors. They will, according to the government, provide B.C. with much-needed capital investment and expertise. But at the same time, the growing role of private interests in the system will have no adverse effects on the existing benefits of the public system. British Columbians will continue to enjoy the benefits of cheap, secure and reliable public electricity for generations to come.

To illustrate how the Liberal government has packaged its reforms, we need only look at some of the major policy statements it has made since its election in 2001. The first page of the Energy Plan sets out in bold type: "Low Electricity Rates and Public Ownership of BC Hydro," and "Secure, Reliable Supply."

The government has made these claims in numerous other statements to reassure the public that nothing much is really changing, and that its policies will continue to deliver the benefits that the people of B.C. have come to expect from their publicly owned electricity company. Similarly, BC Hydro has paid for major advertising campaigns in newspapers, as well as on radio and television stations, all supporting the government's energy policies. According to a Freedom of Information request reported by columnist Bill Tieleman in the tabloid newspaper *24*, the Crown utility spent almost $1.5 million in its autumn 2006 public-relations campaign alone. Its purpose was to "inform" the public of the energy crisis B.C. was facing and explain how the government planned to address this crisis through the purchase of new energy from private power developers (Tieleman 2006).

Another element of the government's rationale for its policies has been its focus acquiring renewable or "green" energy. The government is aware that there is strong public support for the development of environmentally benign energy projects. By banning BC Hydro from building such projects and forcing it to buy new energy from private sources, the government has provided the opportunity for private power investors to claim that they are the real leaders in "green" energy development. In the absence of public sector leadership — which the government has ensured will not take place — the only option that the public sees is that offered by private power developers.

If British Columbians want green energy, under the government's approach, they have no choice but to support private projects.

The government also passed legislation whose purpose and implications are quite different from its official explanation. The 2003 *BC Hydro Power Legacy and Heritage Contract Act* (the "Heritage Contract") ostensibly guarantees to British Columbians that they will continue to receive the benefits of BC Hydro's low-cost energy. However, the energy is already owned by the public, a fact not changed by the *Act*. Arguably, the prime beneficiaries of the Heritage Contract have been major industrial customers who were worried that purchasing new energy from private power developers would add millions, or in some cases, tens of millions to their energy bills. The Heritage Contract effectively shelters pulp-mill and mine owners — who currently pay the bulk industrial rate (formerly known as the 1821 rate), which is much lower than that paid by other customers — from the full impact of the price increases triggered by BC Hydro's purchases of expensive new energy from private power developers. While the initial legislation placed a sunset on the commitment after ten years, in the 2007 Energy Plan it has been extended indefinitely — an enormous gift to pulp mill and mine owners.

Moreover, the Heritage Contract removed the option of using higher prices as a way of encouraging industrial companies — who use over one third of BC Hydro's public energy — to conserve. Absent such a price signal, they have little incentive to reduce their use of BC Hydro's low cost public energy. In turn, this forces the Crown utility to purchase even more energy from private power developers. Thus, far from protecting average residential customers, as the government claims, the Heritage Contract will result in them paying more for their future energy. Yet the government still disingenuously promotes the Heritage Contract as evidence of its commitment to maintain the benefits of public power for the province's future.

A similarly disingenuous approach has been followed with respect to the broader question of privatization of B.C.'s electricity system. The government has stated repeatedly that it is not privatizing BC Hydro. In making these assertions, the government has taken advantage of the fact that most British Columbians equate public ownership of BC Hydro with public ownership and control of the electricity system. However, it isn't necessary to privatize the entity formally registered as BC Hydro in order to privatize the province's electricity system. Nor is it necessary to sell all the Crown utility's assets to transfer control — and the benefits attendant to that control — to the private sector. Rather, this can be done by transforming, over time, the public utility's basic function from that of a producer of B.C.'s electricity to that of a distributor of energy purchased from private sources. The deliberate creation of a split between purchaser and provider recasts — and diminishes — BC Hydro's role as a generator of electricity to that of a purchaser of energy. This constitutes a fundamental — and perhaps irreversible — change to B.C.'s electricity system.

To further consolidate the privatization of the electricity system, the province has implemented major changes to the organization and functions of the transmission grid. Historically, its basic function was to transmit energy generated by BC Hydro to its provincial customers. Since its creation by W.A.C. Bennett, BC Hydro has also traded energy with the United States and Alberta. But such trading was based on mutually beneficial synergies. Temporary shortages in one jurisdiction were addressed by importing energy from another. Similarly, the tie-ins with the American and Alberta systems gave BC Hydro's system additional security in the event of unplanned outages. BC Hydro also used its storage capacity to engage in opportunistic energy trading, buying energy from outside the province when prices were low and selling it back when they rose, a practice enormously beneficial to B.C. ratepayers.

However, under the government's new policy, BC Hydro's use of the transmission system to maximize the benefits of its own energy resources and for opportunistic trading with the United States is being fundamentally curtailed. Energy trading will now be based on American rules (Cohen 2003).

The off-loading of costs to BC Hydro is largely concealed by an approach to pricing transmission services that requires users of the transmission system to pay for their respective shares of the costs of managing the new system. As BC Hydro remains — by far — the system's most significant user, it pays the lion's share of the costs. That BC Hydro did not need these expensive changes, and that it, arguably, could have continued to dispatch its electricity more efficiently without having to accommodate the numerous private interests now joining the system, is a fact that is conveniently ignored. BC Hydro must now use — and pay for — the reconfigured system to transmit its energy.

In sum, the costs of this reorganization are being borne almost exclusively by the public, through fees paid by BC Hydro, while the benefits are almost exclusively reaped by private energy interests. The enormous increase in administrative complexity associated with layering a competitive market structure on top of a physical dispatch system in a manner that avoids outages, maintains high standards of reliability, and recovers all financial obligations from market participants significantly increases the overall cost of operating the system. It also adds considerably to the risks facing BC Hydro, because it cannot allow the system to experience outages that result from the failure of market participants to fulfill commitments to supply energy to the system.

To all this must be added the loss of BC Hydro's flexibility to dispatch electricity on the basis of maximizing the benefits of its own generating capacity. Rather, it now faces the prospect that the transmission access it needs to minimize costs or achieve revenue gains from "opportunistic" energy trading with other jurisdictions, based on the enormous advantages it has from water storage in its reservoirs, may be allocated to other market participants. This is because it now has to bid for access to the transmission system, just like any other private energy supplier or marketer.

In its enthusiasm to promote a private energy market, the government has shown little interest in measuring the lost economic opportunities BC Hydro will experience from system congestion or from the changes to the basic functions of the transmission system. These are now largely hidden in BC Hydro's overall operating expenses and those of the new BCTC. And it simply assumes that the public should handle — and pay for — the risks associated with creating and managing a new private energy market.

The new BCTC — which is independent of BC Hydro — also has a mandate to establish and oversee the development of a competitive energy market within B.C. and to integrate this market with the United States and Alberta. This allows energy generators and energy marketing corporations to access the grids of other utilities on a "non-discriminatory" basis, in order to encourage competition. In this restructured system, BC Hydro is considered just another purchaser of transmission rights in competition with various private interests who wish to use the grid for commercial purposes.

In addition to reconfiguring the transmission system to facilitate its use by private energy interests, the government is also moving, step by step, to integrate B.C.'s electricity grid into the American grid. This is being fostered through participation in the recently formed Regional Transmission Organization (RTO) called Grid West. Grid West is dominated by private American energy interests and is a creature of FERC. Its framework is modeled on the concept of a standard market design developed in the United States by FERC and incorporated into its RTO guidelines (U.S. Federal Energy Regulatory Commission 1999, 2005, 2006). The American energy regulator has advocated the establishment of RTOs in order to implement its electricity deregulation policies. If FERC's RTO policies are fully implemented in Grid West, this new organization will end up overseeing the planning and future development of B.C.'s transmission infrastructure, but B.C. will have only a small minority of seats on its governing body. Provincial policies will thus facilitate the full integration of our electricity system into the American energy grid in a manner that has many parallels with the way our oil and gas sectors have been so integrated. And the outcome — in terms of higher prices for Canadians combined with loss of energy sovereignty — is equally likely over the long term (Cohen 2003).

By opening the transmission system to many new private participants — all of whom have a financial interest in shifting costs to BC Hydro — and giving them a voice in the future development of the system, the government has changed the political dynamic of electricity in B.C. This change is reflected in a dramatic increase in the number of companies now lobbying government, an upsurge in political donations from energy companies to the governing party, and growing pressure from business interests to provide even more favourable terms for their use of the transmission system, including the elimination of what they see as the remaining "unfair advantages" enjoyed by BC Hydro and the citizens who own it.

Yet, the question of how all this will benefit ratepayers remains unanswered. While the government argues that competition will keep rates down, B.C.'s public system has already achieved virtually the lowest rates in North America. And, there is little evidence that the introduction of competition has lowered energy prices in jurisdictions that have experimented with this approach, as ratepayers in California, Alberta, Ontario, and many other jurisdictions can attest. The one thing it will clearly do is provide huge opportunities for profit to private energy developers.

One of the most misleading elements of the government's explanation for requiring BC Hydro to purchase energy from private energy developers within the province is that it will result in long-term energy security. However, government policies do exactly the opposite. Its policy of integrating the province's transmission grid with the United States, while lifting restrictions on private energy exports, undermines B.C.'s ability to remain self-sufficient in electrical energy. Until recently, private sector access to the grid for export purposes was limited by requiring companies to have an energy removal certificate that authorized them to sell their energy to American customers. The certificates were intended to exercise some regulatory control over private exports. But in 2004, through Bill 40, the government abolished this requirement. Energy developers are now free to export at will and to use their enhanced grid access rights to do so. Though the government's stated policy objective is to provide self-security for B.C., this policy change flies directly in the face of that objective.

On top of all this, by giving private interests the option of exporting energy rather than selling it to BC Hydro, the government has undermined BC Hydro's ability to negotiate the best possible terms — from the perspective of the public — for the acquisition of new energy, even within the extremely narrow constraints of its Energy Plan. The EPA approach currently provides a very generous, inflation-protected price floor for private electricity developers. But it doesn't provide any price ceiling once the contracts expire. Given that BC Hydro is paying developers prices far higher than the current market rate at the B.C. border, in the short term this may not be all that significant. But several decades down the road it will mean that B.C. ratepayers will have to compete with — and out-bid — customers from neighbouring American states as far south as California to keep B.C.-generated energy within the province.

While all of this is good news for energy investors, it guarantees that B.C.'s competitive advantage in electricity will largely disappear over time.

As a publicly owned utility, BC Hydro will always be subject to accusations from private interests that its relationship to government gives it an unfair advantage and, therefore, that it must be required to curtail — or completely abandon — aspects of its operations that compete with the private sector. And, from the American perspective, "government monopolies" like BC Hydro are inherently undesirable for two reasons: because they limit the ability of American investors to expand into the Canadian energy market and because they prevent full continental integration of energy. And so the Americans encourage policies that transfer ownership to private investors.

This should not be a controversial point. The United States succeeded in obtaining major concessions in NAFTA to limit the public-policy objectives of Canadian Crown corporations. NAFTA's Chapter Fifteen (titled "Competition, Monopolies and State Enterprises" and including Articles 1501–1505), places major constraints on the operation of public enterprises in Canada, while Chapter Ten (titled "Government Procurement" and including Articles 1001–1025), imposes restrictions on the use of public purchasing for purposes such as regional economic development or small business development through its open tendering requirements. The United States has never been reluctant to push for policy changes in other countries when it has viewed such changes as beneficial to its business sector. And, in recent years, it has been remarkably successful in achieving this objective through NAFTA and other trade agreements.

This highlights another fundamental problem with the government's energy policy: its apparent lack of concern about foreign ownership and control of B.C.'s energy resources. Allowing American energy companies, banks, and investors to acquire power plants in B.C. has profound implications for the province's future energy security and its ability to meet its growing energy needs. While BC Hydro's public energy can readily be kept within the province for use by British Columbians, privately owned energy supplies are quite a different matter.

Lurking in the background of this profound restructuring of B.C.'s electricity system is the fact of NAFTA's Chapter Eleven (titled "Investment" and including Articles 1101-1138). Chapter Eleven's provisions protect American (and Mexican) investors from any government policy or regulation that can be construed as "tantamount to expropriation." This means that once American investors have become entrenched in B.C.'s electricity system — and this is already happening in a major way — future governments will find it difficult, if not impossible, to adopt policies that interfere with their profit-making activities, regardless of whether these activities are in the public interest.

Foreign ownership of B.C.'s new generating facilities will, arguably, result in the profitability of American-owned firms taking precedence over the needs of British Columbians for affordable, reliable, and secure future sources of energy. Unlike the 1960s, when W.A.C. Bennett was able to expand public ownership and control of B.C.'s electricity system to achieve provincial policy objectives, NAFTA's constraints mean future governments will find it extremely difficult to adopt a similar strategy.

Efforts to secure B.C.'s energy supplies by preventing American-owned generating facilities from exporting their energy across the border would likely provoke an international trade dispute. In NAFTA's terms, foreign ownership coupled with opening the provincial grid to energy exports is a one-way street. It may be impossible for future governments to stop private energy exports. This underlines how misleading the government's claims are that its Energy Plan will promote self-sufficiency. And, it highlights how reckless it is for government to abandon the proven, successful public-policy tool of provincial public ownership.

The full extent of the government's changes to B.C.'s electricity system has also been obscured by the long lead-time required for most energy investments, the systems' complexity, and the highly technical nature of many of the issues involved. For example, the private power plants now being built as a result of BC Hydro's 2006 EPA will not start delivering significant amounts of energy until 2012.

Similarly, the enormous financial commitments now being made by BC Hydro are not yet apparent to customers because the large rate increases that will be triggered by the contracts do not take effect until several years into the future. But when the 2006 contracts are fully operational, this one year's energy purchases will increase rates by 8.1 percent after 2012. In fact, if all B.C.'s energy were being purchased at the rates BC Hydro paid for this one block of private energy, ratepayers would now be paying more than double current electricity prices.

Another reason the price impact of the government's policies is not more dramatic is that the increments of new private power are diluted by incorporating them with the huge block of very low-cost public energy already owned by BC Hydro. Consequently, in the short term, the government has been able to obscure the full impact of its policy changes from all but those directly involved in the electricity system. Indeed, the consequences of some of the changes made today will only be clear ten or twenty years from now, by which time future governments will be faced with a *fait accompli* in which their policy choices have been almost totally constrained by decisions made by today's government.

As well, the electricity sector is characterized by difficult technical, engineering, forecasting, and economic issues that are often discussed in arcane terminology largely incomprehensible to the average citizen. While most residential customers deal with energy in the form of watts and kilowatts (or kilowatt-hours), much larger numbers — and acronyms summarizing these numbers — are stock in trade in the industry. The potential output (capacity) of electrical generating plants is normally referred to in terms of megawatts (MW), representing a million watts of power. The actual amount of energy produced is, correspondingly, referred to in terms of megawatt hours (MWh), gigawatt hours (GWh), equivalent to a billion watts, and terawatt hours (TWh), equivalent to a trillion watts. (A rough rule of thumb is that a one-MW power plant will produce enough energy to supply a thousand homes.)

A common analogy to explain the difference between energy and capacity is that energy — MWh or GWh — is like gasoline in a car's gas tank while capacity — MW or GW — is like the horsepower of a car's motor. These terms are different from the kilowatt-hours and kilowatts that the public normally uses in its discussion of energy prices and energy consumption. But these illustrations only begin to reveal the way technical issues — and their corresponding terminologies — can have the effect of obscuring basic policy issues associated with developments in the electricity sector. This is not to suggest that these issues are beyond the ability of most citizens to grasp. Rather, it underlines how relatively easy it can be for the government to utilize arcane terminology to obscure the implications of its policy changes.

One of the other major consequences of the government's new energy policy is its negative impact on the provincial environment. There are several important dimensions to this issue. As we shall discuss in more detail later in this study, the introduction of a competitive market structure in the energy sector undermines previous conservation efforts by BC Hydro through its Power Smart program. Under the old single-supplier, public-monopoly framework, subsidies to encourage conservation were rational because they could help BC Hydro avoid the large capital costs of building new power plants. As long as the reduction in demand — or in demand growth — was sufficiently great, funding energy-saving investments made sense. But this assumes that the policy goal is to limit the growth of energy consumption.

However, in a market-based system, every firm is interested in expanding energy consumption. A stagnant energy market — especially given the amount of public energy BC Hydro already has — would result in minimal opportunities for profitable investment for private energy developers. And in a market system, no individual firm has an incentive to limit growth, because if it does so, it will see its competitors leap ahead as they grab a larger share of the market at its expense. In other words, the dynamic in a competitive energy market is to expand energy production and sales. Conservation simply takes a back seat.

But the environmental impact of B.C.'s energy policy is not restricted to abandoning the benefits of BC Hydro's earlier approach to limiting energy growth. The government's new policy also has a number of quite specific — and negative — impacts. For example, BC Hydro's 2006 EPAs included two major contracts for electricity from new coal-fired plants in the province. This decision was welcomed by the coal industry, and by the owners of some pulp mills who would like to expand their existing production of electricity from wood-waste to additional production from coal. The government sanctioned the use of this controversial fuel source in B.C. for the first time in generations. In the process, it has raised important questions about the extent to which the government is seriously committed both to reducing greenhouse gas emissions and to protecting the public from the negative health consequences of pollution from burning coal. The introduction of coal, however "clean" its proponents now claim it is, can only be seen, from an environmental perspective, as a major step backward. And, while the 2007 Energy Plan imposed new carbon sequestration requirements on future coal plants, the government left open the door to fossil fuel burning through its acceptance of the use of "biomass" (a term coined by the industry to make burning wood seem relatively benign) to generate electricity.

Of equal importance is the environmental impact of the rapidly growing number of run-of-the-river "green energy" projects. Ideally, a run-of-the-river project involves diverting a portion of a river's water through a pipe running parallel to the riverbed down to a powerhouse where it is used to generate energy. The water is then returned to the stream below the powerhouse. The amount of energy produced depends on the volume of water diverted and the difference in height between the pipe's intake and the powerhouse located below it. To minimize environmental damage, there must be sufficient water left in the streambed to allow the normal activities of fish and aquatic life to continue largely unaffected.

Run-of-the-river projects have been energetically promoted by private developers as a clean and environmentally responsible way to generate electricity for our future energy needs. They have also been promoted as much less environmentally damaging than the major dams BC Hydro built in the 1962 to 1984 period, which flooded entire valleys. Such projects thus avoid all the downsides of large hydro.

However, there is an enormous variation in the environmental impact of run-of-the-river projects. Few conform to the ideal noted above. Most involve either a concrete dam or an inflatable weir, creating a large tailpond or even a small reservoir. This allows sediment to settle and thus not be drawn into the power plant's turbines. Whether they use inflatable barriers or permanent concrete structures, they change the pattern of normal stream flows. In fact, one "green hydro" project involves constructing a seventy-six-metre dam to hold back the water. Thus they are more accurately described as small hydro projects (Caldicott 2007).

Many of B.C.'s streams have very little water flow in the late summer, so diversion of even some of the water can significantly affect the amount of water left in a streambed. Diversion can also significantly raise the temperature of the remaining water. Developers can damage the environment both during construction and in the course of ongoing operations. Projects also require transmission lines, which have to be kept clear of brush, as well as access roads to service the power plant and transmission lines. Some projects require new transmission lines more than a hundred kilometres in length, cutting a gash in otherwise pristine forests, with their sixty-metre-wide right-of-ways that have to be trimmed regularly to keep trees from falling on the lines. When taken together, these various impacts can have a very significant — and negative — effect on the environment (Caldicott 2007). It is not self-evident that the total cumulative environmental impact of building a hundred run-of-the-river projects in a region of the province is significantly less damaging than building one major hydro dam, especially if the latter does not have a large reservoir. The point is that constructing dams on these rivers *does* have major environmental impacts that need to be fully assessed.

Indeed, when we look more closely at the environmental practices of private power developers, we see a much less benign picture than the one their promoters portray. While "green energy" projects were supposed to undergo stringent environmental reviews, the government has weakened the environmental assessment process in response to lobbying from private energy developers. The government now only requires a full environmental assessment for projects of more than 50 MW-capacity: smaller projects enjoy a much less stringent review that is largely confined to provincial ministries and agencies. In practical terms, this has meant that the vast majority of run-of-the-river projects no longer need to undergo a full environmental assessment. And, thus far, the government's environmental assessment process has always resulted in approval, regardless of the location and impact of the project. The extent to which environmental concerns have been weakened by changes to the regulatory framework are highlighted by Arthur Caldicott:

> In British Columbia, energy projects are reviewable under the Environmental Assessment Act (EA). It is a time-consuming and costly undertaking for a company. An EA requires more disclosure of details of a project than some companies might want. While a company doesn't face much risk of having its project not being approved — there have been no rejections in the entire ten-year history of the Environmental Assessment Office (EAO) — companies will avoid an

> EA if they can. The easiest way to avoid an EA for an energy project is to make it small enough that it comes in under the threshold for reviewable projects. For energy projects, that threshold is 50 MW. That's why we get small hydro projects like Ashlu Creek (Ledcor, 49 MW), Rutherford Creek (Cloudworks, 49.9 MW), Mkw'alts Creek (Cloudworks, 45 MW), and the original Compliance Energy coal-fired generation plant (49 MW). Deliberately designed to duck the threshold. (Caldicott 2007: 22)

As well, the government's environmental assessment and planning approach is far too narrowly focussed. It fails to capture the overall impact of these projects within a region or river system because it is based on reviewing individual projects, rather than on evaluating the cumulative impact of a number of projects on a wider ecological or geographical area. Environmental impacts are not restricted to the construction of a single power plant itself: they are also caused by interconnected servicing roads and transmission lines needed to move the energy to BC Hydro's main grid.

Once a significant number of projects are located on one river system or in one geographic area, the combination of access roads and transmission lines can create a "spaghetti junction" of development that can dramatically — and permanently — change the formerly untouched character of a pristine valley (Caldicott 2007). Yet the environmental assessment process does not look at the larger picture of what the construction of a series of power plants will do to the habitat and the use patterns of an entire area.

In sum, Victoria's developer-driven approach ignores the need for rational planning of land and water use on a regional basis. Building certain projects may make sense, *if* they are properly evaluated in the context of neighbouring projects and their cumulative impacts on a river system or valley. But approving individual projects in isolation from one another fails to consider the "big-picture" changes that result from unplanned and uncoordinated development.

Yet whether new energy projects go ahead is now largely driven by whether the developer gets an EPA with BC Hydro. Once such an agreement has, in principle, been awarded, the private investor has an enormous financial incentive to get the project up and running as quickly as possible. A month's delay can mean several million dollars — or more — in lost revenue. But encouraging the development of projects purely on the basis of their financial viability to investors only encourages the environmental degradations that such projects can bring about.

There is one further aspect we must analyze in order to complete the picture of the government's privatization agenda: the creation of a financial and ownership framework designed to promote private investment in B.C.'s electricity system. Investments in energy generation are capital intensive and involve long-term financial commitments. However, energy demand and prices tend to fluctuate significantly over time, creating uncertainty — and significant risk — for investors. This makes it difficult for all but the largest developers to borrow the capital they require at reasonable interest rates — if they can borrow it at all. This is why W.A.C. Bennett decided to nationalize the B.C. Electric Company in 1962 and use the vehicle of public ownership, through BC Hydro, to make the investments needed to build the province's electricity system. At that time, the private sector simply did not have the capital required for — and did not want to incur the risks associated with — the huge capital projects Bennett envisaged. Only the provincial government had the fiscal capacity and vision to take on this responsibility.

To facilitate the expansion of the private sector in B.C. in the twenty-first century, the government had to find a way to enable private energy interests to borrow the capital needed to build new projects. It concluded that EPAs could be used to help private investors raise capital. By forcing BC Hydro to acquire all its new energy through EPAs, the government has been able to provide the collateral — in the form of BC Hydro-guaranteed long-term contracts — that private investors need to secure financing.

EPAs provide taxpayer-guaranteed cash flow for private investors, opening the door to investments that would otherwise not get made, while reducing the risk — and therefore the interest-rate premium — faced by private energy interests. The ability of private investors to secure long-term public financing for their new generating facilities — whether they be from "clean coal," biomass, natural gas, run-of-the-river hydro, wind, or other sources — has opened the door to a dramatic expansion of the role of both domestic and foreign energy investors in B.C.

The government has further supported developers of "green energy" by giving them access to B.C.'s untapped water and wind resources. Instead of carrying out a full analysis of the asset value of B.C.'s renewable energy resources, it has been selling them off at fire-sale prices. In the case of run-of-the-river projects, it has provided developers with the information needed to identify the most promising — and potentially profitable — streams and rivers. Similarly, it has given private interests full access to public research on potential sites for new wind farms. And, most critically, it has given its friends in the private sector the opportunity to acquire water licences and wind-farm land tenures for minimal fees on a first-come, first-served basis. As a result, private interests with privileged knowledge about the policy change requiring BC Hydro to purchase all its new energy from private power plants located within the province have been able to stake out claims on the most promising run-of-the-river and wind-farm locations across the province (Calvert 2006a).

The government has also cleared the path for investors to acquire full ownership of the land where "green energy" projects are located by allowing them to acquire land-occupancy tenures and fee-simple ownership of these valuable resources. In doing so, the government has guaranteed to private energy developers the legal right to continue to produce energy — and money — from these sites for generations to come. The government has already sold the most valuable and suitable sites for small hydro and wind projects across the province for a tiny fraction of their asset value. As we shall show later, the amounts paid by private interests for permanent entitlements to water resources and land occupancy are a pittance compared to the future revenues these sites will generate over the coming century. Through its policy framework, the government intends to permanently entrench the private sector into B.C.'s energy system. As if this were not enough, the government has also made changes to property tax, environmental, and other regulatory policies that further reduce the costs of private energy development. Worse still, the public, through the EPA system, is actually financing this acquisition of B.C.'s Crown lands and water resources by private interests. As noted above, BC Hydro is using EPAs to provide revenue streams that enable "insiders" — including former BC Hydro executives, engineering and consulting firms that have worked extensively with BC Hydro, Howe street financiers, and friends of the government — to acquire and fund their new power plants.[3] Many of the most lucrative of these sites have already been awarded to individuals and companies that have links to the government through campaign donations, party membership, and the provision of logistical and other assistance during recent election campaigns.

While these policies are creating numerous "instant millionaires" on Howe Street, the long-term repercussions for those not so fortunate to be first in line to acquire a water licence on a prime run-of-the-river site are the opposite: dramatic increases in electricity prices, loss of public control over the electricity system, and full integration into the energy-hungry American market — a market supported by both the clout of the American government and NAFTA's international trade obligations.

Also, those directly affected by private power projects — First Nations and local communities — have been almost entirely excluded from this corporate bonanza. Only a handful of the 495 water licences awarded by November of 2006 went to First Nations, despite the fact that almost all the projects are on territory subject to their land claims. Similarly, despite both the enormous revenues they generate and the fact that they can have major — and negative — consequences for local tourism, as well as for recreational and community use of rivers and forests, capital-intensive power projects provide very few long-term jobs to local communities.

The changes the government is making to BC Hydro and to B.C.'s electricity system are interconnected. Restricting BC Hydro's ability to build and own new generating capacity is essential to assuring a growing market for private energy investors. Transferring control over the transmission system from BC Hydro to BCTC is necessary to provide guarantees to private energy interests that BC Hydro will no longer have priority of access to the grid. Giving private interests full access to the grid on terms favourable for energy trading, and with no restriction on private exports, further enhances the value of generating facilities now being built by private investors.

As the preceding suggests, there is a pressing need for a comprehensive analysis of the overall costs and risks of the government's electricity policies. Parts of this have already been carried out a by number of energy policy researchers and advocacy organizations (Cohen 2001, 2002a, 2002b, 2003, 2006; Caldicott 2007; Redlin 2002; Shaffer 2004; Richardson 2004; Metcalf 2003; B.C. Citizens for Public Power 2002). Many local communities across the province have also analyzed the impacts of private power developments. However, much more research needs to be done to clarify the long-term implications of the policies now being implemented in B.C. This is especially urgent, because the government is rapidly pushing ahead with further significant changes to the system — including a revised 2007 Energy Plan — that may well be irreversible, regardless of their long-term impacts on the ratepayers and residents of the province.

While we have identified here some of the major policy areas where further research is needed — and, hopefully, have provided an overall framework within which to examine some of the specific elements of these policies — the purpose of this study is more modest: to examine one major dimension of the government's energy policy agenda — turning over B.C.'s future electrical generation investments to private interests, particularly through promoting private run-of-the-river and wind-farm projects.[4] As we shall see, the government has gone to extraordinary lengths to provide a supportive financial, environmental, legal, and ownership framework to assist the growth of private energy investments.

In the following chapters, we will examine, in detail, specific policy measures the government has put in place to implement its privatization agenda. We will begin with a brief history of the path to privatization, examining some of the key events and players that provided the impetus to recent policy changes. Next, we will look at the implications of this agenda in terms of its impact on BC Hydro, future energy prices, future security of supply, and future public control — or, rather, the lack of it — over the development of B.C.'s electricity system. We will then examine how this agenda has impacted on local communities in various areas of the province, including Kitimat, the Squamish-Lillooet Regional District, and the Christina Lake-Kettle Falls area. We will also look at the environmental impacts of the government's policies. And we will discuss how the government has tried to neutralize potential opposition from First Nations, whose treaty rights constitute a risk for private investors and hence a problem for the government to overcome in implementing its private power agenda. Finally, we will discuss the overall consequences for our public system and examine some of the options the government could — and should — have adopted to maintain what, arguably, has been the most cost effective and efficient electricity utility in North America.

NOTES

1. There have been a number of very good studies on the impact of various aspects of the current government's policies in the electricity sector. While it is not possible to list all the contributors to this analysis, some of the key individuals are: Professor Marjorie Griffin Cohen, Professor Marvin Shaffer, Jim Quail, Arthur Caldicott, Murray Dobbin, Malcolm Metcalf, Mark Veerkamp, Charlie Smith, and Trafford Hall. As well, a number of organizations, including B.C. Citizens for Public Power, the Sierra Legal Defence Fund, the Parkland Institute, the B.C. Public Interest Advocacy Centre, and the Canadian Centre for Policy Alternatives, have produced important studies. Finally, there is a wealth of information and data available through the B.C. Utilities Commission's archives, BC Hydro, the recently established B.C. Transmission Corporation, and various provincial ministries.
2. Accenture Business Services for Utilities was founded in 2003. However, the company has been viewed by many as a successor to Arthur Anderson, a firm whose reputation was severely compromised as a result of a number of major accounting scandals in the United States, most notably the collapse of Enron. Accenture maintains, however, that it is a B.C.-registered company and is not connected with these other entities.
3. A quick review of the boards of directors of many of the companies that have acquired water licences over the past six years reveals the extent to which "insiders" have benefited from government policies.
4. While these interests normally describe themselves, innocuously, as "independent power producers," a more accurate description is "private energy interests," the term used consistently — and consciously — throughout this book. While they may be "independent" from government, their objective is to profit from the ownership and marketing of energy generated in B.C. for the benefit of the private investors who own the companies involved. In fact, many of them are definitely not "independent" of foreign control, even though the term suggests they are not constrained by interests outside the province. Indeed, to the extent that language conceals rather than elucidates, an even more accurate description of some of the players, such as Duke Energy or Kinder Morgan, would be "foreign energy interests," because multinational companies are rapidly becoming the dominant players in B.C.'s energy sector, whether it be oil, gas, or, more recently, electricity.

Chapter One

THE PATH TO PRIVATIZATION

> I should be clear that my opposition is to the privatization of BC Hydro, under whatever guise. I have not seen the particular legislation we will be asked to consider. Taken alone, the substance of this particular first piece of legislation may well come across as relatively benign. However, following Minister Neufeld's announcement, I am firmly convinced that this legislation is only the opening move in a strategy whose ultimate goal is the wholesale privatization of the utility. Whether it will be done through the outright sale of core assets of BC Hydro (and I appreciate that the Premier is on the record as specifically rejecting this) or through incremental privatization, the result will be the same. — Former Liberal MLA Paul Nettleton, Letter to Liberal Caucus, Nov. 13, 2002

WHILE THE MAJOR PUSH TO privatize B.C.'s electricity system has taken place since the election of the Liberal provincial government in May of 2001, a number of earlier policy developments laid the groundwork. It can be argued that the first, admittedly small, steps were taken by the Social Credit government at the end of the 1980s. It endorsed the decision of BC Hydro's Board to privatize its natural gas distribution subsidiary, B.C. Gas, in 1989 and thus began the break-up of B.C.'s largest Crown corporation. It also sold its information technology subsidiary, Westech Information Systems, in 1991 (subsequently returned to BC Hydro in the mid-1990s). At the same time, BC Hydro initiated a new policy designed to significantly expand the role of the private sector in the electricity generating system by awarding a number of long-term energy supply contracts (EPAs) to private power developers.

During the late 1980s, the Social Credit government, influenced by Margaret Thatcher's privatization policies in the U.K., began looking for ways to privatize parts of B.C.'s public sector. In its 1987 Speech from the Throne, the government announced it was establishing a Task Force on Privatization, which would review the province's various Crown corporations with a view to determining the best candidates for transfer to the private sector. Its members — including David Emerson, more recently of Parliamentary floor-crossing fame — mapped out a strategy for selling off a number of the government's public assets.

At the time it privatized B.C. Gas, the Social Credit government placed restrictions on the location of B.C. Gas's head office and ownership of shares so as to maintain control of the privatized entity within B.C. However, in 2002, the Liberal government quietly removed these restrictions, a decision that facilitated the sale of the company to American-based Kinder-Morgan under its new name Terasen Gas. The "Kinder" is Rich Kinder, formerly of Enron and a major force in the gas pipeline business internationally (McLean and Elkind 2003; Mair 2005).[1]

While the Social Credit government of the day argued that privatization would not result in foreign ownership and control of B.C.'s gas distribution system, that outcome should have been anticipated, because the best way for B.C. and other Canadian shareholders to maximize the price of their asset, in the event of its sale, is to have it open to international bidders, who are likely to be able to pay much more than Canadian investors. American interests have also acquired the other major gas company in B.C., West Coast Energy, which was purchased by Duke Energy of Charlotte, North Carolina.

As noted, during the late 1980s, the Social Credit government also decided to begin the process of expanding the role of the private sector into B.C.'s electricity system. To do this, it arranged for BC Hydro to purchase energy from a number of private power developers. While the amount of energy acquired was modest, the policy demonstrated how the Crown utility could be used to subsidize the development of private energy projects by awarding their owners long-term energy purchase agreements whose revenue streams would effectively cover the cost of the private investments involved.

The first tender call for energy from private suppliers was made in 1988. It was followed by a second call a year later. In total, the two calls resulted in BC Hydro signing contracts to purchase just over 2,000 GWh of energy annually, from sixteen projects.[2] In 1990, it also entered into a purchase agreement with Alcan in which it agreed to purchase 285 MW of power (roughly 1,230 GWh), annually, through 2014. (This was part of a larger package of commitments associated with the Kemano Completion Project, which we will discuss more extensively further in this study.)

The importance of this development in establishing the private power industry in B.C. was highlighted by the Independent Power Producers Association of B.C. (IPPABC):

> The IPP industry in B.C. was launched in 1989 when B.C.'s Minister of Energy instructed BC Hydro to issue calls for proposals for private power. After a brief initial burst, for the next decade, in general, actual projects were slow to advance due to institutional inertia, changing regulatory practices, sluggish domestic electricity demand

> growth, and, for some projects, the challenges in public perception and financing that face every new industry in B.C.[3]

BC Hydro's decision — endorsed by the government — to purchase energy from the private sector was made despite the much higher costs per MWh of this energy compared with BC Hydro's own costs. BC Hydro was saddled with paying the costs of this energy for the full term of the various contracts negotiated at the time, some of which are still in place.

The election of an NDP government in 1991 put an end to this particular Social Credit initiative. But what proved to be critically important about this early privatization effort is that it created a small, but increasingly influential, private energy lobby — the IPPABC. And it identified the vehicle for channeling public funds to the private sector — long-term energy supply contracts with BC Hydro. What turned out to be a fiscally questionable arrangement for BC Hydro was a financial bonanza for the private energy companies that had managed to get one of the contracts BC Hydro awarded before the 1991 provincial election.

While the policy of contracting to private energy interests was interrupted by the outcome of that election, the NDP honoured projects already in the pipeline. BC Hydro's next call for energy from the private sector — this time under the NDP in 1994/05 — was to deal with the specific problem of Vancouver Island's growing energy needs. Customers on Vancouver Island were consuming about a quarter of BC Hydro's total energy output. But only a small proportion of this was being generated on the island itself. The rest was being imported through underwater high voltage lines from the mainland. The government's interest in getting new energy supplies to Vancouver Island was thus driven not primarily by a desire to support private power developers. Rather, it was to find new energy supplies that would be near the load centre — supplies that would reduce the need to import more energy from the mainland.

To address this problem, BC Hydro entered into two purchase agreements with private power suppliers. It awarded the larger of these, for about 1,500 GWh annually, to Island Co-Generation Project Inc., a partnership at the time between West Coast Energy and Fletcher Challenge. It also awarded a second, much smaller purchase agreement, for approximately 90 GWh annually, to another bidder. Significantly, these were not run-of-the-river or wind-farm projects. Rather, they were contracts for power generated by the forestry industry.[4]

While the NDP government supported the BC Hydro's decision to purchase energy from private energy suppliers, this support was only to address specific regional energy requirements. It did not share the previous Social Credit government's enthusiasm for promoting small privately owned generating projects. This reluctance was reinforced by the fact that the earlier Social Credit-mandated energy purchase agreements were proving extremely expensive compared with BC Hydro's in-house generating costs, a fact that was highlighted in BC Hydro submissions to the BCUC during this period.[5]

Developments in the United States, however, were soon to have a major impact north of the border. The two energy shocks of the 1970s led to a decision by the American federal government to encourage power companies to purchase some of their energy from renewable sources — even if the price was higher than conventional alternatives. Thus began the development of the market for "green energy." In 1980, President Carter deregulated parts of the American phone system by requiring the break-up of AT&T. The rationale was to introduce competition into this economic sector in expectation that it would lead to greater efficiency and lower prices for consumers. The next president, Ronald Reagan soon applied the same approach to other industries, including trucking, airlines, and financial services (savings and loans).

Arguably, the first major challenge to the conventional model of an integrated electricity utility was implemented in the U.K. by Margaret Thatcher. She broke up the Central Electricity Generating Board, carving out the transmission system and creating three separate generating companies, two of which were quickly sold to the private sector. The timing of this coincided with the flood of cheap North Sea gas, which kept prices in check and made the privatization experiment appear — at least initially — quite successful, although critics of this policy have argued that a combination of massive write downs of public assets before privatization, coupled with lower international fuel prices were the key factors (Thomas 2001). But for supporters of deregulation,[6] the U.K. provided an early model of the possibility of fundamentally restructuring electricity systems according to market principles.

The development of the combined-cycle natural gas power plant was also a factor. This technological advance raised the efficiency of gas generating power plants quite dramatically, making them much cheaper to operate. In addition, gas plants could be built more quickly and more cheaply than most other electricity facilities. Construction of new gas pipelines across the United States during the 1980s and early 1990s also made this fuel much more accessible. New entrants could begin generating energy without the long lead times and large capital investments required of other generating systems. Because it lowered the traditional "barriers to entry" that characterized nuclear, hydro, and traditional coal plants, proponents of competition argued that natural gas could play a major role in overcoming the dominance of traditional utilities by assisting in the creation of competitive energy markets. The price of gas soon became a proxy for the price of electricity in many parts of North America.[7]

Until the beginning of the 1990s, the American electricity industry remained highly regulated. This was due to Franklin Roosevelt's Depression-era legislation — the 1935 *Public Utility Holding Company Act* (PUHCA) — which had been enacted to curb anti-competitive practices in the electricity industry. The only significant change in the following years was the enactment of the *Public Utility Regulatory Policies Act* of 1978 (PURPA), which was a response to the oil shocks of the early and mid 1970s. It required American utilities to buy some of their energy from renewable sources. However, with the adoption of deregulation in other sectors of American industry, PUHCA increasingly came under fire because it maintained regulated electricity monopolies — most of which were shareholder owned — and restricted intra-state cross-ownership of electricity utilities. Consequently, from the perspective of proponents of deregulation, it prevented the emergence of a "competitive" national electricity market in the United States.[8]

Enron, in particular, played a key role in this process. The company had developed considerable expertise in the recently deregulated gas-marketing sector, not as an owner of power plants, but as an energy trader. Enron's gas traders had pioneered a wide range of marketing tools and financial instruments that had proved hugely profitable. The company believed it could do the same in the electricity sector if only Washington deregulated the system and created a national electricity trading market. This required the United States to abandon its traditional utility monopoly model in which regulated utilities made investments in electricity generation based on the understanding they would have a captive market, normally within the boundaries of an individual state. Instead, electricity would become a commodity that could be traded, both regionally and nationally. And state-based utilities would be required to open up their transmission systems — and their customers — to energy marketers from across the United States (McLean and Elkind 2003).

Enron believed that the creation of a national market in electricity would open the door to a dramatic expansion in investment opportunities for those with the kind of expertise the company had already developed. Ken Lay and other Enron executives were well connected to the Republican administration of George Bush Sr., and they succeeded in getting his administration to support deregulation of the American electricity system (McLean and Elkind 2003).

On top of this, electricity customers in certain regions of the United States were facing supply shortages and high prices. It was thus tempting to apply conventional economic models to the electricity industry — models that predicted competition would lower prices and trigger new capital investments. Proponents of deregulating the American system also argued that changes in technology — and especially the growing use of combined-cycle gas turbines — reduced the capital cost of new investments and undermined the earlier rationale that it was necessary to provide utilities with a captive customer base in order to justify their long-term investments.

In response to the wave of deregulation initiatives implemented in other parts of the American economy, to high prices in some parts of the country, and to lobbying from energy interests such as Ken Lay of Enron, George Bush Sr. pushed through legislation designed explicitly to begin the process of deregulating the American electricity sector.

The 1992 *Energy Policy Act* fundamentally changed the direction of American electricity policy and greatly enhanced FERC's mandate and powers. The new *Act* explicitly promoted deregulation and competition as the way to address many of the problems facing the American electricity industry. The first Bush administration argued it was necessary to replace the older, regulated, cost-based pricing system with one based on the interplay of market supply and demand. Competition would lower prices and make the industry more efficient. In the process, the *Act* abolished many of the safeguards put in place by Roosevelt — safeguards designed to protect consumers from the predatory practices of unregulated utilities (Cohen 2002a, 2003). The new legislation gave FERC the authority to require states to open their wholesale electricity markets to competition from non-utility generators. It implemented this new authority through Orders 888, 888a, and 889.

Pushed by FERC and lobbied by various private energy interests, a number of American states — most notably California — implemented an aggressive deregulation agenda in the early 1990s (Public Citizen 2002). It restructured existing utilities, forcing them to separate their generating plants from their transmission and distribution systems. It also opened the door to wholesale — and, subsequently — retail competition in some jurisdictions.

This approach was not universally welcomed, however. Many publicly owned utilities, particularly those affiliated with the American Public Power Association (APPA), pointed out the significant drawbacks of attempting to restructure the industry. They felt that the economic theory being applied did not recognize the unique character of electricity and that the changes being implemented would open the door to a wide range of predatory and anti-competitive practices, while failing to deliver on the promise of lower electricity prices for consumers. The Association's longstanding critique of deregulation was summarized by Eugene Coyle in a report commissioned by the APPA that reinforced many of the concerns it had raised in the preceding years:

> Rigorous economic analysis, including a branch of game theory called "the theory of the core," reveals that, rather than textbook competition driving prices down to ever-lower costs and providing

> low-cost electricity to all, what will unfold is price discrimination, redlining of customers, and, ultimately, producer cooperation and/or collusion to frustrate competition....
>
> [E]conomic efficiency will not and cannot result from an unregulated electric power industry... such a market cannot provide rates that will be "just, reasonable, and non-discriminatory," as is now required in the statutes or regulations of most states. (Coyle 2000: 9)

Such concerns — which had been raised by some critics even before the repeal of PUHCA — did not stop Washington from pushing ahead with its deregulation agenda, even after the disastrous experience of states such as California (Hall and Weinstein 2001; Public Citizen 2001, 2002, 2003).[9] Once implemented, there was no turning back to the earlier regime, as the Bush White House remained committed to the deregulation agenda recommended by its key supporters such as Ken Lay of Enron, although many states continued to strongly resist pressure from the American federal government to implement FERC's policy directives.

As deregulation proceeded in the United States — with its subsequently unfulfilled promise of major reductions in energy prices for consumers (and despite the major speculative financial opportunities it provided for private energy investors and energy traders such as Enron) — advocates for this approach, such as former federal Liberal Cabinet Minister and free trade advocate, Donald MacDonald, also emerged in Canada (MacDonald 1996).[10] Alberta, which already had significant private participation in its electricity system, began a major experiment with deregulation in the early 1990s. In Ontario, the Harris government appointed Donald MacDonald of free-trade fame in 1995 to head a commission mandated to review Ontario's electricity system. In his report the following year, MacDonald recommended the break-up of Ontario Hydro and the privatization of most of its electricity generating assets. This was to be accompanied by the introduction of a competitive energy market, including both wholesale and retail competition.

MacDonald's confident prediction that competition would lower prices for customers while improving the efficiency of Ontario's electricity system influenced many in B.C. and particularly those who felt that BC Hydro's monopoly was inconsistent with the shift toward a more market-based economic approach that increasingly characterized many other areas of the province's economy. They felt his views provided a strong case for deregulating the province's electricity system. Similarly, they saw Alberta's experiment in energy deregulation as an illustration of the potential benefits of competitive markets.

Influenced by developments in other parts of Canada, the United States, and internationally, in September of 1995 the BCUC released a report on reforming the province's electricity system, entitled "The British Columbia Electricity Market Review." It advocated the functional separation of BC Hydro's three basic operational divisions: generation, transmission, and distribution. These divisions would remain components of BC Hydro but the transmission system would begin to provide access to other energy suppliers. The BCUC report also advocated the introduction of limited wholesale competition through a power pool, which would allow major energy consumers to purchase their power from companies other than BC Hydro (BCUC 1995).

While the BCUC did not advocate privatization of BC Hydro's assets — a policy that would have likely resulted in a direct conflict with the NDP Government of the day — its analysis claimed that there was no inherent superiority in public ownership. Rather, both public and private ownership had merits. The choice depended on the policy goals government wanted to accomplish. It also argued that while retail competition was not — at least in the short run — desirable, moving some distance toward a deregulated energy market in which prices were established through competition would ultimately prove beneficial to B.C. (BCUC 1995).

B.C.'s right wing Fraser Institute added its voice to the growing number of advocates of restructuring the province's electricity system, although, perhaps not surprisingly, it went much further than the BCUC. It released a major report, "The Case of BC Hydro: A Blueprint for Privatization," outlining how BC Hydro might be broken up and virtually all its assets sold to the private sector. The report was co-authored by Bruce Howe, a former federal Deputy Minister of Energy Mines and Resources (and a former CEO of MacMillan Bloedel) and Frank Klassen, a former Chief Financial Officer of BC Hydro who had been involved in the privatization process initiated by the Social Credit government at the end of the 1980s (Howe and Klassen 1996).

Their report claimed that sale of BC Hydro to the private sector could provide the government with a major cash infusion from its estimated $14 billion in assets. And, they claimed that privatization coupled with deregulation would create a new market framework that would significantly improve the efficiency of B.C.'s electricity system. In the process, it would also result in lower electricity rates for customers over the long term.

Conversely, Howe and Klassen argued, if the government failed to recognize the benefits of this policy change, it would be missing a major opportunity for the province. In their words:

> Electricity markets are in revolutionary change; deregulation, competition, and restructuring are everywhere. A restructured and privatized BC Hydro would enable B.C. residents to benefit from

> these changes. Maintaining the status quo will only result in higher rates and debt levels, and lost economic development opportunities. (Howe and Klassen 1996: 4)

The authors went on to argue that the antiquated monopoly structure of BC Hydro was now unsuited to the rapidly changing energy market in North America:

> The old order of monopolistic power utilities is changing at a rapid pace, and a government-owned, bureaucratically controlled power monopoly is most unlikely to be discerning and swift in response to its changing environment. (Howe and Klassen 1996: 7)

The Fraser Institute report provided a detailed outline for dismembering BC Hydro, arguing for the full separation of generation from both the transmission and distribution systems. Generation would be split into four separate private companies selling energy through a power pool. Transmission would be a regulated monopoly operating like a common carrier in which all suppliers would have equal access. Distribution to residential and commercial customers would be broken up into several regulated distribution entities on a geographic basis. The report also argued that the province should initially permit wholesale competition, with the long-term goal of allowing full retail competition.

Like many other reports advocating deregulation and privatization, the Fraser Institute did not address the possibility that the outcome of its policy recommendations would be the eventual takeover of B.C.'s electricity system by American-based energy corporations, as happened with B.C.'s gas distribution system. Nor did it address the policy implications of integrating B.C.'s electricity system with the American system. Perhaps most importantly, it did not examine the implications of American ownership of B.C. generating assets in the context of Canada's NAFTA obligations (especially those included in Chapter Eleven dealing with investor rights). Nor did it examine the implications of integrating with the United States on the basis of policies promoted by FERC — policies over which Canada would have no control. (It is worth noting that the policy recommendations advocated by the Fraser Institute were challenged by other policy think tanks such as the Canadian Centre for Policy Alternatives at the time. It saw no benefit and many downsides in breaking up BC Hydro or moving to a market-based pricing system.)

Nevertheless, these various provincial, national, and international developments formed the context in which a re-elected NDP government decided in 1997 to carry out its own major review of B.C.'s electricity system. It asked Mark Jaccard, who the NDP had earlier appointed as Chair of the BCUC, to chair the provincial government's new Task Force on Electricity Market Reform. It appointed representatives to participate in the Task Force from major industrial and commercial users, private power developers, environmentalists, public interest advocates, and the two BC Hydro unions.[11] Jaccard believed that B.C. could benefit from the introduction of some elements of a competitive electricity market based, in part, on the approach being promoted south of the border by FERC, as well as on initiatives being implemented at that time in Alberta (Jaccard 1998).[12]

As Chair, Jaccard's mandate required him to achieve consensus among the various stakeholders the government had appointed to the Task Force. However, after a thorough review of various reform options, Task Force members were unable to reach consensus (Jaccard 1998). While some representatives of industry — and particularly the private power developers — wanted to break up BC Hydro and introduce a competitive energy market, others, such as major industrial customers, were not persuaded that such a radical restructuring was warranted. Other participants also questioned whether B.C. should abandon its public-sector, cost-of-production pricing approach in favour of a competitive electricity model, especially as B.C.'s prices were among the lowest in North America, and so did not pose the sort of problems that faced customers in many parts of the United States.

Other Task Force members were disturbed about the emerging evidence of the negative experiences of competition in other jurisdictions — such as the U.K., Australia, and California — where deregulation had been partially implemented. While the full extent of the debacle in California had yet to emerge, there were already signs that deregulation was not a panacea for the electricity problems facing these jurisdictions. In particular, the Task Force's environmental, consumer, and labour representatives did not see how adopting a competitive energy market would improve on BC Hydro's existing system. They were not convinced the system was "broken," and they worried that major changes might undermine BC Hydro's ability to continue to supply the province with low-cost, secure, and reliable energy.

Frustrated with his inability to get a consensus report, Mark Jaccard, in his capacity as Chair, issued his own. This laid out the basic changes he believed would be necessary to restructure B.C.'s electricity system. His recommendations included allowing major industrial customers to purchase energy from suppliers other than BC Hydro; separating BC Hydro's transmission operations from its distribution system; creating a new B.C. Power Exchange to operate a B.C.-based energy market; and establishing a new Grid Oversight Committee with outside stakeholders to oversee the operation of the transmission grid. Further into the future, Jaccard also recommended the creation of a separate entity, B.C. Grid Corporation, to operate the province's electricity grid independently from BC Hydro. The goal was eventually to supplant B.C.'s cost-of-production approach to pricing with one based on a competitive market (Jaccard 1998)

Because his Task Force did not reach a consensus, the NDP government did not feel committed to implementing Jaccard's major recommendations. And, by the late 1990s, there was increasing evidence that deregulation had major downsides, so the case for it was less persuasive than it had appeared only a few years earlier.[13] But while the NDP did not implement Jaccard's key proposals, the government did begin the process of separating the transmission system from the other parts of BC Hydro, while still keeping it within the company. This reflected, in part, its concern that if it did not take some minimal steps toward deregulation, the Americans might retaliate by limiting the ability of Powerex to trade energy in the United States. The existence of B.C.'s huge reservoirs, coupled with an energy surplus during periods when American energy demand was very high, meant that Powerex could sell energy in the American market on highly favourable terms. As a result, Powerex began to generate significant revenues for both BC Hydro and the province. To maximize Powerex's energy trading opportunities, its staff wanted to acquire an energy trading certificate that would enable it to buy and sell energy within the United States — as opposed to simply selling B.C. energy to the south. This required FERC approval. Powerex applied for and eventually received it.

At the time, there was considerable confusion within the provincial government about whether FERC was entitled to demand reciprocity from BC Hydro in return for providing an energy-trading certificate to Powerex. On one hand, critics of the government's position on this issue, such as Professor Marjorie Griffin Cohen, argued that NAFTA does not require reciprocity as a condition for access to the American market. Further, critics maintained that FERC's efforts to have Canadian utilities adopt its policies were inappropriate intrusions into Canadian public policy making (Cohen 2002b, 2003).

On the other hand, a combination of fear that FERC might not allow Powerex to continue its — by then — very profitable energy trading, along with the view held by some government advisors that deregulation was inevitable in any event, resulted in the decision to separate operation of the transmission grid from BC Hydro's other activities, while keeping it within the company. This process required substantial restructuring of the way BC Hydro operated its transmission system: its purpose was to give private interests access to the grid on terms that were no less favourable than those of BC Hydro.

One of the other consequences of the Jaccard Task Force was that it provided a forum for private energy interests to refine their demands for the restructuring of B.C.'s electricity system. While it is true that over the years, the BCUC had also provided opportunities to examine various restructuring options, the Task Force was mandated, specifically, to do research on the costs and benefits of introducing competition into B.C.'s electricity system. Some of the ideas private energy interests developed during this process were reflected in subsequent lobbying by the Independent Power Producers Association of B.C. (IPPABC, later re-named the Independent Power Producers of B.C. — IPPBC), which — correctly — believed that if the Liberals were elected sometime in the future, it would be more sympathetic to breaking up BC Hydro and encouraging the expansion of the private energy industry within the province.

One of the key issues faced by the diverse business interests represented on the Jaccard Task Force was how to reconcile the likelihood that any move toward market pricing would entail significant increases in energy prices for BC Hydro's major industrial customers with the reality that the Crown utility's cost-based approach gave them prices far lower than in any of the neighbouring jurisdictions. While the forest and mining industries, who at the time used about 40 percent of BC Hydro's energy — roughly $400 million worth annually — were not opposed to more private-sector involvement in the province's electricity system, they were worried that a rapid move to international market prices would result in a huge increase in their costs, from about $34 per MWh to $50 MWh, or even more. They were also wary of the potentially high costs of new, privately generated, energy within B.C. — costs that would damage their competitiveness in industries where commodity prices were set internationally and, hence, where loss of their competitive advantage in low-cost energy could have very significant financial repercussions for some major players.

Private power developers understood that they could not compete with BC Hydro's low embedded costs. To justify their anticipated investments, they needed the province to adopt the much higher market prices. But an immediate move to market prices would have a huge downside for major industrial customers. They could face a rate increase of 50 percent or more.[14] And, higher prices would result in a huge windfall for BC Hydro and its shareholder, the public, at the expense of forest and mining interests, a prospect private power producers were determined to avoid.

To resolve this dilemma, representatives of the major industrial customers came up with the concept that they had an historical "entitlement" to BC Hydro's cheap public energy. Their argument turned the normal relationship between shareholders and customers on its head. They claimed that, in their role as customers, they had provided the market on which BC Hydro's expansion during the 1962 to 1984 period was based. This expansion had given BC Hydro its cheap, low-cost electricity, and so they, as major customers, rather than the shareholding public, should be the rightful beneficiaries of this low-cost embedded energy.

Ignoring the fact that the public had taken on the risky — and costly — investments in the Crown corporation at a time when interest rates were high (as much as 18 percent on some long-term notes) and energy prices at the American border were relatively low — meaning virtually no dividends for many years — business interests strenuously argued that if the province were to move toward market-based pricing, it should be done in a manner that did not negatively affect their ability to access BC Hydro's own low-cost energy. They wanted, in other words, continued access at prices based on public investments made in the 1962–1984 period. Even though such an argument would be dismissed as bizarre — indeed, as ridiculous — if it were applied to a private corporation's opportunity to benefit from its investments, business representatives nevertheless proceeded to advance their case for a guaranteed "entitlement."

As we shall see, the Liberal government, elected in 2001, used this entitlement argument to justify its "Heritage Contract" legislation which protected the major industrial customers from exposure to market prices, while the ban on BC Hydro building new generation in its 2002 Energy Plan assured a captive market for private power interests. As a package, this meant that the interests of the two business factions — major industrial customers and private power producers — were reconciled in a manner that gave each major interest group what it wanted — and all at the expense of the public.

Private power interests also faced another problem: how to persuade an NDP government to agree to carve the transmission system out from BC Hydro so that it would become a common carrier similar to the model FERC was pushing American utilities to adopt — a model that involved a complete separation of the management of the transmission grid from the supplier, or generator, of electricity. But the NDP was officially committed to maintaining public ownership of BC Hydro. So they put forward the idea that the transmission system could be separated from BC Hydro and reconfigured as a "public authority" governed by a stakeholder board. This new board would include representatives of private energy interests, major industrial and commercial customers, residential customers, BC Hydro, and the general public. The key point was that the majority on the board would be from the business sector, so they would be able to ensure that the transmission system was operated in a manner that guaranteed equal treatment to private energy developers and marketers, while dramatically reducing the role of BC Hydro in decisions regarding the use and future development of the grid.

On the face of it, such a proposal might not have seemed appealing to the NDP. However, the government of the day was desperate for cash to balance the books and was under constant media attacks for allegedly failing to avoid incurring deficits. Consequently, proponents of this proposal argued that by selling the assets of the transmission system to a newly established "public authority," the government could get a huge, one-time cash windfall. Depending on the assessed value of the system, this could amount to billions of dollars. And, in order to address the government's commitment to the maintenance of public power, the sale could be framed as essentially a transfer *within* the public sector. The NDP government could claim that the new public authority — modeled on the Vancouver Airport Authority — would still be "public" in the sense that it was not a private, profit-making entity.[15] Of course, the fact that such a new entity would no longer be controlled by the government, but rather by a business-dominated stakeholder board, would be downplayed.

In the end, the NDP government chose not to adopt this model at the time, because it recognized the implications that would flow from losing control over the transmission grid. But, as we shall discuss later, the idea of carving the transmission system out from BC Hydro — using an approach different than the public authority model — was eventually adopted by the Liberal government.

This account would be incomplete without a brief discussion of the BCUC, one of the other major institutional players that over the years has provided a key forum for the various private energy interests to develop a made-in-B.C. approach[16] to deregulating and privatizing the province's electricity system. Originally established to provide oversight to regulated private-sector utilities, during the 1980s its mandate was extended to cover BC Hydro.[17] As a result, BC Hydro must seek BCUC approval for a variety of its business decisions, including rate increases, major new investments, and the purchase of new energy from private sources.

As part of this process, BC Hydro is required to submit very extensive documentation to the BCUC on its future plans. The various interests that might be affected by BC Hydro's plans are entitled to seek "intervener" status from the BCUC. BC Hydro, like other utilities reporting to the BCUC, is also required to pay the costs of the intervener process. As a result, private energy companies and major industrial customers, such as pulp mills and mining corporations, can, and do, obtain very substantial funding — amounting to millions of dollars over the years — to pay for their lawyers, consultants, power engineers, and accountants. Though the intervener process was originally set up to enable the public to participate in the regulatory process and voice its concerns about proposals submitted to the BCUC, in reality the major beneficiaries are not members of the public at all: they are corporate interests.

Over the years, private power developers, forestry and mining companies, and other business interests have made very effective use of this publicly funded regulatory process. They have been able to access an enormous amount of financial and business planning information from BC Hydro.

Intervener status allows them to submit detailed questions to the Crown utility about its cost structure, investment plans, and energy trading activities — information that, in the private sector, would normally be protected by the right of owners to maintain business confidentiality and secrecy concerning commercially sensitive activities. But, BC Hydro is public.

In the debate about restructuring B.C.'s electricity system, the BCUC has provided a very important forum for private energy developers and industrial customers to come together to examine various options that would benefit their respective interests. Indeed, it is no exaggeration to say that the BCUC has become a kind of "club" in which private interests have shaped the regulatory process in their favour — a process discussed extensively in the academic literature dealing with regulatory agencies, under the heading of "capture theory" (Bernstein 1955; Peltzman 1976; Knittel 2006). Regular BCUC hearings have also given private energy companies and major industrial customers the opportunity to work through many of the technical issues associated with restructuring B.C.'s electricity system with the aim of resolving potential conflicts within the business sector that otherwise might have impeded the push toward privatization and deregulation.

With the election of the Liberal government in May of 2001, the process of privatization of B.C.'s electricity system accelerated dramatically. While the NDP was ambivalent about how to deal with the pressures for deregulation and competition, the Liberals had no such reservations. They were committed to transforming the system. Far from seeing BC Hydro as a protector of B.C.'s energy independence and a key player in the maintenance of public control and ownership of provincial electricity assets, the Liberals saw it as a barrier to the expansion of private investment opportunities and an anachronistic legacy of an earlier period of wrongheaded state intervention.

Even before the May 2001 election, aspiring Premier Gordon Campbell indicated that he was committed to making fundamental changes in B.C.'s electricity system, including opening the door to a sharp expansion of the role of private energy developers. In a speech on November 29, 2000, to a select group of energy executives, he outlined his policy objectives:

> My goal is greater competition.... Competition requires access to markets.... Greater deregulation in the energy sector is a global reality.... I want everyone to understand this. I am committed to looking at BC Hydro. Indeed we are committed to looking at all Crown corporations.... Whether it's politics, pricing, or just straight economics, independent power producers have been discouraged at every turn in this province. I want to change that and I want to change it big time.... (quoted in B.C. Citizens for Public Power 2002: 7)

Accordingly, the new government moved forward on a number of different fronts to restructure and privatize B.C.'s electricity system. This involved appointing new Board members for BC Hydro and the BCUC, the establishment of a process to develop a new Energy Plan to promote the growth of private investments in B.C. (while protecting the interests of its major mining and forest industry supporters through the Heritage Contract), and major changes to BC Hydro, both internally through contracting out a third of its workforce to Accenture and externally through carving out the transmission system. Here, we will very briefly review some of these key developments, starting with appointments to the BCUC.

Since the 2001 election, the government has replaced most Commissioners as members have retired or have seen their terms expire. The new appointments have reflected the government's commitment to a much larger role for the private sector in crafting its energy policy agenda. Perhaps not surprisingly, given the current government's close relationship with the business community, most — although not all — of its appointees have a business background, and a number have been directly involved in the private energy sector.

For example, the government appointed Robert Hobbes, who had worked as a lawyer for Aquila Networks Canada between 1989 and 2001, as a full-time Commissioner in March of 2003 (BCUC 2003).[18] On August 25, 2003, it then appointed him as BCUC Chair, replacing the outgoing Peter Ostergaard. Hobbes' former employer, Aquila, was the successor company to West Kootenay Power (WKP). Aquila was a subsidiary of Utilicorp of Kansas, a major American electricity corporation. Utilicorp had bought WKP from Cominco, a branch of Canadian Pacific, in 1987 when the Canadian parent firm decided to get out of the electricity business in B.C.[19] As a result of its successful bid to buy WKP, Utilicorp ended up servicing about one tenth of the province's customers, in the southeast corner of the province.[20] Robert Hobbes was one of WKP's representatives on the Jaccard Task Force.

The government's appointment of a new Chair was only part of a quiet reorganization of the Commission that took place in late summer of 2003. It also appointed two more full-time and three temporary Commissioners. According to the official biography posted on the government's website, Robert J. Milbourne, a temporary Commissioner also has a background with the private energy sector, having been a director of Bruce Power Inc. This was the consortium that acquired the Bruce nuclear plant that the Ontario government under Premier Mike Harris sold as part of its own electricity privatization policy. His official government biography notes his past role in the private sector:

> Mr. Milbourne's directorships have included affiliates of Stelco Inc.

> as well as Hatch Associates Ltd., one of Canada's larger international engineering and consulting organizations, and Bruce Power Inc., operator of a substantial portion of Canada's nuclear power generating capacity.[21]

The government made further appointments in 2006, again finding Commissioners with a private-sector energy background. According to the government's biography of Commissioners, Anthony Pullman, appointed in March of 2006, was:

> recently retired as Senior Vice President of ATCO Power Ltd. where he was primarily responsible for financing that company's independent power projects in Canada, the U.K., and Australia on a limited recourse basis. Prior to that he had served as Vice President Controller of ATCO Ltd. and Alberta Power Ltd. [22]

The government's biography of another 2006 appointee, Lisa A. O'Hara, notes the following:

> Lisa O'Hara... recently retired as the Vice-President of Financial Services and Administration from Terasen Pipelines in Calgary.... She has affiliations with a number of organizations, including Encorp Pacific Inc. (Director, Audit Committee Chair)....[23]

While the background of Commissioners should not be interpreted as assuming any bias in the exercise of their judicial functions — and we are certainly not implying that — what is of concern is that the government has chosen not to appoint a more representative group, one that would reflect the many other interests in B.C. affected by the BCUC, including individuals with expertise in consumer and ratepayer matters.

The BCUC's governance changes have been paralleled by major changes to both the Board and management of BC Hydro. One of the government's first decisions after the 2001 election was to appoint Larry Bell as both CEO and Chair of BC Hydro. Bell had been Chair of BC Hydro under the earlier Social Credit government from 1987 to 1991. In this capacity, he had overseen the sale of some of BC Hydro's other assets, including its mainland gas operations (B.C. Gas), Victoria Gas, and its rail operations. Bell had also been instrumental in developing the policy that permitted private energy interests to supply energy to BC Hydro under long-term energy contracts during the final years of the Social Credit administration.

After leaving his position at BC Hydro in 1991, Bell pursued activities in the private sector, becoming a director of both B.C. Gas and TransAlta Corp. Upon the election of the Liberal government in 2001, Bell became a key advisor to its transition team. Once in office, the Liberal government changed the conflict-of-interest legislation to permit directors of Crown corporations to own shares in private energy utilities. Prudently, Bell divested himself of his B.C. Gas and TransAlta shares, thus avoiding further controversy over what some might have seen as a moral, although no longer illegal, conflict with his new duties at BC Hydro. In 2004, he was replaced as CEO by Bob Elton but kept his position as Chair of the Board of BC Hydro.

Bell has made it clear, both through his earlier actions during the Social Credit government and, more recently, under the more recent Liberal government, that he favours a much larger role for private interests in B.C.'s electricity system. In August 2001, he told the *Vancouver Sun*: "I would say Hydro needs to be ready for further deregulation… and that the government wants independent power producers to sell electricity directly to customers rather than sell power to Hydro for resale" (quoted in B.C. Citizens for Public Power 2002: 7) On September 5, 2001, he elaborated his views, again in a *Sun* interview, stating that while deregulation for residential customers was "way out there," he nevertheless saw a need to address B.C. industry's sense of "historical entitlement" to cheap electricity (Nuttall-Smith 2001).

The other members of BC Hydro's Board also reflect the government's business base. Several have been involved in private energy companies or private energy marketing activities. Significantly, there are no longer any appointees with a labour background. (A brief review of the backgrounds of individuals appointed to the Board of the newly created B.C. Transmission Corporation reflects the same pro-business, pro-energy approach to the selection of its membership.)

The new government also moved quickly on the policy front. To test the waters for major changes in the electricity system, in August 2001 it set up an Energy Policy Development Task Force chaired by former provincial Deputy Minister of Energy and Mines Jack Ebbels. The Task Force included Brenda Eaton, one of the Premier's own Deputy Ministers. Her appointment reflected the importance of the Task Force to the government and indicated that its work had the Premier's blessing. The Task Force also included Peter Meekison, a former senior Deputy Minister in Alberta, John Bechtold, a former senior executive with Petro-Canada, and Erik Westergaard, an energy consultant who had been involved in the deregulation of energy markets in New Zealand. As well, the government gave Doug Allen, a former Deputy Minister and a former consultant to Westcoast Energy, the role of helping with the development and implementation of the Task Force's mandate (B.C. Citizens for Public Power 2002).

The objective of the Task Force was to consult the major interests that might be affected by changes to the electricity system and to develop a new policy framework for B.C. (Its mandate was not limited to electricity and covered areas such as oil and natural gas). The Task Force had no shortage of input from various private-sector organizations anxious to ensure that their interests would be boosted by the Task Force's final recommendations. Implicit in its mandate was the objective of reconciling the somewhat divergent perspectives of large industrial and commercial customers with those of private energy developers in a manner that kept both groups happy.

Within months of the election, the IPPABC, representing aspiring private energy developers and, particularly, those interested in building new small hydro or wind-farm generating facilities, submitted a comprehensive set of recommendations to the Task Force. Many of these were subsequently incorporated into the final Energy Plan. The following is a summary of the main elements of the IPPABC's proposals.

First, the government should provide "open access to transmission wires" through the establishment of "an independent, Crown-owned and regulated transmission company" (IPPABC 2001). This change would "avoid conflicts by [BC Hydro] not owning generation or distribution facilities." It would also "operate as a common carrier to provide domestic and export services." The transmission company would have a mandate to facilitate both domestic energy sales and exports by all generators — meaning private power developers and marketers — linked to the grid.

Second, the IPPABC argued that the government should "establish a more competitive wholesale generation market" and "increase the number of electricity buyers by establishing an independent, Crown-owned and regulated distribution company... which would buy electricity directly from IPPs" (IPPABC 2001). As part of this recommendation it also advocated allowing major industrial and commercial users to purchase energy "directly from IPPs." Additionally, "all new generation would be developed exclusively by IPPs until BC Hydro's dominant share of total generation decreased to a level where a truly competitive market could exist."

Third, it proposed that the government give additional powers to the BCUC in order to introduce a market-based approach to regulating B.C.'s electricity system. Within this new regulatory framework, the BCUC would oversee the operation of the transmission grid on the basis of non-discriminatory and open access, monitor the activities of the distribution company, and, finally, set prices for BC Hydro's historical "entitlement" generation (subsequently referred to as the "Heritage Assets").

In addition to these three key recommendations, the IPPABC also recommended a number of other fundamental changes to B.C.'s electricity system:

The IPPABC also recommends that the B.C. government:

- Become directly involved in structuring RTO West;
- Create a comprehensive green electricity policy that would value

low environmental impact and renewability;
- Continue to implement its recently announced plan to reduce the backlog of Water Licence applications by 90 percent in two years;
- Encourage the distribution company(s) to implement net metering;
- Convene a forum to discuss the pros and cons of establishing a market hub to further increase the number of wholesale buyers and sellers;
- Direct the transmission and distribution companies to improve the interconnection procedures with IPP generators by updating interconnection standards and providing a more streamlined, transparent, and disciplined transmission study process. (IPPABC 2001)

The IPPABC argued that the province should encourage private energy development for export markets. Improved access to the United States, it maintained, would provide a stimulus for more private investment within B.C. As noted above, it suggested the B.C. government should support FERC's efforts to establish a cross-border Regional Transmission Organization (RTO West, now Grid West) to further integrate B.C.'s electricity system with that of adjacent American states. IPPABC also advocated privatization of the transmission system itself, in the longer term, because it philosophically supported a greater private role in B.C.'s electricity system and it wanted a guarantee that BC Hydro could never again have preferential access to the grid (IPPABC 2001).

IPPABC argued that BC Hydro should be required to share access to the storage available in its reservoirs with private energy producers, a proposal with profound — and arguably highly negative — implications for BC Hydro's ability to manage its own system and take advantage of its available storage to buy energy from Alberta or the United States at low-demand periods and sell it back during high-demand periods, to the benefit of B.C. ratepayers:

> Consideration should be given to using some of the storage associated with BC Hydro's large hydro-electric generation facilities to increase the value to the province of long-term B.C. IPP exports. Currently, this unique storage asset is used almost exclusively to facilitate Powerex's short-term electricity trade. Making it available to B.C. IPPs might enable them to improve their chances of building for the export market, thereby creating jobs in B.C. and more long-term provincial revenues from taxes.

> For example, the electricity production from most run-of-the-river IPP plants peaks in June and is at its lowest in January. An export buyer may want a constant supply year-round. The storage could be used to shape the profile of the generation to meet the requirements of the buyer. A similar scenario could be developed for an IPP natural gas-combined cycle plant in B.C. BC Hydro would earn a fee for providing the storage service and the provincial and local governments would earn tax revenues and water rental or gas royalty revenues from the corresponding IPP investment and operation. (IPPABC 2001)

Finally, the IPPABC advocated a ban on BC Hydro building any new generating capacity in order to provide a stimulus for new private investment in B.C.'s energy sector. Noting that BC Hydro's share of power generation in the province was about 90 percent, it argued that private energy companies should be encouraged to build all new generating capacity until BC Hydro's share had dropped to less than 60 percent. Strangely, the organization gave no rationale in its document for the 60 percent threshold. But, given that energy consumption has been growing by between 1.5 and 2 percent annually, the implication is that BC Hydro would be barred from new construction for decades to come.

Alcan, the world's second-largest aluminum producer and owner of the huge hydroelectric generating facility in Kitimat, was another major influence on the province's new energy policy (Alcan 2001). With more than 800 MW of capacity that enables it to generate significant volumes of high-value firm energy, Alcan is a significant player in B.C.'s energy industry. In 1950, the provincial government gave it a fifty-year water licence to produce energy from the Nechako River. The District of Kitimat has taken the view that this was for the purpose of smelting aluminum. It maintained that because energy is now so valuable, the company has been trying to reinterpret its original contract to enable it to sell more energy either to BC Hydro or, via Powerex, to the lucrative American market at the expense of aluminum production and to the detriment of the local economy in Kitimat. (We shall return to the Alcan energy issue in a subsequent chapter.)

In order to facilitate a shift from aluminum production to energy sales, Alcan needed a change in government policy that would give it the right to access BC Hydro's transmission grid on an equal footing with BC Hydro and Powerex. This would enable it to transmit energy to potential customers, either within B.C. or to the United States. A close reading of both the Alcan submission to the Task Force (which the District of Kitimat obtained through a freedom-of-information request) and the province's subsequent Energy Plan reveals remarkable harmony on this issue. Alcan outlined its recommendations as follows:

> As power markets throughout North America continue to undergo structural reforms to increase competition and transfer the investment responsibility and risk for new facilities from traditionally regulated utilities to merchant owners, Alcan has become increasingly interested in leveraging its financial strength and utility-operating expertise to participate in these new market opportunities. In British Columbia in particular, Alcan intends to expand its role as an IPP developer and operator by increasing the net electrical output capability of its existing facilities at Kitimat and Kemano through new investments in energy efficiency programs and environmentally responsible reservoir enhancements. Alcan is also interested in considering the development or acquisition of other generating facilities elsewhere in the province. Alcan is embarking on these initiatives for the dual purposes of supporting potential upgrade and expansion programs at its Kitimat smelter, and to supply energy to competitive electricity markets in B.C. and other interconnected jurisdictions. (Alcan 2001: 2)

Alcan's submission focussed on three key areas: access to the transmission system, creation of a competitive wholesale energy market in B.C., and regulatory reform that would include the right to sell energy directly to customers both in B.C. and in other jurisdictions. Regarding transmission, the utility argued that B.C. should increase its capital investment to expand the grid's capacity to accommodate the future needs of private power producers. It argued that this investment should be in the form of "pre-building" in advance of existing needs so private power developers would be assured that new projects would not be held up by transmission capacity issues (Alcan 2001: 3).

Alcan also argued that the government should "de-monopolize" existing transmission access rights, both within B.C. and to "adjacent markets," revise transmission design principles, and establish a separate grid company that would participate in RTO West (now Grid West) (Alcan 2001). The company suggested that "current transmission access rights held by Powerex and BC Hydro be reviewed to determine if a more balanced distribution of these rights amongst several parties" including independent power producers. Regarding the price paid by private energy developers for using the transmission grid, Alcan argued that BC Hydro's tariff structure unfairly penalized the private sector and so should be revised to shift costs back to the public utility. It also proposed that B.C.'s transmission system should be "owned and managed completely separate [*sic*] from the ownership and management of BC Hydro's transmission assets." The new entity should be an "independent transmission company with no continuing affiliation to BC Hydro" (Alcan 2001).

As we noted earlier, one of the impediments to expanding the sale of new, privately generated energy to major industrial customers in B.C. was the very low embedded cost of BC Hydro's public energy. But Alcan, given its own very low embedded cost (estimated to be in the range of $8 to $10 per MWh, including the $5 per MWh provincial water-rental fee at that time), could arguably still make very large profits selling at prices similar to the BC Hydro rate of $35 MWh for large industrial customers. While its 1991 long-term EPA with BC Hydro was priced at about this amount, the company appeared unhappy with this arrangement, which had been negotiated before the sharp rise in energy prices in the West Coast energy market in the late 1990s. This would mean continuing to sell at between $15 and $20 per MWh below the $50–$55 MWh market price at the time. To solve this problem for potential industrial customers, Alcan argued that the province should direct BC Hydro to adopt a "Contract for Differences" pricing mechanism whereby the Crown utility would pay market price for new private energy and resell it at its own, much lower price. BC Hydro would cover the price difference in this arrangement.[24]

Many, though not all, of the IPPABC and Alcan recommendations appeared in the highly controversial *Interim Report of the Task Force on Energy Policy* (Dec. 17, 2001) and, subsequently, in the *Final Report of the Task Force on Energy Policy* the following year (Government of B.C. 2001, 2002). The former recommended the break up of BC Hydro including carving out its transmission grid, in order to address what was seen as its unfair monopoly control over BC's electricity system — control that allegedly discriminated against private power interests. It also advocated that B.C. should be willing to allow construction of new coal-fired power plants. It recommended establishing an "endowment" of BC Hydro's existing public electricity resources. And, most controversially, it urged the government to shift rapidly to a market-based electricity pricing system. In its words: "a fully competitive energy market will attract private capital and bring more energy supply, thereby lowering our energy costs and increasing our energy security" (Government of B.C. 2001). The authors of the Interim Task Force Report misjudged the reception it would get and quickly went back to the drawing board to address some of its most provocative recommendations.

As a result, the final report differed in a number of significant ways from Ebbels' earlier effort. This was most apparent in a revision to the *Final Report* that effectively abandoned the *Interim Report's* ambitious timetable for implementing market prices. Sticking with this timetable would have meant major price increases — estimated at about 30 percent for residential customers, but as high as 60 percent for major commercial and industrial customers.

Needless to say, the latter strongly objected. In addition, the *Interim Report* generated a firestorm of criticism from other organizations including municipalities, the Sierra Legal Defence Fund, the B.C. Public Interest Advocacy Group, and many others who did not feel that there was a "problem" large enough to justify breaking up BC Hydro and fundamentally restructuring the electricity system (Government of B.C. 2002).

Although some of its most questionable recommendations were withdrawn, the *Final Report* still advocated profound changes to B.C.'s electricity system. Like Mark Jaccard's earlier recommendations as Chair of the NDP's Task Force on Electricity Market Reform, Ebbels advocated the separation of BC Hydro's generating and transmission operations. But Ebbels went further than Jaccard, arguing that it was necessary to carve the transmission system entirely out from BC Hydro:

> Therefore, the first step in electricity market reform must be to establish an independent transmission company separate from generation and distribution entities. This would provide independent power producers access to the transmission system to move their electricity to market, which is now continental in nature. (Government of B.C. 2002: 59)

Ebbels wrote that the new transmission company should be entirely independent of BC Hydro and, ultimately, independent of political "interference" (i.e., public policy direction) by the province:

> The new transmission entity must be a commercial operation, charging fully for its services. Initially, the transmission entity should be a commercial Crown corporation. At a later stage, it may be wise to consider some other form of governance, such as a non-share capital corporation, much like many airport authorities in Canada. Whatever the ultimate form, it must be fully independent. Without a modern transmission system that is both effective and efficient, a competitive market for electricity in British Columbia will not be realized. (Government of B.C. 2002: 53)

The idea of structuring the transmission system as a non-share capital corporation was earlier proposed by several participants in the Jaccard Task Force. To sell this idea, its proponents argued that the province could obtain a huge, one-time cash windfall from the sale of the transmission assets to such a "public" corporation.

At the same time, because it would have the organizational characteristics of a public authority rather than those of a private company, the transaction could — misleadingly — be characterized as little more than a corporate reorganization within the public sector rather than privatization of the grid. In its recommendations, the 2002 *Final Report* argued that the BCUC should be given enhanced responsibility for regulating the planning and financial transactions of a newly independent transmission company to ensure it did not unduly favour BC Hydro's generating facilities.

Ebbels' proposed carve-up of BC Hydro did not stop with the transmission system. The Task Force also recommended separating the generating assets from the distribution of electricity to B.C. customers:

> The Task Force further recommends that the provincial government restructure the rest of BC Hydro into at least two legally separate, distinct, and independent entities handling generation and distribution. Generation involves the development, operation, and management of large production assets. Distribution deals with acquisition and delivery of electricity to individual customers and involves connections, service, call-centres and account management. From a competence standpoint, not only are the required skills, knowledge, technology, and processes different, so too are the focus, business strategy development, and performance measures. (Government of B.C. 2002: 54)

Concerned that these changes would still leave BC Hydro with too much influence over the electricity system, the Task Force further recommended that BC Hydro's assets be separated into two broad categories: core assets and non-core assets, each of which would be managed by a separate Crown corporation.[25] The non-core assets would then be spun off to the private sector over time. The core asset Crown corporation would be required to operate strictly on the basis of commercial principles, but to ensure that it did not abuse its dominant market position, it would be subject to tough regulations to prevent it exercising too much market power. Significantly, the costs of this massive restructuring of BC Hydro were not discussed in the *Final Report*; nor were the impacts it would have in reducing the efficiency of BC Hydro.

To further restrict BC Hydro's influence, the Task Force also recommended that all new generating assets should be built by private interests. This represented an enormous policy shift. As the role of private power interests expanded, it would transform BC Hydro from a generator of electricity it owned and controlled into a purchaser of electricity from private energy interests. It would mean a shift from cost-based pricing to market pricing, exposing B.C. ratepayers to the vagaries of the international energy market. Yet curiously, or perhaps deliberately, the long-term financial impacts — and risks — for ratepayers of such a sea change in electricity policy were not examined in the *Final Report* either.

As we noted earlier, the *Interim Report* had recommended a speedy move to market prices. Its goal was to raise rates for residential customers by 30 percent, commercial customers by 40 percent, and industrial customers by 60 percent.[26] The magnitude of the price increases could negatively impact B.C.'s competitive position while imposing significant hardships on large numbers of residential customers, particularly those with lower incomes. Such opposition threatened to derail the bigger project of deregulation and privatization that the Task Force was intent on seeing implemented.

The *Final Report* was still critical of the fact that B.C.'s electricity prices were far below those prevailing in adjacent energy markets. It noted that Toronto-based Pollution Probe was critical of low energy prices because they were a deterrent to effective conservation. Consequently, the Task Force recommended a gradual phase-in of market prices for electricity during the following decade, starting in 2003. This would mean ending the NDP's eight-year price freeze on BC Hydro rates. And it would give ratepayers a chance to "adjust" over time to the new market-based pricing system. In the interim, the government could take a major step toward market pricing by implementing a competitive wholesale electricity market. Given the dominant role of BC Hydro within the province, better tie-ins with the Alberta and American systems would be necessary to reduce BC Hydro's market power and to allow a truly competitive wholesale market to operate successfully.

While acknowledging that there had been problems in setting up competitive energy markets in California, Alberta, and Ontario, the Task Force argued that these were exceptional cases resulting from poor market design and certain unique features of these jurisdictions. Instead, it pointed to what it saw as successful market reforms in other parts of the United States, Europe, and Asia as indicators that it was possible to create a market that would behave according to the principles of supply and demand while benefiting both customers and energy investors.

As noted one of the key concerns of the major industrial customers with Ebbels' proposals for market pricing was the fact that BC Hydro's rates were far below the market rate. While the mining and forest industries may have been ideologically supportive of a move to market pricing, from a practical perspective this would involve major increases in their energy bills. Consequently, they wanted continued access to BC Hydro's low embedded cost energy as part of any restructuring package. They got what they wanted. The *BC Hydro Public Power and Legacy and Heritage Contract Act* was passed in November of 2003, establishing a "Heritage Contract." The government claimed this would maintain the benefits (i.e., low rates and security of supply) of B.C.'s public hydroelectric and thermal generating resources for a minimum of ten years. It required BC Hydro to supply 49,000 GWh of energy annually, at prices based on the cost of generation, rather than on the prevailing market price. It also required BC Hydro to supply 10,700 MW of capacity. In the 2007 Energy Plan, the Heritage Contract was extended indefinitely.

This low-cost public energy would be available to the three major categories of customers in rough proportion to their past consumption share, which meant that roughly one third would be allocated to large industrial customers who paid the bulk rate of $35 MWh. Given that BC Hydro would need to purchase new energy from the private sector at prices that would be far higher than the rates it would be charging large industrial customers, this legislation provided a huge subsidy — at least $400 million annually — to B.C.'s mining and forest industries.[27]

The other major outcome of the Ebbels Task Force was the government's 2002 Energy Plan as articulated in *Energy for Our Future: A Plan for B.C.*, referred to earlier in this study. The Energy Plan outlined both an analysis of the issues facing B.C.'s electricity system and a set of numbered recommendations indicating the actions the government intended to take to address these issues.[28] The enactment of the Heritage Contract was the first of these policy actions. The second was carving the transmission system out from BC Hydro into a separate transmission entity and directing it to offer "fair access to all generators," including enhancing its ability to export energy to the United States. The third set out the government's commitment not to sell BC Hydro's generating assets, acknowledging how central they have been in keeping rates down. (However, the Task Force also said that the benefits of public ownership can be maintained even if private energy developers are permitted to play a much larger role in B.C.'s electricity system.)

Policy action four signaled the government's intention to outsource more of BC Hydro's services, which was quickly implemented through the contract with Accenture, moving roughly 1,500 BC Hydro workers to this private services contractor. Action five restored the jurisdiction of the BCUC to regulate BC Hydro rates, a reversal of the previous NDP policy of setting rates by Cabinet. In the accompanying discussion of this policy action, the government indicated that the BCUC would have to determine how to integrate the new, higher-cost energy from private power developers into B.C.'s rate structure. Arguably, this change was intended to shelter the government from the political fall-out of future rate increases, because it could point to the BCUC as the cause of higher rates.

The sixth policy action committed the government to submitting the proposed 265-MW natural gas plant on Vancouver Island near Duke Point to a BCUC review — a review process that lasted three years and resulted in delays that eventually resulted in cancellation of the project at a cost to BC Hydro of approximately $120 million.

Policy action seven indicated that the government wanted to work with adjacent American utilities to further integrate B.C.'s electricity system with that in the Pacific Northwest, including full participation in RTO West (now Grid West), an organization whose purpose is to plan the future growth of the transmission system on both sides of the border in accordance with FERC guidelines.

Action eight divided BC Hydro's distribution functions into a distinct entity responsible for supplying energy to British Columbians. It would purchase the bulk of its energy from BC Hydro's generating arm at rates to be established by the BCUC. Action nine required the distribution division to acquire new energy from suppliers on a "least-cost" basis, subject to full review by the BCUC.

While actions ten and eleven dealt with oil and gas issues, action twelve indicated that the government would greatly strengthen the BCUC's regulatory powers. In the words of the Energy Plan:

> To fulfill its mandate, the Commission will be strengthened by appointing two full-time Commissioners. The Utilities Commission Act will be amended to focus more on performance-based and results-based regulation, including negotiated settlements, and to define effective consumer participation.[29]

Policy actions thirteen to sixteen outline the government's commitment to expanding the role of the private sector in B.C.'s electricity system. Specifically, policy action thirteen specifies that "the private sector will develop new electricity generation with BC Hydro restricted to improvements at existing plants." It also says that the one remaining major hydro dam BC Hydro might want to construct in future could only be built with explicit Cabinet approval, and it would still be subject to a full BCUC review. Policy action fourteen gives major industrial customers the right to purchase energy from suppliers other than BC Hydro, thus effectively allowing retail competition among such buyers. This encouraged industry to self-generate more of its energy and to conserve through the establishment of new "stepped rates."[30]

The fifteenth policy action signaled the government's intent — subsequently implemented — to establish a completely separate transmission company to operate BC Hydro's grid. It also guaranteed private power developers full access to the grid on a "non-discriminatory basis" and provided assurances that future transmission investments would be made in a manner that would enhance the ability of private power suppliers and their customers to have the transmission access they needed. Policy action sixteen gave the BCUC the authority to determine the prices private energy suppliers would pay for use of BC Hydro's existing grid.

The Energy Plan also noted the government's new categories of environmental standards, in which BC Hydro was committed to having 50 percent of its new energy from "clean" sources, primarily small hydro and wind. But it left a gaping loophole that would permit other, not-so-clean generating technologies, such as coal and biomass (wood waste). It thus opened the door to the purchase of new energy from pulp mills that used wood waste and coal, as well as from dedicated coal-fired generating plants. Arguably, B.C.'s established hydro facilities would meet the much more stringent test of "green" but for the fact that such facilities are not what private energy developers are planning to build. Acknowledging that large hydro is also "green" would also make the new environmental standards appear to be a major step backward. And it would enable BC Hydro to flood the market with its enormous volume of hydro-generated electricity, a development that would have a major, negative impact on the ability of private investors to benefit from "green" energy sales to the United States.

As noted above, the new Energy Plan included many, but not all, of the Task Force's other proposals. Perhaps the most important of the Plan's policy actions was the ban on BC Hydro building new generating facilities coupled with the maintenance of its obligation to plan for future provincial energy requirements, meaning that it would have to purchase all additional energy necessary to meet B.C.'s growing needs exclusively from the private sector.

Significantly, the government has presented no evidence that such a ban is in the long-term interest of ratepayers and the public. There are no studies, that this author is aware of that show that it would be cheaper in the long term for BC Hydro to source all its new energy from private power developers. Nor are there any studies that indicate that abandoning the ownership of generating plants — the very assets that currently produce such low rates for customers — would lead to lower rates in ten or twenty years' time. Despite the lack of evidence supporting this approach, the government has arbitrarily imposed the ban so that it can implement its privatization policy.

The importance of the new electricity framework in driving the government's privatization agenda can only be understood in the context of the way it has manipulated B.C.'s modest need to acquire new energy into a supply "crisis" that justifies buying large volumes of new energy from private power developers. By telling the public that B.C. will soon be desperately short of energy, it has deliberately created an atmosphere in which its privatization policies can be portrayed as the only option available to meet the "crisis." And this is despite the fact that a more careful review of B.C.'s future energy needs reveals that there are much better, more secure, and far less costly options that the government has deliberately chosen not to adopt. We will look at this matter in greater detail in Chapter Two.

NOTES

1. Subsequently, Kinder-Morgan sold most of its Terasen assets to Newfoundland-based Fortis Inc.
2. BC Hydro 2004b, 2005a. (This was BC Hydro's submission to the BCUC for a rate increase). Total energy from the 1988 and 1989 "calls" amounted to 2,015 GWh/yr.
3. Independent Power Producers Association of B.C. (IPPABC) website <http://www.ippbc.com/about_ippbc/history/> accessed January, 24, 2006. The date should be "1988" as this is when the first call was announced. More recently the organization has used the title Independent Power Producers of B.C. (IPPBC) but most of the documents to which we refer in this chapter used the organization's earlier name.
4. Ibid. Table 4-4. Total long-term EPAs contracted before 2001 (including Alcan and Island Co-Generation) commit BC Hydro to purchase 5,914 GWh in 2006.
5. See, for example, the table in BC Hydro 2004a. This information is discussed at length further on in this study, in the section dealing with the cost of energy from private sources.
6. The widespread use of the term "deregulation" can be confusing. It implies the abandonment of government regulations, leaving market participants free to arrange their transactions purely on a voluntary, commercial basis. However, in reality, an extensive regulatory framework is actually required to facilitate the operation of energy markets. Far from an absence of state oversight, deregulated energy markets actually require the adoption of strict — and enforceable — rules on how the various participants conduct their activities. Establishing the appropriate rules to prevent various kinds of predatory practices or market abuses has proven challenging, to say the least. For this reason, other terms, such as "restructuring," "market reform," "re-regulation," or "introducing competition" are commonly used to describe the changes to the electricity sector discussed in this study. Nevertheless, given the widespread and continuing use of the term "deregulation" to describe these changes, our approach will continue using this term, but with the caveat that it is not meant to imply the absence of regulation.
7. Natural gas continues to be a key energy source in the United States and as such a critical determinant of electricity prices. According to the U.S. Department of Energy, natural gas accounted for 39.2 percent of total power plant capacity and 18.2 percent of the energy produced in 2005.
8. The requirements of PUHCA were succinctly outlined by American advocacy group Public Citizen as follows: "PUHCA: (1) limits the geographic spread (therefore, size) of utility holding companies, the kinds of business they may enter, the number of holding companies over a utility in a corporate hierarchy, and their capital structure; (2) controls the amount of debt (thus, cost of capital), dividends, loans and guarantees based on utility subsidiaries (so the parents can't loot or bankrupt the utility subsidiary), and the securities that parent companies may issue; (3) regulates self-dealing among affiliate companies and cross-subsidies of unregulated businesses by regulated businesses; (4) controls acquisitions of

other utilities and other businesses; and, (5) limits common ownership of both electric and natural gas utilities." (PUHCA 2003)

9. In the wake of the California energy crisis FERC was pressured to carry out a major analysis of the various price fixing and market scams of Enron. Its report is very illuminating because it describes the various techniques used by the industry to "game" or manipulate the supply and price of energy (U.S. Federal Energy Regulatory Commission 2002). The names given to some of these scams were truly bizarre, including Death Star, Get Shorty, Ricochet, and Fat Boy.
10. Many of the MacDonald Commission's recommendations were widely known well before the final report was released.
11. Significantly, Enron, which at the time — and before its subsequent collapse — was the "poster boy" of the American electricity sector, demanded that it participate on the Task Force. However, the government turned down its request on the basis that it was not a significant player in B.C.'s electricity system.
12. The author was one of two government representatives on the Task Force.
13. It is not the purpose of this study to review the California energy crisis or the other major energy crises triggered in various jurisdictions by the deregulation and privatization of electricity systems. There are literally thousands of articles and books on what went wrong. This literature includes various — and competing — explanations for the failures caused by deregulation. Among the most thoughtful critiques are those written by the staff of American advocacy group Public Citizen (2001, 2002, and 2003) as well as various papers commissioned by APPA. The Canadian Centre for Policy Alternatives in British Columbia also published a number of studies critical of electricity restructuring (Cohen 2001, 2002a, 2002b, 2003).
14. In fact, as we shall see later in this chapter, the Ebbels Task Force interim recommendations actually recommended a 60 percent increase! (Ebbels, 2002).
15. The idea of reconfiguring the grid on a model based on the Vancouver Airport Authority was subsequently advocated a few years later by Larry Bell, the new CEO of BC Hydro (Curtis 2001). While the current government has not adopted this exact model for the newly created B.C. Transmission System, it could still do so.
16. In 1992, the NDP also set up the B.C. Energy Council, to provide policy recommendations on a variety of energy matters. It held hearings and received submissions on electricity issues, but was disbanded several years later. During its brief existence, it also provided a forum for the development of some of the ideas that subsequently became part of the policy agenda of the major private power producers.
17. All of this begs the question of why a public utility owned by the province needs to be regulated by such a Commission. Legislation already provides a vehicle for democratic oversight of BC Hydro's activities. Unlike private corporations, the activities of Crown corporations are subject to public scrutiny in a variety of ways, including questions raised in the Legislative Assembly, in the Budget Estimates and, outside the Legislature, through freedom-of-information requests. In placing BC Hydro within the scope of the BCUC, successive governments have given private energy interests a very effective vehicle to scrutinize its activities and identify those areas where changes in BC Hydro policies and programs

can result in significant benefits either to industrial/commercial customers or to private energy suppliers.

18. The service plan provides a short biography of Mr. Hobbes.
19. At the time Glen Clark, a recently elected NDP MLA, had argued that BC Hydro should acquire West Kootenay Power to enable it to consolidate its position as the exclusive supplier of energy for the entire province and to keep control of B.C.'s electricity system within the province. But the Social Credit government had no interest in expanding public ownership. It did not see the acquisition of WKP by an American energy firm as a significant problem. Given that it was pursuing an aggressive privatization agenda at the time, it preferred American ownership to any expansion of public ownership in B.C.
20. Utilcorp's West Kootenay operations have subsequently been acquired by Newfoundland-based Fortis Energy.
21. Government of B.C., Board Resourcing and Development Office website <http://www.fin.gov.bc.ca/OOP/BRDO/allBios.asp?Board=5367> accessed May 7, 2007.
22. Ibid.
23. Ibid.
24. A less clearly developed formulation of these ideas was floated during the Jaccard Task Force to address the problem of how to accommodate the demands of private power developers, whose cost of new energy was far higher than that of BC Hydro's hydro dams, with the interests of major industrial customers, who did not want to pay the high price of new private energy. The Contract for Differences approach addressed the needs of both business groups through the simple expedient of a major subsidy from BC Hydro (and taxpayers).
25. In fact, there was considerable evidence that the break-up of BC Hydro was already underway by the time of the November 30 Task Force's *Interim Report.* Larry Bell had already indicated he would be divesting a number of the Crown utility's "non-core" assets, including fleet and customer services, and Westech (its information technology division) in late 2001. Soon after, the scope of the divestiture was expanded to include human resources, computer and financial services, and electricity supplies. The bulk of this ended up in the outsourcing contract signed with Accenture.
26. See, for example, the pointed criticisms set out in the Joint Industry Electricity Steering Committee's document: "Strategic Considerations for a New B.C. Energy Policy: A JIESC Response to the *Interim Report of the Task Force on Energy Policy,*" Vancouver, Feb. 12, 2002.
27. For more than a decade, major industrial customers have raised concerns about the potential downside of moving to a competitive energy market. For example, in the Joint Industry Electricity Steering Committee's final submission to the 1995 BCUC Electricity Market Review, they were sharply critical of B.C. moving to full competition. They also made the case that, as customers, they are entitled to continue to receive low-cost public energy from BC Hydro: "[F]ull competition would not have any protection for embedded costs and would require the full de-integration and privatization of BC Hydro. This model is not acceptable, nor do we believe it has been advocated by any party. The customers have paid for the BC Hydro system and should receive the full benefit of the existing em-

bedded costs. Undoubtedly, BC Hydro's customers would have been required to pay the stranded investment costs of any above-market embedded costs had circumstances evolved differently and, accordingly, fairness dictates that they receive the benefits of the existing embedded costs of generation" (BCUC 1995). Significantly, the Heritage Contract does not contemplate other rate structures that would shift benefits to ordinary residential customers or provide lower rates to small users, such as is the case, for example, in Ontario, where the cheapest residential energy is for the first increments and the price rises as consumption levels increase.

28. To minimize the number of references to this legislation, in the following pages the sections will be cited in the text. As these references are all from the same piece of legislation, there should be no difficulty in identifying them.
29. In contradiction to this change, in early 2007 the government imposed new constraints on the BCUC — constraints which many observers saw as a response to the BCUC rejecting BC Hydro's proposed long-term energy agreement with Alcan.
30. Ironically, when the BCUC eventually approved a stepped-rate structure it did so in a manner that actually reduced the cost of the first 90 percent of energy major industrial customers purchased from BC Hydro under the bulk rate. At the same time, it increased the cost of the last 10 percent in such a manner that the overall impact would be revenue neutral. As a result, some industrial customers have actually been able to reduce their costs by using only the lower-priced 90 percent portion of electricity they are entitled to. If nothing else, this arrangement underlines the effectiveness of the lobbying by major industrial customers in protecting their access to cheap public power while ensuring that the public continues to subsidize their electricity rates.

Chapter Two

Pushing the Private Power Agenda

The nationalization of the B.C. Electric Railway Corporation (B.C. Electric) in August 1961 and its incorporation into the newly created provincial Crown corporation, BC Hydro and Power Authority, the following year enabled the provincial government to take responsibility for the province's overall electricity planning. BC Hydro's resulting obligation to plan for the future energy needs of the province has been a key factor in shaping its more recent decisions to purchase new energy from private power developers. In this chapter we will focus on how the government has utilized projections of future energy requirements to justify its decision to source a growing share of B.C.'s energy from private power developers. Our key conclusion is that its claim that there is a major energy "crisis" that necessitates huge purchases of expensive private energy is a creation of its own policies. The government had many other — and better — choices to better manage the future growth of B.C.'s energy requirements, but rejected them in order to implement its privatization agenda. In the following chapter, we shall focus on the high costs of this approach for B.C. ratepayers. However, before examining how the current provincial government has used BC Hydro to implement its private power agenda, it is useful to provide the background to B.C.'s current energy supply situation by briefly reviewing the reasons for the establishment of BC Hydro as a provincial Crown corporation and its subsequent investments in publicly owned energy.

The Columbia River Treaty lies at the heart of the decision to create BC Hydro. Having completed a number of dams on the Columbia River — dams started under Franklin D. Roosevelt's ambitious public works programs in the 1930s — the United States realized that if B.C. could be persuaded to build major reservoirs upstream on the Canadian side, it could assist with flood control on the lower Columbia. In addition, by storing some of the spring run-off, which otherwise would be wastefully "spilled" by American dams, and releasing the water later in the year, B.C. could also enable Bonneville Power, the federal American corporation that owned the dams, to generate a significant amount of additional electricity. The compensation paid to Canada in return for flood control could provide much of the capital to build the new dams, which could also provide B.C. with a major new source of hydro-based electricity.

While the potential benefits of such an arrangement were obvious long before the Treaty was signed, negotiations, involving both federal governments and the province of B.C., dragged on for a number of years during the late 1950s (Tieleman 1983). They also indirectly included some of the major private energy companies that might be affected by construction of the dams. The Treaty itself was initialed in 1961, but the details were only finalized in 1964. This was, in part, because B.C. held out for "up-front" financial compensation from the Americans to enable the province to pay for the huge projects the Treaty would commit it to.

Under the terms of the Treaty, B.C. agreed to build three major dams on the Columbia River to create the huge storage reservoirs the Americans needed. After lengthy — and frustrating — discussions with B.C.'s major private electricity company, B.C. Electric, and its owner, the B.C. Power Corporation, Premier W.A.C. Bennett decided that the only viable course of action to achieve his objectives was to nationalize B.C. Electric, creating a new Crown corporation and using it as the vehicle for developing electricity in the province.

Bennett was a staunch free-enterpriser. He did not make the decision to expropriate because he was an advocate of expanding public ownership, even though some critics called him the "Castro of the North" at the time. Rather, he saw public ownership as a practical measure necessary to ensure that B.C. would have the energy needed to exploit the province's largely untapped resource sector. Cheap electricity was essential to fulfill his ambitious industrial strategy, which was based on the view that the energy potential of the Peace River had to be developed simultaneously with that of the Columbia River. This was referred to as Bennett's "two-river strategy." He successfully linked it to the finalization of the Columbia River Treaty by obtaining an advance payment from the Americans of $274 million for the first thirty years of the "downstream benefits." These were B.C.'s half-share of the additional energy the United States could generate as a result of the new reservoirs on the Canadian side of the border. Without this funding, it would have been very difficult for Bennett to raise the capital needed to carry out development of the Peace River at the same time the province was financing dams on the Columbia (Tieleman 1983).

Among the factors leading to Bennett's decision to expropriate B.C. Electric was the company's inability to enter into an agreement with another private firm, the Peace Power Development Corporation, to purchase the energy that could be developed on the Peace River. B.C. Electric had earlier announced it would build the Burrard Thermal station to serve customers in the lower Mainland and felt it would have enough energy for its future needs from Burrard and the proposed Columbia River development. It was also concerned that energy from the Peace River would cost more and end up being surplus to B.C.'s future needs, meaning that it would have to be exported.

Yet at the time, there was no guarantee that the United States would need this energy, or that Ottawa would provide an export permit for it. So, B.C. Electric saw power development on the Peace River as too risky to support (Tieleman 1983). Without a commitment from B.C. Electric, which owned the lion's share of the province's electricity distribution system in the major load centres — and hence access to the province's customers — development of the Peace River's energy potential was unlikely to proceed.

Bennett reasoned that if the resources of the B.C. interior were to be profitably exploited, the mining and forest industries would need the energy that could be generated from the Peace, as well as that of the Columbia. Failure to develop the Peace would limit the expansion of these industries and frustrate Bennett's vision of a development strategy for the province based on rapid growth of the resource sector (Swainson 1979; Tieleman 1983). And so B.C. Electric's fiscally conservative, shareholder-focussed approach conflicted with Bennett's larger vision of using cheap electricity for industrial development. As well, the fragmentation of both ownership and corporate objectives in the private sector undermined the possibility of creating a coherent province-wide electricity strategy. In the absence of agreement within the private sector on energy priorities, Bennett saw expropriation of B.C. Electric as the only reasonable answer to the achievement of his larger vision.

Once established as a provincially owned Crown corporation, BC Hydro proceeded to make major investments in large hydro facilities and the transmission system required to deliver this new energy to the major load centre in the lower Mainland. The W.A.C. Bennett Dam at the head of the Peace River canyon was completed in 1967, creating the huge Williston reservoir. In the following years, turbines were installed to produce energy from this huge power project. The Peace Canyon Dam was subsequently built fourteen miles downstream. Together, these projects resulted in 3,425 MW of new capacity for BC Hydro's system. On the Columbia River, three major dams were built under the terms of the Columbia River Treaty: Duncan (1968), Keenleyside (1969), and Mica (1973). These were primarily for storage and flood control, although the Mica Dam was also designed to generate energy, with rated capacity of 1,736 MW. Revelstoke, completed in 1984, was the last of the major dams BC Hydro built. And so the construction phase of B.C.'s hydroelectric development was largely finished by the mid-1980s (B.C. Hydro Pioneers 1998).

From the completion of the Revelstoke Dam in 1984 until the turn of the century, these major hydro projects provided the province with a significant, although diminishing, surplus of energy. The one major project BC Hydro still wanted to build — Site "C" — was eventually mothballed due to widespread public opposition, particularly from communities and First Nations in the region that that had been so significantly — and adversely

Figure 1: Increases in B.C.'s Installed Capacity, 1920–2006 (MW)

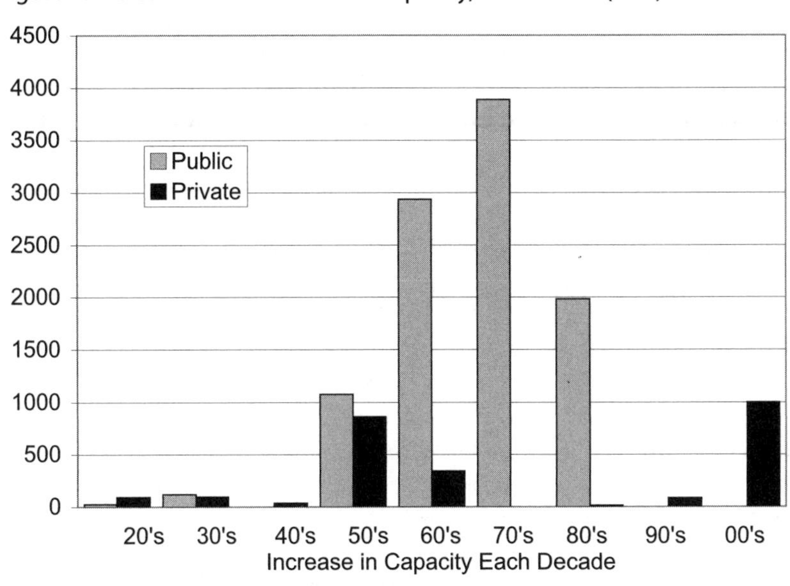

Note: Excludes Alcan but includes Burrard. Source: Heywood 2006.
Source: Statistics Canada: Electric Power Generating Stations 2000 and BC Hydro

— impacted by other dams above and below its proposed location. In addition, the energy it would have generated was surplus to the province's needs at the time and so would have been exported to the United States or Alberta. Given the environmental impact of the project, and the high cost of borrowing the capital needed at that time, the reluctance of the public to support another mega-project, largely for export, was understandable.

The NDP government's 1995 announcement that it would not go ahead with Site "C" was triggered by the decision of the Liberal opposition, in the run up to the 1996 provincial election, to include cancellation of the project in its election platform. Faced with the prospect of Site "C" becoming a significant election issue in constituencies where it was electorally vulnerable, the NDP decided to preempt the Liberals by canceling the project. As a result, BC Hydro has not built any major electricity-generating project in the province since 1984. But, with the growth of B.C.'s population and the expansion of its economy, BC Hydro's energy surplus gradually diminished.

Figure 1, based on data from Statistics Canada and BC Hydro illustrates additions to B.C.'s installed generating capacity over the past century. It shows how rapidly BC Hydro expanded the capacity of the system during the 1960 to 1985 period, the absence of new public investment from 1984 onwards, and, finally, the growth of private energy investments since the Liberals were elected in 2001.

Although BC Hydro's surplus was eroding during the 1990s, the fact that its energy was largely derived from hydroelectric dams, with their enormous storage reservoirs, enabled BC Hydro to continue to supplement its own energy through opportunistic energy trading with the United States and Alberta. This enabled it to deal with the diminishing surplus and put off the need for major new generation investments, at least in the short term. And, along with BC Hydro's own energy, the province also had access to the large block of downstream benefits associated with providing flood control and storage for the American side of the Columbia River. This amounted to about 4,300 GWh of energy annually and 1,200 MW of peak capacity, which, under the terms of the Columbia River Treaty, could be returned to B.C.

However, given that BC Hydro did not need this energy in earlier years due to its energy surplus, W.A.C. Bennett decided to sell the initial thirty years of downstream benefits to the United States, an arrangement that provided cash to cover much of the construction costs of new dams.[1] But, having become became dependent on the resulting income, subsequent governments have been reluctant to return the energy to BC Hydro, even though it could be used to supply B.C. customers as an alternative to purchasing more energy from private power developers. Currently, the province, through Powerex, continues to sell the downstream benefits provided by the Columbia River Treaty to American utilities. The amount it receives for this energy has varied dramatically in recent years due to fluctuations in American electricity prices, reaching a peak of $621 million in 2001 and dropping back to an average of about $250 million in recent years.[2]

However, the government's decision to continue to sell the downstream benefits in the American market has exacerbated the energy supply situation within the province, forcing BC Hydro to purchase additional energy from private power developers in order to meet the terms of the government's Energy Plan.

As noted earlier the government's rationale for requiring BC Hydro to purchase more and more energy from the private sector is based on the assertion that B.C. has a looming supply shortage, and so BC Hydro must acquire large blocks of new energy from private power developers in the coming years to address this shortage. A brief review of the province's current energy supply situation will put this claim into context and will illustrate how the government has manipulated the options available in order to force the Crown corporation to source more energy from private power interests.

As of 2006, BC Hydro was supplying about 57,000 GWh of energy to its provincial system, annually. Of this, roughly 47,000 GWh was generated from its publicly owned hydro facilities. Another 3,300 GWh came from a combination of market purchases and natural-gas generating facilities (prin-

Table 1: BC Hydro Electricity Purchase Agreements (Status as of 2005)

Electricity Purchase Agreements	Firm Energy (GWh)	Dependable Capacity (MW)
Columbia Power Corporation	772	120
Alcan Long-Term Energy Purchase Agreement	1,228	147
Calpine Island Co-Generation Project	1,900	235
Pre-2001 Energy Purchase Agreements	2,115	210
2000 Expressions of Interest	153	2
2001 Green Call	1,054	39
Customer-Based Generation	300	52
2003 Green Call	1,054	39
Duke Point Power Project (Subsequently Cancelled)	(2,000)	(252)

Source: BC Hydro 2005c

cipally Burrard Thermal).[3] It purchased the remaining 6,700 GWh through long-term EPAs. Table 1 shows the status of purchases from private power interests before the major escalation of purchasing from developers in the 2006 block of EPAs (which we shall examine in more detail shortly).

As noted, BC Hydro's storage capacity has made — and continues to make — market purchases very cost effective.[4] Storage capacity gives it the flexibility to determine when to buy and sell on the international energy market. Unlike most other commodities, the price of energy fluctuates dramatically on a daily, weekly, or seasonal basis, depending on short-term supply and demand. Thus, for example, energy purchased in the middle of the night when demand is low may be half or even one-third the price of energy purchased during the late afternoon when demand is normally much higher. The price of energy also varies significantly on a seasonal basis and in the Pacific Northwest is also significantly affected by annual variations in rainfall.

When the energy prices are high, BC Hydro can supply domestic customers with energy from its reservoirs, thus avoiding having to pay high market prices. It can also sell energy back into the market during periods of peak demand — and high prices — in the United States or Alberta. Storage enables BC Hydro to "buy low and sell high." Other forms of electricity generation, such as coal-fired power plants, do not have this flexibility because they lack storage. And, because they cannot easily expand or contract energy output on an hourly, or even daily, basis, they may be forced to sell their energy at whatever price the market establishes (assuming they are dependent on the spot market for their sales).

The gains resulting from BC Hydro's storage capacity have contributed to ensuring adequate supplies of energy while keeping prices low for B.C. customers. The availability of storage has also made it much more economical to operate the Burrard Thermal natural-gas plant, because BC Hydro can usually choose to minimize its operations when gas prices are high, relying instead on hydro-generated electricity from its reservoirs. While natural-gas plants in other jurisdictions tend to operate near full capacity day in and day out, thus making them vulnerable to fluctuations in the price of gas over which they have no control, BC Hydro has the ability to take advantage of the capacity of its gas-powered plant when demand is high in the lower Mainland, while minimizing its use when its much cheaper hydro-generated electricity is sufficient to meet customer requirements.

One other aspect of B.C.'s reservoirs is worth noting. Some of the year-to-year fluctuations in imports are not based on domestic consumption. Rather they may reflect decisions made by BC Hydro to replenish its reservoirs when energy is cheap on the market. This can mean importing 3,000 or 4,000 GWh in some years and exporting it in others. To have a clear picture of the supply situation in B.C., it is thus necessary to look at water levels in the reservoirs in conjunction with the annual import and export figures.

The gradual erosion of BC Hydro's energy surplus would not be a significant problem if B.C.'s economy could continue to function with the amount of energy BC Hydro now generates. Nor would the expansion of private power be a significant public policy issue, because without additional demand there would be little opportunity for new private investment. But, if B.C.'s energy requirements continue to grow as BC Hydro anticipates, the province will need additional energy and capacity to meet the increased demand over the coming decades. It is the projected future growth of energy consumption and the choices about how to meet this growth that have provided the government with its opportunity to reshape B.C.'s electricity system to the benefit of the private sector.

Although BC Hydro is not permitted to build new generating facilities under the government's Energy Plan, it still has responsibility for ensuring that the lights go on. To guarantee that it has adequate supplies of energy, it must make projections of future energy consumption and, based on these projections, acquire the additional power the province will need. New energy projects have a long lead-time — in some cases as much as a decade. This is not only because of the time required for planning and construction, but also because there are a number of other legal requirements, such as environmental assessments (both federal and provincial), which can significantly delay start-up of new facilities. Because the lead-time for new energy investments is so long, BC Hydro must make long-term estimates of future demand and acquire the additional supply it will need, normally on the basis of a twenty-year planning cycle.

BC Hydro's long-term energy forecasts are based on a number of assumptions including population, projected economic growth, estimates of future natural-gas prices, electricity market price trends, and various other factors. To ensure that its forecasts are as accurate as possible, it also incorporates data from a number of outside forecasting agencies, both public — such as the U.S. Department of Energy — and private — such as Calgary-based Confer. This information enables it to develop high, medium, and low estimates of future energy demand. Because so many variables are involved, projections need to be updated regularly. But, despite the increasingly sophisticated models, forecasting future energy demand remains a challenging activity. Not surprisingly, BC Hydro's projections have varied considerably in recent years. In its submission to the 2005–06 Integrated Electricity Planning process, it forecast that the province would require up to an additional 25,000 GWh of energy and 4,200 MW of capacity by 2025, based on a high-load forecast generated in December of 2004.

However, as a result of a new forecast developed in February 2006, BC Hydro revised its estimates significantly upwards. It concluded that B.C. might require as much as 33,200 GWh of additional firm energy by 2025, based on high-load forecast. Its new mid-range forecast was just under 29,000 GWh (BC Hydro 2006b). The timing of this additional demand is also significant: much of it will be needed, according to BC Hydro, within the next decade.

While some of this additional energy might not, in the end, be needed if energy conservation initiatives (principally through BC Hydro's "Power Smart" program) are aggressively implemented — or if concerns about climate change lead to fundamental shifts in energy usage — BC Hydro argues that most will still have to come from new power plants in the province. It assumes that it will need between 900 and 1,300 GWh of new energy, on average, every year for the next two decades, depending on whether the low- or high-load forecast proves correct. Table 2 is a mid-range forecast that includes the impact of BC Hydro's potential demand-side management (DSM) conservation initiatives on B.C.'s future energy requirements. It also takes into account adjustments for line losses.

Faced with the task of meeting the growing demand for energy, BC Hydro has a number of options for achieving this objective. However, as we have seen, the Energy Plan dramatically reduces these options because it requires BC Hydro to source its new energy from private power plants located within the province. While the 4,300 GWh and 1,200 MW of downstream benefits could be used, the government has ruled out this option, preferring to sell this energy in the United States and place the proceeds into general revenues. Site "C," with its estimated annual 4,000 GWh of new energy,

Table 2: BC Hydro Projections of Total B.C. Energy Requirements, February 2006 Estimates (including losses), Demand-Side Management Factored In

Fiscal Year	Forecast with DSM and Adjustments (GWh)
2006/07	58,159
2007/08	58,913
2008/09	59,581
2009/10	60,415
2010/11	61,413
2011/12	62,347
2012/13	63,311
2013/14	64,359
2014/15	64,516
2015/16	65,635
2016/17	66,690
2017/18	67,684
2018/19	68,617
2019/20	69,831
2020/21	71,089
2021/22	72,514
2022/23	73,611
2023/24	74,691
2024/25	75,771
2025/26	76,879

Source: BC Hydro 2006e

requires Cabinet approval, but no such approval has been forthcoming. True, the government's revised 2007 Energy Plan indicates that it will finally ask BC Hydro to review the costs and benefits of this project. But it remains very unlikely that Site "C" would receive approval before BC Hydro has signed many more contracts with private power developers. In the process it will ensure that they are able to develop virtually all B.C.'s easily accessible small hydro and wind projects. Thus, delays in evaluating Site "C" ensure that BC Hydro will continue to rely on major new energy purchases from private power interests in the coming years.

Increasing the price of energy to encourage conservation — especially among large industrial users who pay the bulk rate for just under a third (31 percent in 2006) of the Crown utility's energy — is precluded by the

Heritage Contract, which guarantees that residential customers will continue to access to B.C.'s low-cost public power. As noted in the previous chapter, it also gives a similar entitlement to large industrial customers that pay a much lower rate for their energy, arguably reducing their incentive for conservation.[5] Reliance on market purchases from the international energy market is also limited by the government's policy of sourcing new energy from within the province. And, BC Hydro's tendering process has made it difficult for Columbia Power, a regional Crown corporation set up by the NDP a decade ago, to sell BC Hydro more energy.

All these restrictions have narrowed BC Hydro's options, effectively forcing it to acquire the new energy it needs from B.C.-based private power developers through long-term energy supply contracts. Doing so involves issuing a tender call, normally about once a year, for bids from B.C. private energy developers who wish to supply part of BC Hydro's future needs.[6] BC Hydro evaluates the bids and ranks them by price, location, and a variety of other factors. It then offers contracts to private power developers whose bids are below the cut-off line for the total amount of new energy required in the tender.[7]

By 2005, BC Hydro had concluded sixty-one EPA contracts with private developers, including both those it had inherited over the previous decade and those it had entered into because of the current government's Energy Plan. In its 2005 submission to the BCUC for its 2005 Resource Expenditure and Acquisition Plan, BC Hydro outlined the status of private energy purchase contracts at that time:

> BC Hydro has an ongoing acquisition program and continues to acquire electricity from private producers of power generation. This activity is consistent with Policy Action #13 of the Energy Plan. Currently, 34 IPPs provide approximately 7,000 GWh of electricity to BC Hydro's system. A further 27 IPPs are contracted to bring on over 4,100 GWh of supply in the future. BC Hydro has incorporated the voluntary Energy Plan goal (Policy Action #20) of acquiring 50 percent of new supply from "B.C. Clean Electricity" sources developed in-province into its energy acquisition processes. Of the total of 61 contracts, 37 are for green energy, providing over 2,900 GWh. (BC Hydro 2005a-1: s2, 3)[8]

The 2006 energy call, issued in December 2005, sought tenders for 2,700 GWh of new energy. BC Hydro received sixty-one tenders from thirty-seven bidders for fifty-three projects before the deadline of April 7, 2006. This included 6,500 annual GWh of energy and 1,800 MW of capacity. The bids were spread among five sources of generation: small hydro, waste heat, wind, biomass, and coal (BC Hydro 2006b).

When the results of the tender call were announced on July 27, 2006, BC Hydro made a stunning announcement: it had decided to purchase more than three times the energy requested in the original tender. It awarded contracts for thirty-eight projects totaling 7,125 GWh of new energy from private power developers (BC Hydro 2006b). Fully 40 percent of this energy was from small hydro projects and another 14 percent came from wind. (We will look in more detail at the financial implications of these energy supply contracts in the following chapters.) Significantly, BC Hydro decided to accept two contracts for coal-based energy that included an estimated 2,032 GWh of energy, representing 28 percent of the total call award. Finally, 1,185 GWh, 18 percent of the total, went to purchases of energy generated from biomass (primarily wood waste). In other words, power plants burning fossil fuels accounted for roughly 46 percent of the total. This was a major and, some would argue, very regressive environmental precedent for the province (Calvert 2006b, 2007a).

As noted earlier, the province's Energy Plan effectively bans BC Hydro from building new power plants, including run-of-the-river, wind, geothermal, and other "green" or innovative types of generating facilities. Of the three limited exceptions to the ban — adding new turbines to existing dams, re-powering the Burrard Thermal natural-gas plant and building Site "C" — BC Hydro has acted on only one. It is now retrofitting existing dams with additional turbines under the "Resource Smart" program. Arguably, this is necessary to accommodate the increasing amount of non-firm energy BC Hydro is now purchasing from small hydro and wind-farm projects. Because the energy generated by these projects fluctuates dramatically, either on a seasonal (small hydro), or daily (wind), basis it needs to be augmented with capacity from another energy source. By adding new turbines to its existing dams, BC Hydro can provide the needed capacity. Without it, the non-firm private energy could negatively affect the reliability of the grid. In short, the decision to pursue the "Resource Smart" option was not only a way to extract more energy from its existing hydro facilities: it was also a way to facilitate additional purchases of non-firm private energy. (The decision to purchase coal and biomass energy in the 2006 tender, some might argue, also reflects the need to provide additional capacity to balance the low-capacity energy from run-of-the-river and wind-farm contracts.)

The second exception to the ban on BC Hydro building new power plants was that it might be allowed to maintain, or upgrade, the old Burrard Thermal natural-gas plant, located near the lower Mainland load centre. The Burrard plant uses relatively inefficient single-cycle gas turbine technology. Retrofitting it with modern combined-cycle turbines would significantly increase its efficiency, an important consideration given the cost of natural gas.

Historically, Burrard has served several functions in BC Hydro's system. In addition to generating energy, Burrard acts as a back-up supply for the lower Mainland, where about half of B.C.'s electricity is consumed. This is important, because if a natural disaster were to interrupt the supply from the main transmission lines connecting the lower Mainland to the Peace and Columbia hydro facilities, Burrard would still be available to provide some energy to customers. Its location near the load centre and its significant capacity makes it an important "insurance policy."

At the time of writing (early 2007), Burrard operates at a fraction of its potential because gas prices are high and it is much cheaper to supply the lower Mainland from BC Hydro's hydro-based energy or from market purchases. Consequently, Burrard is used primarily to meet peak load requirements in the lower Mainland. However, its significant capacity — 950 MW — and its ability to meet peak load demand is an important supplement to the energy BC Hydro buys on the open market and to the much cheaper energy it generates from its hydro facilities. Burrard adds flexibility to the system without having to be operated primarily as a source of expensive energy.

However, in 2006 — perhaps under government direction — BC Hydro decided to mothball the Burrard plant by 2013 (BC Hydro 2006b).[9] To compensate for this major loss of supply, BC Hydro must acquire an equivalent amount of new energy from other sources, and, under the Energy Plan, this will have to come from private power developers. In other words, by choosing to close Burrard, BC Hydro has created a future shortage. It then used this projected shortage to justify acquiring a much larger amount of new private energy in the 2006 tender call, and will presumably continue to use the shortfall as a justification for additional purchases in subsequent tender calls.

The third exception to the province's ban on BC Hydro building new generating capacity was Site "C." At the time of the 2002 Energy Plan, the government indicated that BC Hydro could only build Site "C" with explicit Cabinet approval. It assured BC Hydro that if Site "C" were to be built, it would be owned by the Crown utility.[10] However, in November of 2006, the government announced that all major capital projects valued at more than $20 million would have to be public-private partnerships. It is not clear at the time of writing whether the province's earlier commitment to BC Hydro regarding Site "C" would be exempt from this policy, but the likelihood of BC Hydro proceeding with this project on its own remains an open question. Perhaps more importantly, by indefinitely delaying a decision on Site "C," the government has forced the Crown utility to purchase even more energy from the private sector.

The Energy Plan's arbitrary ban on BC Hydro building new generating facilities was not evidence based. It was not accompanied by reference to any studies that demonstrated that it would be cheaper in the long run for ratepayers to acquire energy from private power interests. It ignored the long-term public policy consequences of private ownership and control of B.C.'s renewable power generating assets.[11] As a result, the true cost to ratepayers of buying all future energy from private energy developers is simply unknown. And, because BC Hydro is not building new projects, it no longer has its own benchmarks with which to compare the prices it is paying to the private sector. While the government and BC Hydro maintain that the highly restrictive competitive tendering process provides sufficient protection for the public, as we have seen, the Energy Plan limits the basis for competition to new private power projects in B.C. and follows a costing methodology that fails entirely to consider the long-term value of hydro assets.

The latter point illustrates the questionable nature of the province's claim that purchasing power from private developers is no more expensive than having BC Hydro provide it. In the 2005 Integrated Electricity Planning process, in which the author participated, BC Hydro costed various energy resource options on the basis of twenty-year price projections. Thus, for example, the cost per MWh from Site "C" (if BC Hydro were to build it) was compared to the cost of purchasing energy from various private suppliers, including coal-fired plants, wind and small private hydro projects, geothermal projects and other options. The methodology looked at the cost per MWh of each alternative and assumed it would be supplied over a twenty-year period, either as an energy purchase contract with the private-sector supplier, or, in the case of Site "C," as a project owned by BC Hydro.

However, this costing methodology gave no consideration to the ownership — or asset value — at the end of the period. It simply ignored the fact that Site "C" — or small hydro or wind if built publicly — would be owned by BC Hydro and would provide low-cost energy for many decades into the future once the capital cost had been paid down. Conversely, in the case of privately owned energy projects, it took no account of the fact that on expiry of its EPAs, BC Hydro would own nothing. Therefore it would have to renew the contracts at the prevailing price twenty or thirty years into the future and continue to do so as long as it required this energy. According to a 2003 study prepared for the B.C. Ministry of Sustainable Resource Management, many small hydro projects can be expected to operate for roughly 100 years (Stothert Engineering 2003).

To illustrate the fundamental problem with this approach to costing energy, an analogy may be helpful. Suppose two individuals are offered housing at the same monthly payment for twenty years. In one case, the payment takes the form of rent. In the other, the payment is to pay down a twenty-year mortgage. The monthly payments are identical. For the first twenty years, each individual pays the same and enjoys the same quality of accommodation. However, at the end of the period, the renter has nothing and must renew the rent at levels prevailing at that point in time. In contrast, the individual who paid down the mortgage now owns the property and will no longer have to incur a monthly payment to continue enjoying its benefits. A rational costing of these two options would not lead to the conclusion that it is just as beneficial to rent as to own. But this is exactly the conclusion BC Hydro draws from its methodology. Ownership of assets — in this case hydro generating facilities — is entirely ignored in its approach to costing energy options. It is only by ignoring the question of asset ownership that BC Hydro can come up with numbers that make purchasing energy from private interests seem comparable to building public projects.

This costing methodology is fundamentally misleading — and fiscally irresponsible — because it fails to incorporate the normal "due diligence" required to protect the public's financial interests — due diligence that would take into account all relevant financial issues, including asset ownership. Instead, BC Hydro has justified its purchases of private energy on the basis of comparing only the short-term costs of different options, deliberately excluding all the historical evidence that public ownership of assets does, in fact, significantly impact electricity prices over the long term, to the benefit of B.C. ratepayers.[12]

The problematic economics of many of these small private hydro projects — in the absence of generous public subsidies — is also confirmed by the findings of a 2003 research study on small hydro sponsored by the Ministry of Sustainable Resource Management. In it, the government consultants acknowledge that "the vast majority of projects will sell power to BC Hydro under long-term contract" (Stothert Engineering 2003).[13] In other words, these projects depend on the public sector to buy their energy: otherwise they do not get built.[14] To put it more bluntly, without a BC Hydro energy supply contract, most are uneconomic at prices currently prevailing in the Pacific Northwest energy market.

While BC Hydro could continue to supply some of its future energy needs through purchases on the international energy spot market, the government has rejected this approach. Its rationale for this policy is threefold. First, it would expose ratepayers to the unpredictability — and risk — of this market, and so it is preferable to lock in contracts at known prices than face the price risk of the market. However, as we shall see in the next chapter, evidence from various forecasting agencies indicates that international energy prices are not likely to increase from current levels for many years. Second, it argues that buying from within the province will provide greater long-term security of supply. However, sourcing from private energy developers in the context of a policy framework that has opened the door to private energy exports from B.C. does not increase security of supply for B.C. ratepayers. Third, the government maintains that sourcing new energy from "green" projects within the province avoids the negative environmental impacts of energy imports from fossil-fuel burning power plants in neighbouring jurisdictions. However, this ignores both the fact that BC Hydro is continuously buying and selling energy on a daily basis in the American and Alberta spot markets and that much of the energy in the Pacific Northwest is hydro-based.

An alternative explanation for the government's policy is much more persuasive: allowing BC Hydro the option of purchasing a greater share of its future energy from the international energy market would lower the volume of energy BC Hydro needs to acquire from private power developers within the province and thus reduce the likelihood of many of the projects actually getting built in the first place. Also, having the option of purchasing from the energy market would give BC Hydro more leverage in negotiating prices with private energy developers within the province. While this would benefit ratepayers, it would reduce the profitability of private power plants.

Even within the context of those who advocate a competitive energy market in B.C., the policy is difficult to justify, because it effectively exempts B.C.-based private energy generators from price competition with other neighbouring jurisdictions — in both the short-term and long-term markets — and exempts them from competition from other public options. Private developers can thus obtain prices through BC Hydro contracts that are much higher than either the price BC Hydro would pay if it generated the energy itself or the price it would pay to out-of-province suppliers if permitted to rely on this market for some of its future energy requirements. In short, the government's policy framework has resulted in a very sweet deal for private power interests in B.C.

Another factor further sweetens the arrangement. BC Hydro is paying small hydro and wind-farm developers premium prices for non-firm energy.[15] To understand why this is so it is necessary to understand the difference between "firm" and "non-firm" energy and how this difference is reflected in the price of electricity. In purchasing energy from small hydro and wind projects, BC Hydro has to consider both the total amount of energy it needs (GWh) and the "firmness" of the energy; that is, the capacity (MW) of the generator to provide a minimum constant supply to meet load requirements day in and day out. Firm energy is particularly valuable during peak demand periods.[16] Energy that is reliably available when it is most needed is considerably more valuable than energy that is only available intermittently. Consequently, firm energy normally commands a significant price premium in energy markets.[17]

As noted earlier, two of the most important variables that determine the value — and the price — of energy are its quantity and its availability when needed. Its quantity is the total amount of energy, expressed in kilowatt hours (for domestic use), megawatt hours for larger commercial users, or in the much larger denomination of gigawatt hours for system-wide calculations. These numbers represent the total amount of energy used over a period of time.

The second variable is capacity. It refers to the instantaneous availability of energy when needed. Electricity needs to be there when the lights are switched on. It is not helpful if there is little or no energy available during periods of peak demand (either hourly, daily, or seasonally) and in great surplus at other times. In periods of high demand, it is essential that the system has the ability to provide all the energy that customers require: otherwise, they will have to limit their consumption or, worse, face blackouts if there is not enough energy in the system to meet peak demand.

Capacity is normally measured in megawatts. Electricity systems require a balance between the total energy produced over time and the instantaneous, or rated, capacity of the system. Firm energy is energy that is properly balanced with capacity. Non-firm energy is intermittent and may not be available on a reliable basis when needed.

While capacity varies significantly from one power facility to another, run-of-the-river and wind generating facilities are generally low in capacity, and much of their energy is non-firm.[18] Energy production from run-of-the-river projects varies according to the location, annual rainfall, and timing of the spring run-off. Normally, the bulk of energy from small hydro is generated in a short two-to-three-month freshet "window," with very little produced the rest of the year. The variation between production at the height of the freshet and at its annual low point can be a ratio of ten to one, or even more. This means that, for most of the year, they produce little, or no, firm energy, a problem particularly acute during low-flow periods if there is competition for water use for irrigation, fish spawning, or tourism activities.

Wind generation varies significantly both during time of day and from week to week. While, ideally, wind farms are located in areas of strong, constant winds, the fact remains that weather is unpredictable. Hence, wind is low in capacity and much of the energy it generates is not firm. One of the major challenges in incorporating wind energy into an existing grid is the need to have adequate back-up to deal with sudden changes in wind-energy production. Without back-up, the dramatic swings in wind-based output can destabilize the system. This, in turn, can lead to reliability problems and unplanned outages, so a number of utilities have raised concerns that having too much wind energy entering their systems could undermine system reliability. They have argued that the share of wind energy entering the system must be limited.

In contrast, large hydro projects, which have storage reservoirs, as well as natural-gas and coal systems, all have high capacity. To achieve the right balance between energy and capacity, BC Hydro must augment its purchases of low-capacity, small hydro energy with energy sources of high capacity. It has normally done this by using the capacity in its reservoirs to balance the "capacity-lite" energy from wind and run-of-the-river sources.[19]

The reason BC Hydro can offer to purchase large volumes of non-firm energy from private run-of-the-river or wind-farm projects is because it can store this energy in its large hydro reservoirs (and, as noted earlier, with additional investment it can also create additional capacity to match this energy by adding, or upgrading, turbines in existing dams). In doing this, it adds enormously to the energy's value, because it then can be used as firm energy on a year-round basis.

All of this may not matter in years of low rainfall. However, if natural rainfall in a high-precipitation year is sufficient to raise BC Hydro's reservoirs up to their maximum level, the utility may not need this run-of-the-river or wind-farm energy. It may, as a consequence, end up "spilling" water, or exporting energy at a time when energy prices are low because the Pacific Northwest energy market has a surplus due to its high proportion of large hydro-based energy generation. This means foregoing the potential energy — and revenue — from this water.

But if BC Hydro has committed to paying private energy developers a fixed amount for their energy each year — and to accepting large volumes of non-firm energy as part of its EPAs — it may end up buying energy it doesn't need and can't store because its reservoirs have no more storage available. It is not easy to predict how great this financial risk is for BC Hydro and its ratepayers, but it is certainly one that suggests that the final costs of these contracts could be significantly higher than BC Hydro asserts.

Consequently, BC Hydro's storage may end up being used, indirectly, to further subsidize private energy interests through a pricing structure that effectively pays far too generously for non-firm energy, thus assuring a market for energy that otherwise might be difficult to sell — or difficult to sell at prices that would give investors a suitable profit. Indeed, without a contract with BC Hydro, many developers would have difficulty selling their energy to other customers precisely because it is not firm. And, even if they were able to sell it, they would have to do so at the much lower prices commanded by non-firm energy.

Using BC Hydro's storage to accommodate the energy production of private run-of-the-river and wind projects has another cost. It reduces the utility's ability to use its storage to maximize the benefits it obtains from energy trading with the United States and Alberta. Long before Powerex was established as an energy marketer in the United States, BC Hydro was using its storage capacity to buy and sell energy at the border. When hourly energy prices in Alberta or the United States were low, it would conserve its water in favour of purchasing cheap out-of-province energy, and then sell it back when prices were high. Similarly, it would use Burrard's capacity to generate energy if the price of natural gas made doing so economical, or it would buy out-of-province energy when gas prices were too high.

However, committing large amounts of storage to accommodate non-firm energy purchased from private generators in B.C. through long-term contracts greatly reduces the flexibility and economic benefits of this storage capacity for both BC Hydro and its ratepayers. Instead of buying energy cheaply when it is available in the United States or Alberta and re-selling it at higher prices, BC Hydro is increasingly committed to using its storage to fulfill its contractual obligations to private run-of-the-river projects.

This raises the question of whether the costs of this arrangement are being properly factored into the calculation of the impact of long-term energy purchases that the province's Energy Plan commits BC Hydro to. An analysis of the 2006 tender process suggests that BC Hydro is buying too much of the wrong type of energy — and paying far too much for it.

The same concerns apply to energy purchased from wind farms. Locating wind farms near the large reservoirs on the Peace and Columbia Rivers is beneficial to wind-farm investors because these areas are among the most suitable locations to maximize output of their turbines. But this energy is far from load centres. And it is very expensive — far more so than it would be to simply acquire energy from the international market during non-peak periods. Wind farms on Vancouver Island have more promise, but are still very expensive to build and suffer from the critical weakness that their energy is not reliable and must be backed up by other suppliers that have capacity. From the perspective of both BC Hydro customers and the general public, all this raises fundamental questions about the advisability of the government's energy acquisition strategy.

One other issue needs to be raised in this context. As noted earlier, private energy interests view BC Hydro's large storage capacity as an untapped resource that could enable them to obtain far higher prices in the American energy market for their low-capacity energy. However, BC Hydro, for reasons explained above, has been reluctant to allow private interests to use its storage capacity, because doing so would seriously compromise its ability to use its storage for opportunistic energy trading. However, lobbying by private interests for access to storage, which began in a modest way during the 1990s, can be expected to escalate dramatically as more and more private energy interests in B.C. develop run-of-the-river and wind-farm energy. This could change the political dynamic, because these interests can be expected to increase their demands for access to storage so that they can sell firm "green energy" to the United States at premium prices.

Of course, they could also try to match their low-capacity energy with other private generators that have capacity-rich resources such as coal, natural gas (less likely given the unpredictability of future prices), or co-generating plants in pulp mills or other industrial facilities. (Co-generating facilities normally combine production of heat or steam for manufacturing or processing materials with the use of this heat for production of electricity.) Indeed, some private developers may try to do this, but it is still less attractive than BC Hydro's storage because it doesn't provide the flexibility to sell at premium prices — one of the key benefits of large hydro storage. While private power companies have solved this problem for the immediate future through the contracts they now have with BC Hydro, the issue will arise again once the EPAs expire.

The key concern, from the perspective of ratepayers, is that at some point, the province may cave in to the demands of private energy developers and allow them to use BC Hydro's storage. Most customers will not likely appreciate the significance of such a decision — until it shows up in the form of higher electricity bills and reduced dividends resulting from BC Hydro's revenue losses. Additionally, if BC Hydro's storage is made available to some private energy developers, it may be impossible to deny it to others seeking similar opportunities. And, it may also be impossible to stop providing storage, because BC Hydro will be required to adhere to Canada's investor-rights obligations under NAFTA's Chapter Eleven. These obligations may force it to maintain policies favourable to private American investors, regardless of the impact on B.C. ratepayers and taxpayers.

We have argued here that the provincial government has used the projected growth in B.C.'s energy demand to create opportunities for private power developers to sell increasing volumes of energy to BC Hydro. To do so, it has adopted policies that have forced BC Hydro to reject a number of much better options. These include bringing back the downstream benefits, re-powering the Burrard Thermal plant, fast-tracking the evaluation of Site C, raising the very low prices charged under the Heritage Contract to major industrial customers who use a third of BC Hydro's energy, continuing to rely on market purchases when they make economic sense, and, finally, allowing BC Hydro to build small hydro and wind-farm projects. By rejecting other alternatives, the government has manufactured an "energy supply crisis" to facilitate the expansion of private power developments within the province. This has resulted in BC Hydro making commitments to purchase increasing volumes of high-priced energy from private power producers under long-term contracts that expose ratepayers to major price risks during the contracts and both price and security-of-supply risks once these contracts expire. The government is forcing BC Hydro to purchase far too much of the wrong type of energy, a practice that may limit its future ability to make full use of the opportunities it enjoys from the storage capacity in its major reservoirs. As we shall see in the following chapter, the financial costs of this policy to ratepayers will be extremely high.

NOTES

1. The downstream benefits were allocated on the basis of the completion of the three dams and were originally scheduled to come up for renegotiation in 1998 (9 percent), 1999 (46 percent) and 2003 (45 percent). The basis of the calculation of energy was that Canada would get half the additional amount of energy generated in the United States as a result of B.C. dams holding back water in its new reservoirs during the spring flood, which could be used later in the year by American power plants to generate extra electricity.
2. Source: BC Hydro response to a request from the Joint Industry Electrical Steering Committee during the BCUC hearings on the 2005/2006 BC Hydro Revenue Requirement Application, March 29, 2004. For more recent data and future projected revenues from downstream benefits sales, see Government of B.C. 2007b. The downstream revenue amounts are as follows: F2003/04 – $230 million; F2004/05 – $258 million; F2005/06 – $319 million; F2006/07 – $235 million, and projected F2007/08 – $285 million.
3. Under the Heritage Contract, approximately 49,000 GWh of BC Hydro's public energy is earmarked for B.C. customers at prices based on BC Hydro's historical cost of supply (that is, considerably below current market rates). This amount actually varies somewhat depending on annual rainfall and snow-pack conditions. It is worth noting that the amount of energy generated within the province is more than that delivered to customers, largely due to line losses on the transmission grid. Depending on line capacity, voltage, distance, and other factors, a portion of the energy put into the system is lost. This sometimes leads to confusion, because the numbers associated with energy produced at the source of generation may be as much as 10 percent, or even more, higher than the energy actually delivered. For example, in 2006, the amount of energy delivered to customers was 52,440 GWh, somewhat less than the 57,000 GWh total cited above. Using the delivered volume, the breakdown among categories of customers was as follows: Residential, 16,261 GWh (31 percent); Light Industrial and Commercial, 17,913 GWh (34 percent); Large Industrial, 16,428 GWh (31 percent); and Other, 1,838 GWh (4 percent) (BC Hydro *Annual Report* 2006f).
4. Short-term market purchases are not to be confused with long-term energy supply contracts. The former are based on the spot market price of energy, which, as noted, can vary quite dramatically on a daily, weekly, and seasonal basis. The latter involves commitments to purchase fixed amounts of energy every year over a long-term period at prices specified in the contract. Normally, they are "take or pay," which means the purchaser must take the specified amount of energy at the agreed price. If the purchaser ends up not needing the energy, it still must pay the agreed amount.
5. Although large industrial customers used 31 percent of BC Hydro's delivered energy in 2006, their share of BC Hydro's revenues from domestic sales only amounted to 22 percent of the total, largely because of the very low bulk-rate

schedule, which offers them a rate of roughly $37 per MWh.

6. However, in the spring of 2007, the government announced that BC Hydro would also accept contract proposals from private projects of less than 10 MW on an ongoing basis, meaning that proponents did not have to wait for the next tender call to submit a bid.
7. Tender calls include both firm and non-firm energy. Estimates of the amount of additional energy required each year vary. Projections for 2006 were for 800 GWh of firm energy, up to 800 GWh of non-firm energy, and 200 GWh of energy from small hydro. The estimated requirement for the following year was 1,000 GWh of firm energy (BC Hydro 2005a-1).
8. It should be noted that although BC Hydro has signed contracts for this amount of energy, a number of the private power developers have not been able to deliver the energy they promised at the price BC Hydro offered. Consequently, the total amount of energy that will be delivered is somewhat less than these numbers indicate.
9. This was confirmed by the author in a telephone call to BC Hydro staff in January 2007.
10. The author, who was a member of the 2005 Integrated Electricity Planning Committee, asked Vice President Bev Van Leuven specifically whether the government had committed to BC Hydro that Site "C," if built, would be public and owned by BC Hydro. She assured the author and other members of the IEPC that the government had written to BC Hydro formally making this commitment.
11. Interestingly, in promoting public-private partnerships in other areas of the public sector, the government normally uses a "public sector comparator," a concept borrowed from Thatcher's Private Finance Initiative. This "comparator" is used to estimate the cost of public provision of infrastructure for purposes of comparing with a public-private, or entirely private, alternative. Setting aside the question of whether this approach is being utilized in a fair and balanced way, the fact is that in the area of electricity, the government does not even require BC Hydro to attempt to estimate what the costs would be for it to build new small hydro or wind-farm generation as a benchmark with which to compare private-sector costs.
12. It should not be inferred from this that the cost estimates of small private hydro projects were as low as Site "C." In fact, they were actually considerably higher, even though the costing numbers for of Site "C" included paying down the capital cost of building the facility and paying a $4 premium per MW on the water rental fee, compared with small private projects. (This subject is explored in a later chapter dealing with private hydro projects.)
13. The length of these long-term contracts can vary significantly. In the 2006 call, BC Hydro provides options in five-year intervals ranging from a minimum contract length of fifteen years to a maximum of forty years.
14. BC Hydro distinguishes between small hydro and micro-hydro. The following is the utility's definition of each, taken from BC Hydro's website: "While definitions of the terms "micro" and "small hydro" vary significantly, Hydro considers micro-hydro developments as ones with an installed capacity of less than 2 MW (2,000 kW). We apply the term "small hydro" to developments with installed

capacities between 2 and 50 MW."

15. BC Hydro uses the term "firm energy" to describe much of what it is purchasing, but this applies to the total package, which is composed of a few projects — particularly coal and biomass — that have significant capacity, along with many wind and run-of-the-river projects, which have little or no capacity.
16. Firm energy is electrical energy supported by sufficient capacity, interruptible only on conditions agreed upon by contract. In other words, it must be fully available at all times and cannot be interrupted due to fluctuations in the generation supply.
17. To give a simple illustration, the American energy publication *BTU Weekly* has separate tables for off-peak and peak energy prices — prices that reflect capacity as well as energy. The price spread fluctuates significantly from week to week, but using the first week in July 2005, we find that the price of "on-peak" electricity at COB (a major hub for energy trading in the United States) fluctuated from $53.29 to $56.50, while the "off-peak" price varied from $33.40 to $42.16. The ability to supply energy during peak demand periods carries quite a significant price premium. While "on-peak" and "off-peak" designations are slightly different from "firm" and "non-firm," they illustrate the importance of having energy available whenever it is required, as opposed to simply generating energy in varying amounts during any specific timeframe.
18. Because the freshet occurs at different periods in different locations in the province, it is possible to develop a mix of run-of-the-river projects that expand the period when high volumes of energy are being generated and thus reduce the capacity problem to some degree. But without storage, there is little that can be done to compensate for major reductions in stream flows — and energy generation — in late summer and autumn.
19. Thus, in modeling portfolios of energy for the 2005 IEPC process, BC Hydro had to balance the most "green" portfolios — that is, those containing the largest component of run-of-the-river and wind energy — with additional capacity from its major hydro dams. To do this it had to assume that it would install additional turbines in existing dams to make up for the lack of capacity of run-of-the-river projects.

Chapter Three

The High Cost of Private Power

IN THIS CHAPTER, WE TURN our attention to the cost of purchasing energy from private power developers. We will illustrate how much more expensive it has been, historically, for BC Hydro to rely on private energy purchases compared with generating its own energy. We will then examine the costs of the very large purchases that BC Hydro has made in its more recent energy contracts — costs that will dramatically increase the price of electricity for ordinary ratepayers. These contracts also force BC Hydro's ratepayers to accept major price risks while providing no guarantees of either security of supply or price once the expensive EPAs have expired. However, to provide an appropriate context for this analysis, we will begin with a discussion of the reasons why BC Hydro's own energy now costs so much less than either market purchases or contracts with private power developers.

There are two key reasons why BC Hydro's public energy has provided ratepayers with low and very stable energy prices in recent years. First, in owning its energy generating facilities, BC Hydro's cost structure is based on the historical price of investments made thirty or forty years ago. Like the homeowner who has paid off a mortgage, BC Hydro and its ratepayers have been able to enjoy the benefits of assets whose costs have been largely written down. Second, BC Hydro, as a matter of policy, has chosen to charge its customers rates based on its very low cost of production, rather than prevailing prices in the energy market. The maintenance of a cost-of-production rather than a market approach to setting prices has been — and remains — enormously beneficial to the province's ratepayers.

To get a sense of how successful public ownership of energy resources has been for all categories of B.C. customers, it is helpful to compare the province's electricity prices with those in other jurisdictions in both Canada and the United States. Every year, Hydro Québec does a detailed analysis of prices across North America and publishes them in its annual *Comparison of Electricity Prices in Major North American Cities*.

Hydro Québec includes a breakdown among various customer categories, including residential and small, medium, and larger power customers. In every category, B.C. ranks in virtually a dead heat for the lowest prices in North America. And the other two low-price utilities, Manitoba Hydro and Hydro Québec, are also publicly owned. Figure 2 compares residential rates, using Montréal as the basis-of-comparison benchmark (that is, assigning it a value of 100 and ranking the others higher or lower depending on their

Figure 2: Hydro Quebec 2006 Residential Customer Rate Comparison

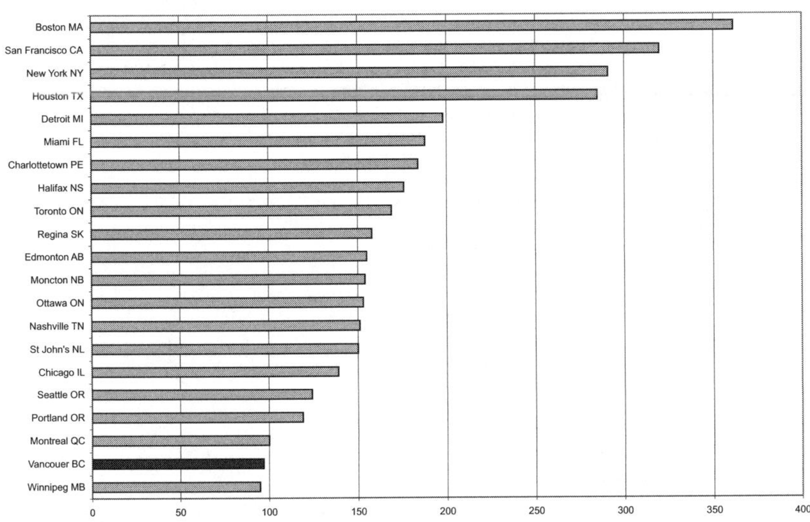

Source: Hydro Québec 2006 Comparison of Electricity Prices in Major North American Cities

Figure 3: Hydro Quebec 2006 Medium Power Customer Rate Comparison

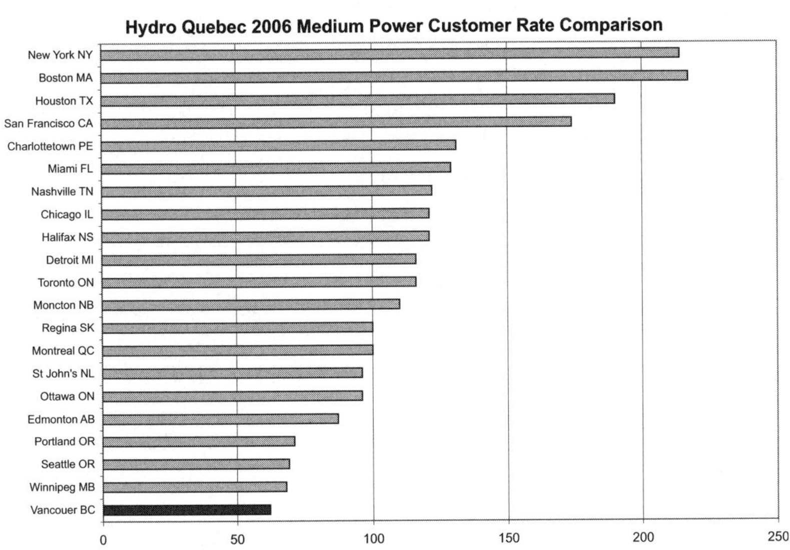

Source: Hydro Québec 2006 Comparison of Electricity Prices in Major North American Cities

Figure 4: Hydro Quebec 2006 Comparison of Electricity Rates: Large Industrial Customers (over 3 GWh monthly, 5000 KW capacity)

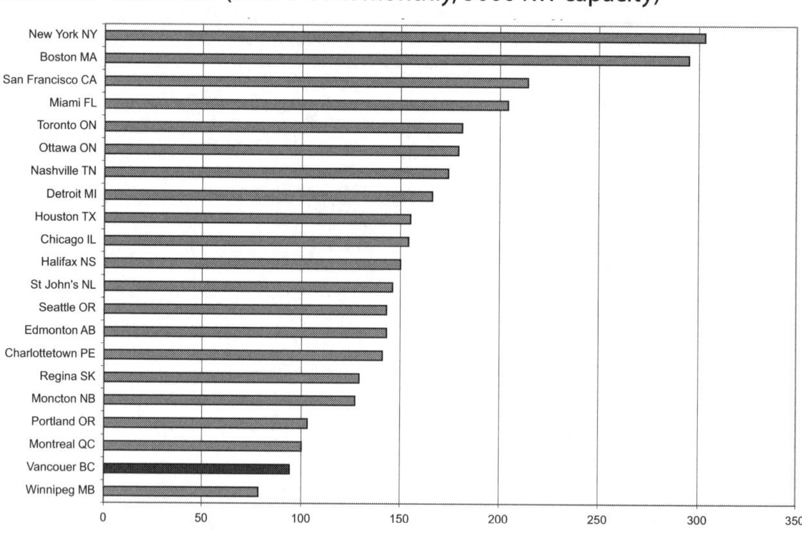

Source: Hydro Québec 2006 Comparison of Electricity Prices in Major North American Cities

relative price). B.C. has the second-lowest prices in the residential survey, only marginally above those of Manitoba.

When we turn to commercial and industrial customers, the pattern is broadly similar. Figure 3 shows the rates paid by medium-sized customers using more than 100 MWh a month, again using Hydro Québec rates as an index of 100. In this case, B.C.'s rates are actually lower than those of its nearest rival, Manitoba, and still below those of any jurisdictions in which energy is supplied by the private sector.[1] Figure 4 shows a similar pattern in the rates charged to large power customers in the various jurisdictions.

Hydro Québec also includes in its comparisons several intermediate categories of medium-sized power users, with similar results. Depending on the amount of energy the customer uses, B.C. is either the lowest, second-lowest, or third-lowest in comparison with other jurisdictions, principally Manitoba Hydro and Hydro Québec.

While these data are from 2006, comparisons among jurisdictions for the period when the 2001/02 Ebbels Task Force was developing its policies were broadly similar: B.C. did not have an energy price problem compared with other parts of North America. And, the evidence was clear: public ownership had been enormously beneficial to the province's ratepayers. In light of the much higher prices in other jurisdictions where energy generating facilities were privately owned or where deregulation and competition had recently been introduced, there was no evidence that the kind of "reforms" proposed

Table 3: Comparison of Energy Sources (GWh)

Energy Source	F 1994	F 2003	Change
BC Hydro Generation	40,101	47,665	7,564
Independent Power Producers and Other Long-term Purchase Contracts	2,791	4,950	2,159
Other Energy Purchases	0	896	896
Thermal Resources	3,248	251	(2,997)
Non-Integrated Energy	62	96	34
Net Purchase from Powerex	0	1,113	1,113
Net Storage Returns (Exchange Net)	131	(1,605)	(1,736)
Sub-Total	46,333	53,366	7,033
Line Loss and System Use	(4,315)	(4,698)	(374)
Domestic Sales Volume	42,018	48,677	6,659

Source: BC Hydro 2004b, Chapter 4, "Energy Supply Costs," Table 6

by Ebbels — and subsequently implemented by the provincial government — would result in lower prices for B.C. customers. All the evidence pointed in the opposite direction.[2]

Further evidence of the long-term advantages to B.C of public ownership of generating assets was also available from BC Hydro's earlier experience of purchasing energy from the private sector. In its 2004 Resource Expenditure Acquisition Plan (REAP), which BC Hydro submitted for approval to the BCUC, the Crown utility provided a series of three tables showing changes in the cost of energy produced at its own hydro facilities and the cost of energy purchased from the private sector through energy purchase agreements between 1994 and 2003.

It is worth examining the data in these tables because it underlines how much more expensive it has been in the past for BC Hydro to buy energy from private power developers rather than building its own generating facilities. Moreover, the data also highlights how relying on EPAs for new electricity exposes ratepayers to significant risks of future price increases.

Table 3 is from the BC Hydro Revenue Requirements Application 2004/05 and 2005/06. It documents the growth in the volume of electricity purchased from private power developers between 1994 and 2003. The volume of energy acquired from private sources rose by 77.4 percent, from 2,791 GWh to 4,950 GWh over the ten-year period.[3] By fiscal 2003, BC Hydro was acquiring roughly 10 percent of its energy from the private sector. More significantly, the increase in the volume of energy purchased from private power developers was also accompanied by a major increase in the total price paid by BC Hydro for each MWh it purchased. Table 4 reveals

Table 4: Comparison of Energy Costs ($ millions)

Source	F 1994	F 2003	Change
Hydro	$217	$259	$42
Independent Power Producers and Other Long-term Purchase Contracts	$92	$290	$198
Other Energy Purchases	0	$54	$54
Natural Gas for Thermal Generation	$48	$28	($20)
Non-integrated	$11	$14	$3
Transmission charges and other expenses	$1	$13	$12
Net Purchases of Powerex	0	$50	$50
Domestic Energy Costs	$369	$708	$339

Source: BC Hydro 2004b, Chapter 4: "Energy Supply Costs," Table 7

Table 5: Average Energy Price ($ MWh)

Energy Source	F 1994	F 2003	Change
Hydro	$5.41	$5.43	0.02
IPPs and Other Long-term Purchase Contracts	$32.97	$58.59	25.62
Other Energy Purchases	0	$60.27	60.27
Natural Gas for Thermal Generation	$14.78	$111.55	96.77
Non-Integrated	$177.42	$145.83	(31.59)
Net Purchases of Powerex	0	$44.92	44.92
Weighted Average Cost	$8.78	$14.54	5.76

Source: BC Hydro 2004b, Chapter 4, "Energy Supply Costs," Table 8

Table 6: Cost of Energy to BC Hydro in Fiscal 2006

	Gigawatt Hours	$ Millions	$ per MWh
Hydro Generation	46,219	$272	$5.81
Private Power Developers	6,741	$449	$66.61
Other Domestic Purchases	5,853	$343	$58.60
Gas for Thermal Generation	375	$53	$141.33
Transmission Charges	71	$79	N/A
Totals/Averages	59,259	$1,196	$20.18

Source: BC Hydro 2006d

the astonishing fact that by 2003, BC Hydro was already spending more to buy approximately 10 percent of its energy from private power developers than it spent to generate the other 90 percent from its own hydro facilities.[4] BC Hydro's in-house energy production costs totaled $259 million while its purchases from private energy developers amounted to $290 million. The reason total costs went up so dramatically was that the price per MWh of energy BC Hydro acquired under long-term purchase agreements almost doubled during this period, rising from $32.97 per MWh in 1994 to $58.59 in 2003. Significantly, energy purchased under these agreements was more than ten times more expensive by 2003 than energy generated from BC Hydro's own facilities (see Table 5). In contrast, the energy generated from BC Hydro's own dams remained at almost exactly the same price — $5.41 in 1994 and $5.43 in 2003 — despite a decade of inflationary price increases in the province.

As noted above, the cost of energy from private power producers had reached $290 million by 2003, and costs have continued to climb in the years since. In its 2005/6 REAP application to the BCUC, BC Hydro acknowledged that its short-term commitments for energy purchases for the years 2006 to 2008 were anticipated to grow substantially from the $290 million indicated in 2003. The numbers cited were as follows: 2006 — $425 million (subsequently revised to $449 million); 2007 — $456 million; 2008 — $476 million.

Table 6 shows the cost of energy from various sources. Even in 2006, the cost of energy from BC Hydro's own dams was only $5.81 MWh, or roughly 9 percent of the cost per MWh of purchasing energy from private power developers through long-term contracts. In light of the unequivocal evidence of the escalating prices and increasing total costs of purchasing energy from private power developers, the government should have recognized that continuing to use this approach was not a cost-effective way to supply the people of B.C. with their future electrical energy. But it did not.

Since the provincial election of May 2001, the current government has issued three major tender calls, asking that a major share of "green" energy be included, along with tenders for several other localized energy purchases. The first, referred to as the "2001/02 Small Hydro" or "Green Call," was relatively modest. A total of fifteen projects were approved with a combined capacity of 172 MW. Many of the projects were located in or near the lower Mainland.[5] Table 7 indicates the successful bidder, project location, and capacity involved. Although the price offered at the time was just over $55 per MWh, the tender call was only moderately successful, as more than 30 percent of the energy offered by private developers did not materialize, presumably because the costs of production were too close to, or above, the anticipated selling price.

The following year, the "2002/03 Green Power Generation Call" was

Table 7: Successful Bidders BC Hydro 2001/02 Call for Energy: Small Hydro

Developer	Project Name	Location	Energy Source	Capacity MW
Raging River Power & Mining	Raging River Project	Port Alice	Water	1.75
Pacific Cascade Hydro Inc.	HPS Eagle Lake C2	West Van	Water	0.2
Rockford Energy Corp.	Brandywine Creek Project	Whistler	Water	7
Renewable Power Corp.	McNair Creek Project	Gibsons	Water	5
Morehead Valley Hydro	Siwash Creek	Lytton	Water	0.5
Synex Energy Resources Ltd.	Mears Creek	Gold River	Water	3.8
Lorenz Holdings	Tete Creek	Tete Jaune	Water	2.4
Eaton Power Corp.	Furry Creek	Howe Sound	Water	6.9
Ledcor Power Inc.	Fitzsimmons Creek	Whistler	Water	3.4
Innergex Inc.	Tsable River	Courtenay	Water	4.5
East Twin Creek Hydro Ltd.	Hystad Creek	Valemount	Water	6
Cdn Hydro Dev. & Brascan	Pingston Creek	Revelstoke	Water	30
Cdn Hydro Dev. & Brascan	Upper Mamquam River	Squamish	Water	25
Rutherford Creek Power Ltd.	Rutherford Creek	Pemberton	Water	50
Epcor Power Development	Miller Creek	Pemberton	Water	26
Totals (MW Capacity)				172.45

Source: BC Hydro website. Note: BC Hydro does not list the energy tendered in its summary of these 2001/02 contracts.

announced. This was somewhat more ambitious, as Table 8 illustrates. This tender call provided a bit less than 3 percent of B.C.'s annual energy supply and represented a small, but still significant, expansion of the government's privatization agenda. Again, there were problems with some bidders not fulfilling their initial contractual commitments.

In 2004, BC Hydro began planning for a major new tender call. Initially, it was to be completed in mid-2005. But for a variety of reasons, such as the unresolved status of its application to construct the large Duke Point natural-gas plant on Vancouver Island, BC Hydro delayed issuing the call until December of 2005. (It is customarily referred to as the "2006 tender call.")[6]

Table 8: Successful Bidders BC Hydro's 2002/03 Green Power Generation Call

Developer	Project Name	Location	Energy Source	Capacity MW	Energy GWh/yr
Ledcor Power Inc.	Ashlu Creek Hydro	Squamish	Water	42	200
Regional Power Inc.	Bear Hydro Project	Sechelt	Water	16	77
Princeton Energy Inc.	Berky Creek Hydro	Hope	Water	1.5	6.5
Brilliant Expansion Power	Brilliant Expansion	Castlegar	Water	120	203
Hupacasath First Nation	China Creek Hydro	Port Alberni	Water	5.6	25
Synex Energy Resources	Cypress Creek	Gold River	Water	3.1	11
Coast Mountain Hydro	Forrest Kerr R-of-R	Stewart	Water	112	541
Stothert Power/ Global Renewable Energy	Holberg Wind Energy	Holberg	Wind	58.5	176
Princeton Energy	Hunter Creek Hydro	Hope	Water	2.4	10
Maxim Power (B.C.)	Maxim Landfill Gas Cogen	Delta	Landfill Gas	1.85	15
Cloudworks Energy	Mkwaits Creek Hydro	Mount Currie	Water	45	154
Larson Farms Inc. No. 593815	Pierce Creek Hydro	Chilliwack	Water	0.77	3
Advanced Energy Systems 1	South Cranberry Creek	Revelstoke	Water	6.6	33
Interpac Resources	Spuzzum Creek	Boston Bar	Water	29	90
Ucona River Joint Vent	Ucona River	Gold River	Water	35	125
Pacific Rim Power	Zeballos Lake	Zeballos	Water	21.85	93
TOTALS				501.17	1763

Source: BC Hydro website

The 2006 tender call asked private power developers to bid on providing a total of 2,700 GWh per year of electricity (BC Hydro 2006b). This was a larger block of energy compared to previous calls — roughly 5 percent of BC Hydro's annual energy sales. Forty-eight potential suppliers placed their names on the initial bidders' list. They proposed to provide a total of

13,500 GWh per year of energy and 2,800 MW of capacity from eighty-one projects. However, after reviewing the tender documents, a number of these bidders decided to drop out of the competition. Consequently, by the April 7 deadline, thirty-seven proponents had submitted sixty-one bids involving fifty-three proposed power projects. They offered to supply approximately 6,500 GWh per year of energy combined with a total capacity of 1,800 MW (BC Hydro 2006b).

There were two broad categories of bidders. Those submitting projects generating more than 10 MW were defined as "large bidders," while those with projects generating less than this, but with a minimum of 0.5 MW, were defined as "small bidders." Presumably, this was to appease private power developers wanting to develop smaller — and generally higher cost — hydro projects. BC Hydro allocated 200 GWh of the 2,700 GWh per year total to this category of bidders, a decision that would ensure that even if their prices were higher than bids submitted by proponents with larger projects, some of them would still get contracts. The tender call was "open," meaning that bids from any type of power generation would be accepted, so long as the overall package met the province's "green" and "clean" requirements. As a result, the bids spanned a variety of different generating technologies, including small hydro, waste heat, wind, biomass, and — for the first time in B.C. — coal.

The inclusion of coal as an acceptable source of new energy marked a major change in B.C.'s approach. Previous governments had ruled out coal because of environmental concerns, popular opposition to introducing a major new source of pollution, and the surplus of hydro-generated electricity. However, the Liberal government's carefully nuanced distinction between "clean" and "green" energy, in which the thresholds were set to accept a portion of new energy from non-renewable sources, opened the door to purchases of coal-derived energy. The voluntary commitment to acquire at least half of its new energy from "clean" sources was, in reality, a way of packaging the introduction of coal and biomass as the other half.

The change in policy reflected, in part, pressure from the Joint Industry Electrical Steering Committee (JIESC). Its industrial members — primarily the mining and forestry industries — were concerned about the potentially high cost of energy from small private hydro and wind-farm projects. As noted earlier, they did not want to subsidize the owners of such facilities, which they might end up doing if these sources were given preference over lower-cost sources such as coal. As well, some JIESC members were themselves interested in selling energy to BC Hydro from thermal generating plants that burned both wood waste (biomass) and coal. Lobbying by the coal industry has been intense since the Liberals were elected. In the August 25, 2005, issue of *Georgia Straight*, editor Charlie Smith noted that a number of mining companies had made substantial donations to the provincial Liberal Party in the run-up to the 2005 election. The two largest mining-sector donations were Fording Inc. ($132,990) and Teck Cominco Limited ($112,210). Smith went on to say:

> the second- and fifth-largest B.C. Liberal donors, Fording Inc. and Teck Cominco Ltd., have benefited from the Campbell government's support for the coal industry. In their first term, the B.C. Liberals ended requirements for coal companies to pay royalties for the use of gravel for road-building. In addition, the government has aggressively promoted coal-fired electricity in general, and refused to include greenhouse-gas emission targets in B.C.'s climate-change plan. (C. Smith 2005)

The government also accommodated JIESC demands for an "open" tender call process — that is, one that would accept bids from all types of generation, including coal — with the singular exception of nuclear.

As we noted briefly in the previous chapter, when BC Hydro announced the outcome of the 2006 tender call, it unveiled a big — and nasty — surprise for ratepayers: the total amount of energy it had agreed to purchase from private energy suppliers was over three times more than it had solicited the previous December, when the call had first been announced. The Crown utility signed contracts for 7,125 GWh per year of electricity from private power developers.[7]

Table 9 shows the contracts awarded in the 2006 tender call, as well as the energy sources, project locations, and amounts of energy and installed capacity. BC Hydro made an enormous purchase of private energy in its 2006 tender award. Its explanation for this decision was that it needed to acquire a much larger volume of energy because B.C.'s forecasted energy requirements had risen significantly since the previous load forecast study of December 2004. More recent projections indicated that there could be a significant shortfall unless BC Hydro increased the amount of energy it purchased. Given the lead time before new projects come on stream, the Crown utility argued that it had to move quickly to ensure that it would have enough energy to satisfy provincial needs in the coming decades (BC Hydro 2006b).

Again, as we noted in the previous chapter, energy forecasts are based on a variety of complex factors, including overall economic growth, the anticipated price of various fuel inputs, the extent to which demand may be mitigated by successful energy conservation measures, population growth, and so forth. One of the forecasting models BC Hydro uses is referred to as the "Monte Carlo Model," which uses six major simulation factors in its projection mix.

Table 9: Successful Bidders BC Hydro 2006 Energy Tender Call

Developer	Project Name	Location	Energy Source	Capacity MW	Energy GWh/yr
Plutonic Power	East Toba-Montrose	Powell River	Water	196	702
AES Wapiti Energy	AES Wapiti Energy	Tumbler Ridge	Coal Biomass	184	1,612
Dokie Wind Energy	Dokie Wind Project	Chetwynd	Wind	180	536
Bear Mountain Wind	Bear Mountain Wind Pk	Dawson Creek	Wind	120	371
3986314 Canada	Can. Glacier/ Howser/E.	Nelson	Water	90.5	341
Green Island Energy	Gold River Power	Gold River	Biomass	90	745
Kwaisa Energy	Kwaisa	Mission	Water	85.9	384
Anyox Hydro Electric	Anyox and Kisault R.	Alice Arm	Water	56.5	242
Compliance Power	Princeton Power	Princeton	Coal Biomass	56	421
Upper Stave Energy	Upper Stave Energy	Mission	Water	54.7	264
Mackenzie Green Energy	Mackenzie Green	Mackenzie	Biomass	50	441
Kwoiek Creek Res.	Kwoiek Creek Hydro	Lytton	Water	49.9	147
Mount Hays Wind Farm	Mount Hays Wind Farm	Prince Rupert	Wind	25.2	72
Canadian Hydro Dev.	Bone Creek Hydro	Kamloops	Water	20	81
Songhees Creek	Songhees Creek Hydro	Port Hardy	Water	15	61
Plutonic Power	Rany River Hydro	Gibsons	Water	15	51
Hydromax Energy	Lower Clowhorn	Sechelt	Water	9.99	48
Hydromax Energy	Lower Clowhorn	Sechelt	Water	9.99	45
Highwater Power	Kookipi Creek	Boston Bar	Water	9.99	39
Cogenix Power	Log Creek	Boston Bar	Water	9.99	38
Canadian Hydro	Clemina Creek	Kamloops	Water	9.85	31
KMC Energy	Tamihi Creek	Chilliwack	Water	9.9	52

Valisa Energy	Serpentine Creek	Blue River	Water	9.6	29
Synex Energy	Victoria Lake	Port Alice	Water	9.5	39
Second Realty	Fries Creek	Squamish	Water	9	41
Renewable Power	Tyson Creek	Sechelt	Water	7.5	48
Hupacasath FN	Corrigan Creek	Port Alberni	Water	6.65	19
Axiom Power	Clint Creek	Woss	Water	6	27
EnPower	Savona ERG Project	Savona	Waste Heat	5.89	41
EnPower	150 Mile House ERG	150 Mile House	Waste Heat	5.89	34
Maroon Creek	Maroon Creek	Terrace	Water	5	25
Spuzzum Creek	Sakwi Creek	Agassiz	Water	5	21
Canadian Hydro	English Creek	Revelstoke	Water	5	19
Synex Energy	Barr Creek	Tahsis	Water	4	15
Raging River Power	Raging River 2	Port Alice	Water	4	13
Synex Energy	McKelvie Creek	Tahsis	Water	3.4	14
Advanced Energy	Cranberry Creek	Revelstoke	Water	3	11
Dist of Lake Country	Eldorado Reservoir	Kelowna	Water	0.8	4
Totals				1,438.6	7,124

Source: BC Hydro (2006b). Note: Brilliant Expansion Project energy contracts have been excluded from the table.

However, forecasts are less and less reliable as we attempt to predict energy requirements further into the future. Various unanticipated "shocks" to supply or price can dramatically affect future energy consumption. Economic growth can also vary quite significantly from forecasts as a result of major — and unanticipated — changes that affect Canada's relatively open economy, such as a slump in the United States, declines in Canadian export commodity prices, or fluctuations in international interest rates, to cite only a few of the many influences on future growth. And, growing evidence of the deeply worrisome impact of greenhouse gas emissions on the global environment may make many predictions redundant if global temperatures rise as quickly as some are now predicting. In that proves true, it will no longer make sense to assume that the province will experience steady, incremental growth of energy use.

This is not to deny that the province's short-term energy needs have increased in recent years more than BC Hydro anticipated. However, it can be argued that this is partly due to the Olympics-triggered economic boom in the province — a boom that has coincided with a major increase in oil-

and-gas production, particularly in the northeast corner of the province. B.C.'s proximity to Alberta's booming tar sands project has also driven up demand — and costs — particularly for major construction and infrastructure projects. But, it remains to be seen how long this growth spurt will last: there may be a significant "hangover" from the 2010 Olympics.

The extent to which the oil-and-gas sector has the reserves to maintain current levels of growth also remains an open question, as does the issue of whether Alberta will be able to continue to expand the highly polluting tar-sands development in the face of international pressures to reduce greenhouse gas emissions. All of this is to say that energy growth forecasts may significantly over-estimate future needs. If this proves true, BC Hydro's rush to lock in thirty- and forty-year contracts during the current economic boom may prove, in hindsight, to have been an extremely unwise decision, even within the narrow constraints of the government's Energy Plan.

Setting aside the issue of whether BC Hydro's projections on the growth of energy consumption are likely to prove accurate, the fact is that much of the additional demand for new energy from private power developers is a direct result of the government's own policy decisions. These have clearly limited the options available to BC Hydro and thus forced it to purchase more energy from the private sector.

BC Hydro's decision to triple the amount of energy being purchased from private power developers was also a surprise to many of the participants in the Crown utility's own major stakeholder consultative process, the 2005 Integrated Electricity Planning Committee — familiarly known as the IEP — of which this author was a member. The first IEP, appointed not quite two years earlier, had been mandated to provide a single set of recommendations, but had failed to reach agreement.

The 2005 IEP was composed of a group of individuals representing various stakeholders interested in the province's future electricity needs. These included large industrial users, private power developers, environmentalists, business organizations, regional representatives, local governments, consumer advocates, and First Nations. Selected by the Board of BC Hydro and constrained in its mandate by the Energy Plan and other provincial electricity policies, BC Hydro asked the IEP to assess the province's future energy requirements. It spent more than a year examining the issue in a very intensive process that aimed to determine the appropriate portfolio of new energy the province should acquire. Different options were developed with varying mixes from small and large hydro, gas, coal, biomass, and conservation measures such as "Power Smart."

After lengthy deliberations, the 2005 IEP — which was appointed in December of 2004 and completed its work in late spring of 2006 — failed to arrive at a sole recommendation for the province's best energy portfolio.

Rather, its stakeholders ended up recommending a number of possible energy portfolio options.

During the period when the IEP was carrying out most of its work, its members assumed that the amount of energy to be purchased in the 2006 tender would be roughly what had been solicited in December 2005. While the IEP was not part of the process used to evaluate the various tenders — this was entirely managed by BC Hydro — its members were not aware until late in their deliberations that such a large energy purchase would likely be made. The IEP made no recommendation to increase the proposed volume of energy purchased beyond that indicated in the original call.[8] Indeed, given that the average annual increase in B.C.'s growth of energy use was projected to be between 1.5 and 2 percent, some of which might be offset by "Power Smart" savings — and given that other options such as Site "C" (which would be owned by BC Hydro) were possible energy sources — the decision to acquire three times the previously indicated requirement from private energy interests constituted a remarkable policy shift between the time the IEP finished its work in the spring of 2006 and the July 27 announcement of the large volume of energy to be purchased in the 2006 energy call.

It should also be noted that the government deliberately delayed the release of the IEP's final report. BC Hydro executives were understandably circumspect about the reasons for the delay. Some IEP members felt that the reason was that the government was unhappy with its results. Several of the portfolio options presented in the first drafts of the IEP report were quite different from the course of action the government wanted BC Hydro to follow. Specifically, the inclusion of Site "C" in some portfolios may have raised an issue the government did not want to flag at the time.

As well as acquiring a much larger volume of energy in its 2006 tender call, BC Hydro also agreed to pay private power developers much higher prices than earlier projected. When the tender process was first being developed in early 2005, the market price of energy was in the $50–$55 per MWh range. Previous EPAs with private power developers in the 2001–2004 period had resulted in prices in the $56–$61 MWh range. During BC Hydro's IEP process, Hydro staff attempted to estimate the likely costs of various options for acquiring new energy. Table 10 shows the range of price options for various energy resources. The unit energy costs of options varied from a low of $36 MWh for the most cost-effective energy conservation projects to $60 MWh for the fourth bundle of small hydro projects. The estimate for Site "C" included a $5 MWh water-rental charge to the government, so its most likely estimated cost would actually be about $42 MWh, while its highest estimated price would still be only $57 MWh once the $5 water licence charge was deducted. The IEP also developed estimates for the cost of energy from a re-powered Burrard natural-gas plant that averaged $57

Table 10: Resource Options: Unit Energy Cost Summary

Resource Type	Project Name	Average Annual Energy (GWh)	Unit Energy Cost (UEC) $ MWh	Range of UEC $ MWh
Demand Side Management	Energy Efficiency level 3	2576	36	32–50
Demand Side Management	Energy Efficiency level 4	2534	44	40–62
Large Hydro	Peace River Site "C"	4600	47	43–62
Geothermal	South Meager Geothermal Project	800	47	44–60
Wind	Peace Region Wind Bundle 1	1510	49	45–63
Small Hydro	Medium Hydro 1st 1,000 GWh/yr Bundle	1000	50	47–63
Small Hydro	Small Hydro First 1,000 GWh/yr Bundle	1000	50	47–63
Demand Side Management	Energy Efficiency Level 5	2164	54	49–76
Wind	Peace Region Wind Bundle 2	1430	54	50–70
Small Hydro	Small Hydro Second 1,000 GWh/yr Bundle	1000	55	52–69
Small Hydro	Small Hydro Third 1,000 GWh/yr Bundle	1000	55	52–69
Natural Gas	Greenfield CCGT — 500 MW	3954	57	48–80
Natural Gas –Resource Smart	Burrard Re-powering 500 MW — First 2x1 F-series	3954	57	48–80
Biomass	Bundle — Biomass Wood waste	1256	59	56–71
Small Hydro	Medium Hydro Second 1,000 GWh/yr Bundle	1000	60	56–75
Small Hydro	Small Hydro Fourth 1,000 GWh/yr Bundle	1000	60	56–75

Source: BC Hydro 2006a. Extracted from the first 16 options set out in Table 5-1

MWh (with a high level of uncertainty over future gas prices), and for coal, which averaged $61 MWh, but with a big question mark associated with the cost of greenhouse gas offsets.

However, the bids submitted to BC Hydro — which it accepted — were

Table 11: Large Project Portfolio Blended APB Components ($MWh)

Levelized Plant Gate Price	74.0
Green Credit	(1.6)
Hourly Firm Credit	(1.5)
GHG Adder	4.0
CIFT Adder	2.8
Network Upgrades Adder	0.9
Losses	8.9
Adjusted Bid Price	87.5

Source: BC Hydro "Report on the F2006 Call For Tender Process." BC Hydro Submission to BCUC August 31, 2006.

far, far higher than these estimates. In its August 31 filing with the BCUC, BC Hydro stated that it was going to pay an average price in its new EPAs of $74 per MWh at the plant gate — roughly 50 percent higher than projected market rates, 50 percent higher than the estimates developed for the most attractive options by the IEP, and about 25 percent higher than previous tender calls.

But this $74 MWh price is not what BC Hydro will end up paying, due to various adjustments for transmission losses, greenhouse gas emissions, hourly firm energy requirements, and inflation. The actual cost to BC Hydro when delivered to the lower Mainland will be much higher. About 90 percent of the energy BC Hydro purchases from private energy developers will come from large projects where the adjusted price is roughly 75 percent higher than market rates.

Table 11, taken from BC Hydro's August 31, 2006, submission to the BCUC, outlines the various factors that contribute to this higher price. The table shows the average cost of energy from large projects and indicates that the delivered price will end up averaging $87.50 MWh, far above the BC Hydro price projections submitted to the IEP. (The adjusted price for smaller projects is a bit lower than for large projects, but they represent only a small part — roughly 10 percent — of the overall purchase.) And, not unimportantly, this price is inflation adjusted, so the private power developers supplying this energy will see their price per MWh increase steadily during the term of their contracts.

Not only are the preceding prices far higher than BC Hydro earlier predicted, even more disturbing is that they are far, far higher than most estimates of future energy prices. Figure 5, which BC Hydro included in its submission to the BCUC, shows the estimates by different professional forecasting agencies of future energy prices in B.C. and the Pacific Northwest. The data provided by the American Energy Information Administration

Figure 5: F2006 Call Annual Adjusted Gate Price vs. Price Forecast Scenarios

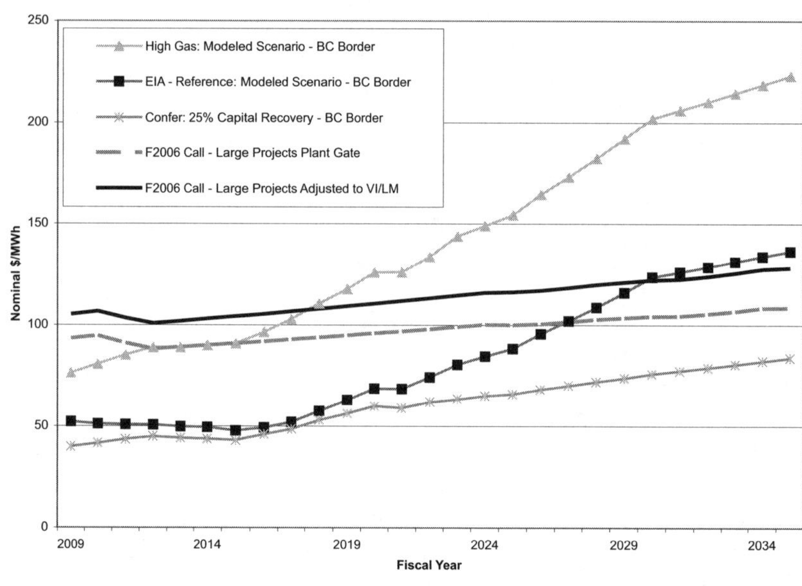

Source: BC Hydro submission to BCUC August 31, 2006

(EIA, part of the U.S. Department of Energy) projects that energy prices at the B.C. border will be in the range of $50 per MWh until roughly 2018, and they are unlikely to increase to the level being paid in the EPAs for almost two decades. Confer, a well-respected Calgary firm, had projections that are even lower than the EIA forecasts. Even the highest price energy projection — natural gas — does not reach the level of the 2006 EPAs until about 2018. It would still take roughly fifteen years for the total payments under this worst-case scenario to equal those BC Hydro is now committed to paying.

If we stick, instead, with the more likely EIA projections, it will take more than twenty years for the estimated market price to catch up with BC Hydro's 2006 EPA prices. But even twenty years is a long time in the energy business. To commit to paying as much as 75 percent more than projected market prices — prices that will still be higher two decades from now — in order, allegedly, to guarantee future supply, seems extremely risky, and perhaps downright reckless, for B.C. ratepayers.

This raises fundamental questions about why BC Hydro is choosing to buy so much expensive private energy in its 2006 call. BC Hydro's explanation is that it will provide long-term energy security. As we have discussed elsewhere, this is a problematic argument, because the "security-of-supply" guarantee is only a short-term one. Once the contracts expire, the private

Table 12: BC Hydro Expected Annual Energy Payments

To Private Energy Developers, F-2006 Call (2009–2051)			
Fiscal Year	Payment ($mm)	Energy GW/yr	Unit Price ($MWh)
F2007	$0	0	$0.00
F2008	$0	0	$0.00
F2009	$8	93	$84.80
F2010	$94	1,019	$92.10
F2011	$305	3,389	$90.00
F2012	$438	4,987	$87.80
F2013	$442	4,987	$88.70
F2014	$447	4,987	$89.50
F2015	$451	4,987	$90.50
F2016	$456	4,987	$91.40
F2017	$460	4,987	$92.30
F2018	$465	4,987	$93.30
F2019	$470	4,987	$94.30
F2020	$475	4,987	$95.30
F2021	$480	4,987	$96.30
F2022	$486	4,987	$97.40
F2023	$491	4,987	$98.40
F2024	$496	4,987	$99.50
F2025	$496	4,987	$99.50
F2026	$498	4,987	$99.90
F2027	$504	4,987	$101.00
F2028	$510	4,987	$102.20
F2029	$509	4,939	$103.10
F2030	$508	4,898	$103.80
F2031	$484	4,654	$104.00
F2032	$469	4,463	$105.00
F2033	$474	4,463	$106.30
F2034	$477	4,424	$107.90
F2035	$435	4,034	$107.90
F2036	$402	3,731	$107.70
F2037	$406	3,728	$109.00
F2038	$411	3,728	$110.30
F2039	$416	3,728	$111.70
F2040	$385	3,404	$113.10

F2041	$271	2,431	$111.50
F2042	$191	1,682	$113.60
F2043	$193	1,682	$114.90
F2044	$195	1,676	$116.10
F2045	$192	1,646	$116.80
F2046	$145	1,311	$110.50
F2047	$126	1,155	$109.30
F2048	$128	1,155	$110.60
F2049	$129	1,155	$112.00
F2050	$115	1,013	$113.70
F2051	$62	498	$124.00
Total/ Average	$15,595	154,878	$100.69

Source: BC Hydro submission to BCUC. August 31, 2006. (Figures include attrition and outages.)

owners of this power will be free to export it to the United States if they can get a higher price

The high bid prices, combined with the acquisition of three times more energy than originally planned, has resulted in a financial commitment between four and five times higher than indicated in BC Hydro's original 2006 tender call, and the resulting financial obligations — and risks — for B.C. ratepayers are enormous. According to BC Hydro, the total potential cost of contracts between 2009 and 2051 will be a staggering $15.6 billion.

This is illustrated by the Table 12, taken from BC Hydro's 2006 submission to the BCUC. Not surprisingly, BC Hydro, in its submission to the BCUC, estimates the impact on electricity rates of this one tender call to be about 8.1 percent, once the projects are on stream in 2013. Projected annual costs between 2012 and 2139, in which the bulk of the energy will be purchased, range from $400 million to $508 million. But, incredibly, the figures are based on the assumption that there will be a 30 percent attrition rate in the contracts it has signed. The $15.6 billion total cost has been adjusted to reflect this assumption. But if the attrition rate is lower, the total could actually be considerably higher. While previous BC Hydro energy calls resulted in the delivery of significantly less energy than initially contracted — because a number of successful bidders subsequently backed out of their deals — these earlier contracts were at much lower prices, in the range of $56 MWh to $61 MWh. Whether a similar proportion of bids will fail to deliver the contracted energy volume is unclear, given the much higher price BC Hydro will be paying for energy purchased in the 2006 call. Thus a 20 percent attrition rate would push the total financial obligation to almost $20 billion.

BC Hydro has also estimated the potential costs of the 2006 EPAs according

Figure 6. Nominal Expected Annual Energy Payments to IPPs

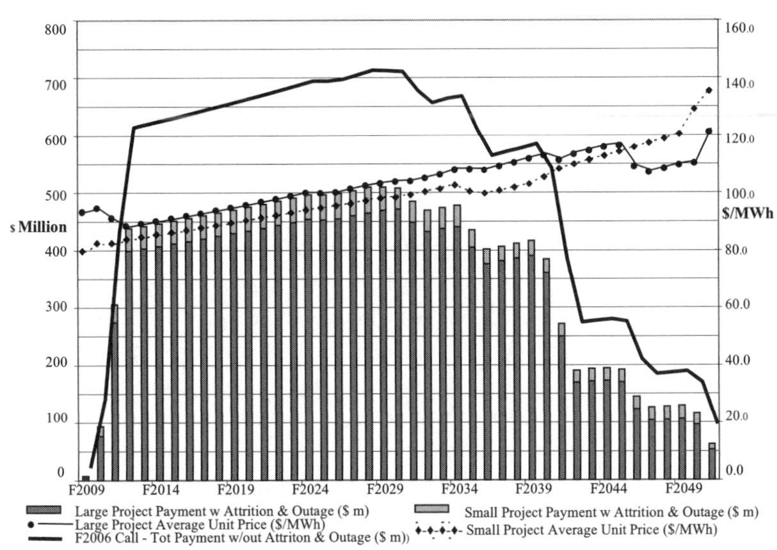

Note: The solid black line is the 2006 call's total potential payments without attrition or outages. Source: BC Hydro submission to BCUC August 31, 2006

to a number of different assumptions. What is significant in a graph from BC Hydro's 2006 submission to the BCUC (see Figure 6) is that the potential cost in some years — without the 30 percent attrition figure — is actually more than $700 million. But the 2006 energy call is not the end of the story. As noted earlier, BC Hydro was already committed to both $1.8 billion in EPAs signed up until the end of 2003 and for an unspecified — but significant — additional amount for the two tender calls immediately preceding the 2006 call.

The huge financial obligation BC Hydro is making on behalf of ratepayers has been confirmed in a letter dated October 2, 2006, from Carl Fisher of the Ministry of Finance in the B.C. government in response to a freedom-of-information request from Keith Reynolds, a researcher with the Canadian Union of Public Employees. Attached to the letter is a table outlining the contractual obligations of various entities owned by the provincial government, including BC Hydro (Fisher, 2006). The numbers for BC Hydro read as follows:

Energy Purchase Contracts
July 2006: $5.249 billion
Corrections: $8.147 billion
September: $13.396 billion

While the September figure is slightly less than the amounts cited in our review of the 2006 tender awards, they may not include all these contracts due to delays in completing text of the legal documents for some of the awards.

On top of all this, BC Hydro, following the direction set out in the province's current Energy Plan, has already announced a 2007 tender call for a yet another block of private energy. The government has also amended the tender call process under the 2007 Energy Plan to enable power developers with projects of less than 10 MW to approach BC Hydro with proposals on an ongoing basis. In other words, they will no longer even have to wait for BC Hydro's periodic tender calls. And the government has announced that its goal is not only to make B.C. self sufficient by the middle of the next decade, but also to have a surplus — a surplus that will be created, presumably, by even more lucrative contracts for private power developers.

All this raises the question: why the rush to have BC Hydro buy so much energy, so quickly, from private developers? Given that market projections indicated that it would still be possible to purchase energy for more than a decade at prices far, far less than the $87.50 MWh BC Hydro is now paying, and given that energy forecasts are less and less reliable the further out in time the estimates are, it seems highly questionable to lock B.C. ratepayers into such high-priced energy contracts, in some cases until 2051.

As we noted in the previous chapter, there are many other options that make more sense for B.C. ratepayers. The government could have chosen to make full use of the 1,200 MW of downstream benefits from the Columbia River Treaty rather than treating this energy as a separate source of provincial revenue and forcing BC Hydro to make up an equivalent amount through much more expensive EPAs. Site "C" could produce almost as much energy — 900 MW and 4,600 GWh — as the 2006 tender provides, but at an estimated capital cost in 2004 dollars ranging from $2.3 to $3.2 billion, depending on interest rates and construction costs (BC Hydro 2006c). Even with a substantial cushion for inflation, interest rate risks, and construction cost overruns, Site "C" would cost ratepayers far, far less, for a comparable amount of energy. BC Hydro could have re-powered Burrard thermal, again at a cost significantly less than the 2006 tender, and this would have had the added benefit of providing 950 MW of capacity at the load centre in the lower Mainland — an insurance policy in the event a major disaster cut off lines from the major dams in the interior. BC Hydro could have continued to rely on the energy market, using its storage capacity to cushion ratepayers from fluctuating international energy prices. And, it could have chosen to be much more aggressive with its "Power Smart" program by investing in energy conservation.

Alternatively, the government could conserve energy by simply allowing BC Hydro to raise the price — currently about $37 per MWh — of Heritage

Contract energy sold to industrial customers to market rates. This would send a clear signal to major pulp mills and mining companies that they need to conserve energy. These industries are price sensitive when it comes to energy, and a major increase in prices would provide a huge incentive for them to reduce energy use. Given that they use about one-third of the energy BC Hydro generates, there is little doubt that they would be able to reduce energy consumption quite significantly, given the right price signal. Selling energy at $37 MWh while buying it at $87.50 is hardly smart business practice.

The government could have chosen not to open the transmission grid to allow Alcan and Cominco to export energy to the United States, thus ensuring that these significant sources of existing supply would be retained for use in B.C. Had the government not squandered the best water for power licences by giving them to private energy interests for virtually nothing, it could have had BC Hydro develop many of these sites. As a Crown corporation guaranteed by the government, BC Hydro has access to much cheaper financing, as well as the huge advantage of being able to avoid the needless duplication inherent in allowing numerous private companies to develop sites on their own, paying for the costs of their learning curve by boosting the price of energy they sell to BC Hydro.

In short, there were a number of better choices than BC Hydro's 2006 tender call. A combination of these options would have been far more rational than signing long-term agreements at such high prices. There appears to be no immediate crisis that would justify locking BC Hydro into the very large future expenditures that will have to be made under the terms of these contracts — payments that will have to be made even if changes in B.C.'s economy result in lower energy demand in coming years.

However, one consequence is very clear: the decision on the 2006 tender call dramatically speeds up the privatization of B.C.'s electricity system. It increases the share of private ownership in B.C.'s system and saddles the Crown corporation with enormous financial obligations that will significantly constrain future public options for BC Hydro and its ratepayers.

Our discussion, thus far, has looked at financial costs we have already undertaken. However, as noted, the government plans to continue this approach indefinitely. If we assume, as the IEP committee did, that B.C. will require about 20,000–25,000 GWh of additional energy over the next twenty years, and if we further assume that the government will continue with its current strategy of energy purchases from the private sector, the financial obligations involved will be enormous. The 2006 tender call will satisfy less than a third of the province's projected future energy needs, at a cost of $15.6 billion. If we add the two-thirds of energy yet to be purchased, as well as the energy from EPAs made prior to 2006, the sums are truly staggering: they could amount to as much as $50 or $60 billion. Even if we assume significant savings from aggressive "Power Smart" conservation programs and the impact of higher prices on demand, we are still looking at huge financial commitments on the part of ratepayers.

One final issue also merits attention. BC Hydro's purchase agreements are being treated as "off the books" financial transactions rather than as government debt. Yet EPAs commit BC Hydro, and the public, to providing a revenue stream to the private energy sector that is analogous to the payments that would have to be made on a loan if BC Hydro were to borrow the money to build these facilities itself. This payment stream represents just as clear a financial obligation as if the government were paying down a debt in regular installments. Arguably, it should be included as part of the province's long-term debt obligations.

Just as the off-the-books approach of early public-private partnerships have been questioned by the accounting community for not providing an accurate picture of the government's debt obligations, keeping EPAs off the books is equally problematic, because future governments will have no choice but to meet these financial obligations. While it is true that BC Hydro may choose to flow through the price increases associated with these obligations to its customers by raising rates, it is also possible that public resistance to price increases may mean that the government will swallow all, or part, of these increases in the form of lower dividends from BC Hydro, or no dividends at all. Clearly, this will impact negatively on provincial finances, regardless of whether it shows up in BC Hydro's or the province's books. If BC Hydro chooses to flow through the full costs to ratepayers, the resulting higher energy prices will negatively affect many other aspects of B.C.'s economy.

The key point is this: for all its additional annual expenditures, BC Hydro will get no assets. Ownership of the new generating capacity is completely private, and so the cost of buying energy will continue to rise indefinitely, despite the fact that BC Hydro's EPAs are effectively financing the private acquisition of these assets.

This is the critical flaw in the government's energy policy. Ratepayers effectively fund the construction of private power projects through the long-term contracts BC Hydro awards. These contracts provide the revenue stream — the collateral — that private energy interests need to borrow the capital to develop the projects. Virtually all of them are dependent on EPAs for their construction. But, having provided the generous revenue streams to fund these projects, B.C. ratepayers get no equity: when the contracts expire, they own nothing. Private power developers will then be free to sell to the highest bidder, either in B.C. or south of the border. This approach gives no long-term price protection to ratepayers either, despite the fact that they have paid the full costs of these lucrative private investments.

NOTES

1. Interestingly, the only American jurisdictions with energy prices that are even in the same ballpark as those of BC Hydro are Portland and Seattle, where prices are significantly influenced by publicly owned Bonneville Power Corporation.
2. We could cite the disastrous experience of California, the price spikes in Alberta, or the experience of a number of other American states that decided to introduce competition into their electricity systems. But what is interesting about this issue is how the early proponents of deregulation who had predicted major price decreases associated with reform gradually abandoned that rationale, substituting other alleged benefits, such as providing new capital investments, opening up opportunities for investors, eliminating utility "monopolies," and/or following the global trend toward reducing regulations and freeing markets.
3. BC Hydro's year-by-year generation numbers are contained in its response to the first round of BCUC requests. The numbers show significant variations largely as a result of annual changes in rainfall.
4. These tables also show significant increases in some other costs, such as the price of natural gas. At the same time, BC Hydro was able to shift its resource mix to minimize the impact of higher gas prices on the overall cost of its energy, a reflection of the flexibility possible with a hydro-based system in which storage can be used to offset short-term fluctuations in the price of other energy sources.
5. Descriptions of the various calls can be found on the BC Hydro website. The first call also included a five MW bio-gas project as well as the fifteen small hydro projects mentioned above.
6. The Duke Point fiasco illustrates the questionable approach to long-term planning that now characterizes the relationship between the government, BC Hydro, and the BCUC. The original Duke Point proposal was developed before the Liberals were elected in 2001. It was intended to address the projected energy shortage on Vancouver Island and to facilitate the construction of a new natural-gas pipeline to the Island, which would also be utilized by private gas interests. At the time, some critics saw this as an indirect subsidy by the NDP to the gas industry, which wanted a new pipeline to the Island. In the event, BC Hydro's application to construct Duke Point as a public project was rejected by the BCUC — a decision that fitted well with the new government's policy of placing limits on any further expansion of BC Hydro's publicly owned generating facilities. Instead, the BCUC directed the Crown utility to come back with a public-private partnership, and BC Hydro proceeded to do this. But, during the interim, gas prices rose substantially. A number of major industrial customers on the Island signalled their opposition to the project, which they saw as likely to increase their energy bills substantially. It would also limit their future opportunities to sell their own energy from sources such as wood waste to BC Hydro. Many community and environmental groups were also opposed to the project. A court challenge to the way the BCUC had conducted its hearing resulted in further delays. As a result, the project was unlikely to be able to fulfil one of its other key objectives: bridging the anticipated gap in energy supplies before a new transmission line to the Island was built. So, in June of 2005 BC

Hydro ended up scrapping the entire project, at a cost to ratepayers estimated to be in the range of $120 to $130 million.

7. It also agreed to purchase another 226 GWh from Columbia Power, the regional, publicly owned utility.
8. The 2005 IEP met roughly every six weeks over a period of eighteen months. The process included a number of the most senior BC Hydro staff and involved regular attendance by a Vice-President, along with numerous analysts, forecasters, energy policy experts, and consultants either employed by or on contract to BC Hydro. The IEP's deliberations were prominently highlighted on the BC Hydro website and in its news releases.

Chapter Four

Insecurity of Supply

WHILE ESCALATING ENERGY PRICES are one key weakness of the government's energy policy, another, hinted at earlier, is its failure to protect the public from future supply shortages. One of the government's most frequently cited rationales for purchasing high-priced energy from private, B.C.-based developers is that sourcing it from within the province will guarantee future security of supply for provincial customers. In its Energy Plan, as well as in numerous public statements, the government emphasizes that obtaining energy from within the province will restore B.C. to energy security. In fact, during the autumn of 2006, BC Hydro ran a multi-million-dollar media campaign, including expensive advertisements on television and in the print media, claiming that the policy it was following would restore our energy security within a decade (Tieleman 2006).[1]

Setting aside the fact that B.C. had energy security before the current government came to power over six years ago and that the ban on BC Hydro building new publicly owned generating facilities has been a major factor in prejudicing future energy supplies, the claim that purchasing energy from private power developers would protect B.C. residents from future shortages is itself specious. Reliance on private interests to supply all new energy will lead to less, not more, energy security.

One of the fundamental advantages of public ownership of our electricity generating facilities is that it does not impose any constraints on the ability of BC Hydro to supply energy to customers within B.C. The province has the authority to direct BC Hydro's to sell our publicly owned energy only to domestic customers. Depending on provincial requirements, BC Hydro may, or may not, choose to export energy. But, because it owns the energy, there are no restrictions — such as those that might be posed by NAFTA or the WTO — on its ability to keep its publicly owned energy within B.C. for the exclusive use of British Columbians.

The question of whether B.C.-generated energy will be used for B.C. customers has not been a major area of concern precisely because it is public. When the current government came to power, the private sector was supplying about 10 percent of B.C.'s energy through long-term contracts. However, as the private sector's share of B.C.'s energy production grows, this issue will become increasingly important. When we add the energy from past tender calls to the purchases included in the 2006 award, we can see that now close to one-fifth of B.C.'s future energy supply will be sourced from private power developers. Moreover, the current policy will force BC Hydro to continue to issue new annual tender calls indefinitely into the future. Acquiring all new energy supplies from private power developers could result in as much as 35 to 40 percent of B.C.'s energy being supplied by the private sector within two decades, depending on how fast energy demand grows (and assuming no change in current policy direction).

Looking at this purely from the supply perspective — and ignoring the issue of cost — the most effective way for the government to ensure that purchases from private power developers provide enhanced energy security would be to maintain stringent controls on private energy exports. However, as we noted previously, the government has systematically removed all regulatory barriers to the export of privately owned energy. Through Bill 40 in 2004, it abolished the former requirement that owners of power generating facilities had to have "Energy Removal Certificates" to export energy from the province. This was part of its larger deregulation agenda, in which it opened up the transmission grid to allow private developers full access to international energy markets.It is true that before it abolished this requirement, Removal Certificates were readily given out. Arguably, the previous NDP government also gave them out too freely and without adequate concern for the long-term implications of permitting private energy exports. But the policy framework at the time was also very different. At the time, there was no restriction on BC Hydro building new power plants and it wasn't then required to purchase large quantities of new energy from private interests. So, the growth of private power projects remained minimal at that time.

The existence of the requirement to apply for the right to export energy gave the government a tool to regulate exports and protect B.C. customers, even if it was not always used as effectively as it might have been. Getting rid of this regulatory tool entirely was neither necessary nor prudent from the perspective of energy self-sufficiency.

It can be argued that the federal National Energy Board can still exercise some control over electricity exports. But, influenced by the export commitments already in place through NAFTA with respect to the oil-and-gas sector, the Board has shown no interest in limiting private electricity exports. So, the only other governmental body that could conceivably exercise control in this area — the provincial government — has actually eliminated the one provision that gave it at least some regulatory oversight over energy exports.

Aside from the provincial government's commitment to markets, private ownership, and the (unsubstantiated) belief that deregulation and privatization are sound public policies, there is another reason for the government's willingness to open the floodgates to private energy exports: its key corporate supporters know that the ability to export energy dramatically raises the value of the generating assets they are now acquiring across the province.

If private energy developers were restricted to selling their energy only to BC Hydro, their options — and their negotiating power — would be quite limited. Having no other purchaser for their energy, they would be forced to pay what BC Hydro and the province felt was a fair and reasonable price, given the cost of the investments they had made. They might have faced an approach to pricing that parallels that used, historically, in many American states where utility regulators limit the rate of return to private utilities to what is deemed a "reasonable" profit for investors. Under such a regulatory regime, private energy developers in B.C. would have little room to gain the enormous windfalls they anticipate they will get from their newly acquired water licences and wind-farm tenures.[2]

As well, there is already considerable evidence that many of the local players in the energy "gold rush" are not in it for the long haul. While they may be well connected with the provincial government — well enough connected to know to apply for water licences before the general public knew that BC Hydro was going to be purchasing all its new energy from private power developers — they remain tiny players in the North American energy market. They know they do not have the economies of scale of large energy corporations, nor do they have the marketing skills and outlets for their electricity that will be needed to capture the full benefits of their investments once their BC Hydro contracts terminate. Consequently, they plan to capitalize on the windfall gains arising from their water licences, wind-farm tenures, and lucrative BC Hydro EPAs, which, once signed, become extremely valuable — and saleable — assets.

For example, Plutonic Power, which claims that its East Toba Inlet hydro project near Powell River is the largest new hydro development in B.C. in recent years, sold 49 percent of the project to GE Capital of Canada, an affiliate of the giant American financial corporation, within a month of getting its 2006 EPA from BC Hydro. According to a Plutonic press release, GE paid $100 million for a 49 percent share of ownership of Plutonic, and will receive 63 percent of its revenue stream. It has also undertaken to lend another $400 million to build the project (Plutonic Power 2006).

A number of other projects currently under construction, or about to deliver energy to BC Hydro under EPAs signed after 2002, have already been "flipped'" to other owners. This is a subject that has been of considerable concern in areas such as Whistler-Squamish, which experienced both the first major wave of private power projects and the first major wave of project re-sales. Many of these new investors are large international energy companies, private equity funds, or international banks. Selling power plant assets to these outside investors would be far less lucrative if they were required to sell their energy to BC Hydro. A guarantee that they will be able to export their power hugely increases the amount developers can charge any prospective purchaser.

This explains, in part, why private power developers lobbied the government so energetically to get it to separate the transmission system from BC Hydro. They did not want to be forced to sell their energy to the Crown utility. By restructuring the transmission system into a common carrier obliged to provide unrestricted access to any power developer or marketer — including exporters — they have strengthened their bargaining power with BC Hydro. The rhetoric about the need to provide "non-discriminatory" access to the grid conceals the developers' financial calculation that freedom to export will increase the asset value and future re-sale price of private power projects. But by giving them such access, the government is undermining the Crown utility's ability to negotiate fair prices for B.C. ratepayers.

As the share of domestic energy production in the hands of private energy developers increases, the province will become increasingly vulnerable to potential supply constraints if these developers choose to export their energy. All EPAs have a fixed term and will, in time, expire. When this happens, private owners will be free to sell their energy to the highest bidder. If B.C. customers want access to this energy in future, they will have no choice but to pay American market prices to keep it in the province.

There is a clear parallel here with natural gas prices. The federal government's decision to allow unrestricted gas exports means that B.C. customers have to compete with American customers for natural gas produced within the province. As a result, prices in B.C. have been driven up by American demand, and the fact that it is produced in the province is now irrelevant. While natural gas is specifically covered by provisions in NAFTA's Chapter Six, including the guarantee that Canada can only reduce its exports to the United States in a manner proportional to reductions in domestic consumption, Chapter Eleven provides strong protection for any investment in B.C. by American and Mexican private power developers. Given that B.C. is now locked into NAFTA and WTO obligations, and given the changes made to the transmission system, it is not clear how the province could prevent private investors from exporting their energy.

Even the assumption that B.C. customers will be able to purchase all the electricity produced by B.C.-based power developers, albeit at prices determined by the American market, may not hold. There is no guarantee that developers will be willing to sell to B.C. Hydro. To the extent that large multinational energy companies acquire run-of-the-river and wind-generating facilities — a development consistent with both what has already happened in the oil-and-gas sector and in the recent consolidation of the American electricity sector — the owners' primary focus may be to meet the needs of their American customers.

It is notable, for example, that the California Public Utilities Commission has provided US$14 million to Pacific Gas and Electric, one of the largest utilities in the world, to investigate the feasibility of acquiring renewable energy from B.C. Part of the funding is to be allocated, as well, to examining the options for new transmission lines linking B.C.'s wind and water renewables with the California grid. This is due to new legislation in California mandating that utilities operating within the state increase the share of renewable energy in their portfolios. Under the constraint of having to reach a specific renewable target, they may view the issue of price as less important than that of meeting their quota (Calvert 2007b).

If the experience of foreign takeovers in B.C.'s gas industry — in which West Coast Energy was acquired by Duke Energy of Charlotte, North Carolina and Terasen (formerly B.C. Gas) was purchased by Texas-based Kinder Morgan — B.C.'s run-of-the-river and wind-farm facilities are also likely to end up being acquired by foreign or out-of-province corporations. The government's policy is likely, over the long term, to result in the loss of provincial ownership and control of the private portion of B.C.'s electricity system. Far from enhancing future security of supply, the policy will lead to precisely the opposite outcome.

All of this is to underline the fact that BC Hydro's growing reliance on buying energy from private developers does not guarantee security of supply for B.C. customers. Electricity is not like other commodities: a small shortfall of energy can have dramatic — and very harmful — effects on the province, an observation to which customers in California, Alberta, Ontario and a number of other jurisdictions can readily attest. Being unable to meet demand during peak periods could entail significant curtailments of service to customers and, in the worst-case scenario, major blackouts, as have been experienced in other jurisdictions.

Uncertainty about future energy supplies can also affect B.C.'s comparative advantage as a location where new businesses can invest, secure in the knowledge that they will have access to the energy required for their production facilities. Thus far, security of supply has not been an issue affecting such decisions. Rather, the fact that B.C.'s electricity system has been so reliable and secure has been a positive factor. But, down the road, if B.C. ends up having to contend with supply constraints resulting from private exports, this could negatively affect investment decisions, especially if such constraints were accompanied by major increases in energy prices.

In sum, the government's new policies are creating additional risks, rather than greater security, for B.C. customers. They ignore the province's recent historical experience, which demonstrates very clearly that the key to B.C.'s successful energy policy has been public ownership of generating assets — ownership that has enabled the government, through BC Hydro, to guarantee an adequate supply of energy for B.C. customers.

NOTES

1. It is true that the diminishing energy surplus discussed earlier was not entirely due to the policies of the current government. But the fact is that it has had over six years to address the problem during which time it has prevented BC Hydro from building new generating facilities. The previous NDP government should also come in for some criticism: it largely avoided dealing with the province's future generating needs, preferring to rely on past investments. And, its eight-year rate freeze, while of considerable benefit to customers, also negatively impacted BC Hydro's finances and, arguably, its ability to build new capital projects. Had BC Hydro built additional capacity under the NDP, it would have been considerably more difficult for the Liberals to expand the role of private energy developers.
2. Of course, as we noted earlier, historically, private American utilities were regulated under PURPA to obtaining a rate of return that was seen as "reasonable" given the investments their shareholders had made. A process for determining a "fair" rate of return was in place. This was to ensure that utilities did not use their monopoly position to gouge the public. But in B.C. nothing like this is in place in the electricity industry. Even if companies are making 50 or 100 percent profit — or more — on their investments, the EPA approach conveniently sidesteps any regulation of the companies' rates of return. The BCUC simply assumes that the truncated competitive process the government has put in place through BC Hydro's competitive tender calls is sufficient to protect the public's interest.

Chapter Five

Alcan and Cominco

IN ASSESSING THE LONG-TERM impact of the government's policy of requiring BC Hydro to purchase its future energy requirements from private power developers, it is instructive to examine earlier examples of private ownership of energy facilities in the province. There are two major private hydro generators in B.C. that clearly illustrate the problems the government will face in future if the current Energy Plan continues to be the basis of new electricity investments. They are Alcan, based in Kitimat, and Teck-Cominco, based in Trail. In both cases, earlier B.C. governments granted these firms — or their predecessor companies — the right to use public water resources to generate electricity primarily for their mineral smelting operations. And, in both cases, the companies have taken advantage of the fact that they have been permitted to generate energy to sell part of this energy, rather than using it for mineral production, when it was more profitable to do so.

Alcan is currently the world's second-largest producer of aluminum. It is also owner of a very significant hydro generating facility near Kitimat that has perhaps the lowest production costs of any power plant within the province — lower even than BC Hydro's own hydro facilities.[1] A brief history of the Alcan experience illustrates how allowing private interests to own energy generating facilities undermines the province's ability to maintain control of its water-for-power resources. It also shows how difficult it is for the government to obtain a fair economic rent for the electricity produced once private interests have acquired water licences and built power plants. And, it highlights how transferring control over water resources to corporations also undermines the government's ability to control prices or ensure that privately generated electricity is used to meet the needs of the people of B.C. Although the Alcan experience has been seen largely as a concern for the people in the District of Kitimat, it underlines the challenges future governments will face as more and more of B.C.'s electricity generating facilities are acquired by the private sector.

In 1949, Premier W.A.C. Bennett entered into negotiations with Alcan to allow it to use the water resources of the Nechako River to build and operate a major aluminum smelter in Kitimat. This initiative was enshrined in the 1949 *Industrial Development Act,* as well as a separate contract negotiated between the province and the company the following year.[2] The deal provided Alcan with a water licence to run for fifty years, expiring in 1999. In return for the use of the public water resource, the company agreed to use the energy to smelt aluminum, with provision for local sales of electricity.

Alcan chose the Nechako River because it promised to be a very good water source for cost-effective development of hydro power, a fact that had been well known for many years before the project began in 1950. The company proceeded to dam the river to stop most of its water from flowing into the Fraser River during the annual spring freshet. The dam flooded over 50 hectares of land and displaced roughly 200 members of the Cheslatta First Nation, who got virtually nothing from the government for the loss of their territory and way of life (Larsen 2003; Girard 2005). The resulting reservoir was seen as a way to ensure that there always would be at least a minimal flow into the Fraser during dry periods (Girard 2005).[3] The remainder of the water from the reservoir was to be diverted back across the coastal mountain range and used for energy production. Alcan proceeded to build a sixteen-kilometre water diversion tunnel from the reservoir to a new hydro generating station to provide electricity for the smelter in Kitimat it had agreed to construct.[4] The new power plant, situated 335 metres below the reservoir, had an installed capacity of 790 MW, sufficient to support a major, energy-intensive aluminum smelter.[5]

The government of the day believed the smelter would create the base for economic development in Kitimat and the surrounding region. In the view of many observers at the time, the essence of the deal was that the government provided Alcan with the public water resource in exchange for investment, jobs, and the regional economic development associated with aluminum smelting. To sweeten the deal, the government also ceded Alcan ownership of very large tracts of land in the vicinity of the project.

Alcan proceeded to build the generating facility, a smelter in the new town of Kitimat, and a fifty-kilometre transmission line to connect the two. The province, in turn, funded major investments in municipal infrastructure and services to support the proposed new city of Kitimat, which it believed would eventually have a population of 20,000 once the smelter was in full operation. Kitimat's economy was thus directly — and almost totally — dependent on the jobs and investment associated with the smelter. It is also worth noting that until 1978, Alcan's electricity grid was not connected to BC Hydro's transmission system. Consequently, energy from its power plant could not be exported out of the region.

However, the smelter built in the 1950s was only part of the project as originally envisaged. The water licence permitted Alcan to expand the capacity of its power plant, using more of the public's water resource on condition that it completed an upgrade of the smelter by 1999. If it failed to do so, the extra water would no longer be available as part of the contract. Consequently, during the 1980s, the company proceeded to begin work on the controversial Kemano Completion Project so it could take full advantage of the provisions of its water licence.

But by that time, public concerns over the environmental impact of diverting more water from the Nechako River (and other tributaries feeding into the reservoir) had become quite significant. Environmentalists took the company to court, challenging its right to continue with the project. The court battle dragged on for a number of years. An initial decision went against Alcan, but the company succeeded in having the decision reversed on appeal. Given the project's uncertain legal status, Alcan proceeded cautiously with its construction timetable.

On September 14, 1987, a controversial settlement was reached among three parties: Alcan, the province, and the federal government to clear the way for the project to be completed (Girard 2005). Alcan succeeded in separating the expansion of the hydro facility from the expansion of the smelter, arguing that the expanded hydro facility had to be completed before work could begin on the new smelter. It maintained that if the new smelter was finished before new energy was available; it wouldn't be possible to begin operations, so the new power plant had to come first. The understanding Alcan reached with the province was that it could build the power plant and sell the resulting extra energy to BC Hydro until the new smelter was complete, when it would then use the new energy for smelting aluminum.[6]

Then, during the final years of the Social Credit administration, Alcan persuaded the government to allow it to sell to BC Hydro any energy from its existing power plant that was "surplus" to its needs at the smelter. It argued that fluctuations in the aluminum market and certain operational constraints meant that during certain times of the year it did not require all the energy it could generate.[7] On this basis, in 1990 BC Hydro negotiated a long-term energy purchase agreement with Alcan. Once Alcan upgraded its smelter, it would again be able use the full capacity of its generating facilities to produce aluminum. The energy purchase agreement was thus essentially a stop-gap measure.

The 1990 agreement stipulated that the company would only sell energy to BC Hydro that was "surplus to its needs until required by Alcan for its own industrial purposes" (Kunin 2002). Surplus sales would constitute a temporary deviation from the original condition of its 1950 water licence. And, if Alcan found that its own smelter required this "surplus" energy for aluminum production, it would meet its obligations to BC Hydro by purchasing an equivalent amount on the energy market.

Alcan's interest in selling surplus energy to BC Hydro at the time can be explained, in part, by the extremely low cost structure of its generating facilities. Alcan was benefiting from investments made at prevailing construction prices in the 1950s, which meant that its cost of producing electricity was now extremely low compared with other generating options. By the beginning of the 1990s, energy prices were beginning to rise across North America. Selling energy had become far more profitable than making aluminum.

The 1990 EPA was based on the assumption that the Kemano Completion Project, due to be completed in 1995, would go forward. The twenty-year EPA signed in 1990 was to run from 1995, when the energy was due to come on stream, until 2014, and during this period, Alcan would complete construction of Kemano. The parties assumed the smelter would be in production before then, but the 2014 date provided a cushion in the event Alcan faced unanticipated problems.

The 1990 EPA included inflation indexing based on a price of approximately $30 MWh for 285 MW of capacity and 1,225 GWh of energy annually. Given that the company didn't know precisely when the smelter would be completed and, hence, when it might need the additional energy from Kemano, a provision was included enabling Alcan to "recall" the energy by giving the province five years' notice at any time once the first five years of the agreement had been fulfilled. The assumption was that the recall would be triggered by the completion of the new smelter.

But opposition to Kemano did not abate. One of B.C.'s best-known media personalities and former Social Credit Cabinet Minster, Rafe Mair, championed the opposition cause. By 1995, in the run up to the next year's provincial election, the Liberals — desperate to get votes in the north — indicated they would stop the project if elected. The NDP government then cancelled it, thus eliminating the possibility it would be a critical election issue. But by this time, Alcan claimed it had invested over half a billion dollars in the project and felt that the province had an obligation to make the company whole, that is repay Alcan for the development costs it had already incurred.

Confronting the prospect of lengthy litigation, the government negotiated a revised agreement with Alcan in 1997 that resolved the lawsuit between the parties. Alcan promised to expand aluminum production using the energy generated in Kitimat. This new investment would maintain jobs in the community. (The District of Kitimat has subsequently argued that this was a renewal of Alcan's commitment to build a "full-sized" smelter.)

In return, the government agreed to compensate Alcan for its expenditures. Rather than paying the half a billion dollars the company was demanding, it changed the terms of the original 1950 water licence, due to expire in 1999, to one that ran in perpetuity. While this enabled the government to avoid adding another half billion dollars to the province's official debt — and the political costs associated with being hounded by the media as a spendthrift administration — it also represented an enormous policy change in the government's relations with Alcan. On one hand, it meant that it could never again use the lever of not renewing the water licence as a bargaining chip in negotiations with the company. On the other hand, the government assumed that this amendment to the water licence would give Alcan the security it required to justify major new investments in upgrading its smelter.[8]

The agreement also allowed Alcan to continue to sell surplus energy as long as it kept the existing smelter running at capacity. And it guaranteed Alcan that the province would bridge the gap in the energy the company had expected to receive from the Kemano Completion Project, had it not been stopped. Because the Kitimat smelter used about 620 MW of the 780 MW capacity and line losses to the smelter took up 20 MW, there was a residual amount of 140 MW of energy left over.

Under the terms of the new (1997) Replacement Electricity Supply Agreement, negotiated in return for the smelter being upgraded, the province agreed to provide Alcan with 115 MW of base load electricity and an additional 60 MW of "firming" electricity annually, to enable Alcan to construct the larger smelter at Kitimat.

The 1990 long-term EPA anticipated that Alcan would have 285 MW of additional energy available once the Kemano Completion Project was in place. But as noted, this did not happen. Hence there was a gap of about 145 MW between the amount available for sale by Alcan and the amount it had committed to selling to BC Hydro. (The actual amount was adjusted from 145 MW to 167 MW by shortening the duration of the twenty-year contract by about eighteen months).

Alcan went to the energy market to purchase what it had agreed to supply to BC Hydro. Unfortunately, the company it chose to provide the energy was Enron, which eventually reneged on its commitment to deliver the 167 MW of energy to BC Hydro. BC Hydro's subsidiary, Powerex, sued Alcan and eventually received $100 million plus $10 million in accrued interest in compensation for the energy Enron had failed to deliver[9] (*New York Times* 2004).

The 1997 long-term purchase agreement with BC Hydro required Alcan to "return any idle capacity at its existing smelter at Kitimat, B.C., to full capacity on a priority basis relative to other idle aluminum smelting capacity controlled by Alcan and, in any event, not later than January 1, 1998" (District of Kitimat 2002). However, there were delays in returning to full production. The District of Kitimat grew increasingly upset because it believed that the company was diverting electricity from the production of aluminum — and the maintenance of jobs — in Kitimat so that it could benefit from highly profitable energy sales: "It is now April 2002 and there is plenty of idle capacity at Alcan's Kitimat smelter" (District of Kitimat 2002). Other critics have subsequently voiced similar concerns (McLaren 2006b).

By 2000, energy prices — particularly in California — skyrocketed, and Alcan had a long-term EPA to supply energy to BC Hydro at rates negotiated before those prices rose. If it were forced to purchase energy at market prices and sell it to BC Hydro at the price to which it was committed, it could lose money — a lot of money. Instead, according to the District of Kitimat, it used the low water flows in the Nechako River to justify shutting down part of its smelter operations. But it continued to sell energy (District of Kitimat 2002).

In the summer of 2001, after the provincial election and using the justification of ongoing low water levels, Alcan shut down approximately 40 percent of its smelting capacity (District of Kitimat). This enabled it to sell additional energy through BC Hydro's subsidiary, Powerex, and take advantage of the high prices created by the California energy crisis. While it maintained there would be no lay-offs and that everyone on the payroll would continue to be paid, it shortly afterwards announced that it would reduce employment at the Kitimat smelter by 200 jobs.

The District of Kitimat argued that, having established the principle that it could reduce its smelting operations in order to sell energy, Alcan then developed a plan to refurbish its smelter and, in the process, make it much more energy efficient. By doing so, it could produce as much aluminum as in the past, using less energy and approximately 1,000 fewer workers. The District of Kitimat described this plan as the "half-sized" smelter (District of Kitimat 2005). While the more efficient smelter would produce slightly more aluminum than the older operation, it would use much less energy. It would thus free up additional electricity for sales either to BC Hydro or the American market.

From the perspective of the District of Kitimat, this was unacceptable. It felt the energy should be used for increasing aluminum production, thus adhering to what it believed was the original intent of the province's 1950 agreement with Alcan. The District commissioned studies to show the negative impact on the local economy of this approach and to support its position that the government should enforce the original terms of the 1950 deal (Kunin 2003).

However, Alcan proceeded to put in place the infrastructure needed to implement its new focus on energy sales. It established a new division within the company with specific responsibility for energy marketing. It set up a new American subsidiary to sell electricity south of the border. And, most significantly, it successfully applied to the Federal Energy Regulatory Commission for a licence allowing it to sell energy in the United States.

A major impediment to expanding Alcan's energy sales was the limited capacity of the transmission line linking Kitimat with BC Hydro's major transmission corridor. This 380 MW line was built in the 1970s, not to facilitate energy exports by Alcan, but primarily to enable BC Hydro to provide service to that region of the province. Although both Alcan and BC Hydro have since invested in upgrading some of the electrical components used in the transmission system, line congestion still imposes clear limits on the amount of energy Alcan can export from the region.

This may explain why the issue of expanding investment in the transmission grid and separating its operation from BC Hydro were two key policy recommendations in Alcan's 2001 submission to the Energy Policy Task Force chaired by Ebbels, which we discussed earlier (Alcan 2001). While Alcan did not reference the issue of specifically expanding the capacity of this line, it would likely be easier to persuade an independent transmission company operating separately from BC Hydro to upgrade the line to carry more energy. If this did occur, Alcan would be able to sell a significantly greater quantity of energy either to BC Hydro or to the American market. And, as we have also seen, the government has created such an entity: the B.C. Transmission Corporation.

The District of Kitimat, on behalf of the local community, has vigorously opposed any reduction in the company's energy consumption at its smelter that would allow Alcan to expand energy sales. The District has attempted, on its own, to get its interpretation of the 1950 contract honoured by taking both the company and the provincial government to court. Its dispute with the province is partly a result of what it sees as the government's unwillingness to support Kitimat's position. But in attempting to force Alcan to utilize the full quantity of energy it generates in its Kitimat smelter, the District confronted a major roadblock: it is not a signatory to the original agreement with Alcan. This raised the legal question of "standing," that is, the right of Kitimat, as a non-signatory, to ask the court to rule on whether Alcan is violating the terms of the contract.

According to Kitimat's mayor, Richard Wozney (citing a 2003 study by Roslyn Kunin): "Every hundred jobs lost in aluminum cost B.C. $56 million annually in lost GDP. Already, since power sales started in 2000, Alcan has cut almost 370 jobs" (District of Kitimat 2005).

The public policy concerns of the District were reflected in the following analysis:

> [E]lectricity generated at Kemano by the use of the public's water resource will be used more and more for power sales to be exported out of the region. This will, over time, eliminate or severely contract the use of that electricity for industrial development in the Northwest, specifically aluminum production in Kitimat.
>
> Alcan's operations, before the recent shut down to sell power, had sales in excess of $500 million and supports about 1,800 direct

> high paying jobs and another 4,200 closely linked jobs. The community of Kitimat was built specifically to support industry, which would rely on the Kemano power. The community has developed infrastructure for about 20,000 persons. Municipal, provincial, and federal taxes are substantial. Smelting operations, using Kemano cost electricity input price, are consistently profitable.
>
> If Alcan was to eventually sell all the Kemano power, it would employ about 50 to 100 persons. Federal and provincial corporate taxes may be the same but all taxes dependent on personal income and property ownership would be severely reduced. Huge personal costs would be assumed as property values, already depressed by about 30 to 40 percent from 1998 values, would plummet. For every 10 percent loss in property value there is an aggregate personal loss of approximately $38 million from residential and small business owners. Personal and retirement savings would collapse and the livelihood of 6,000 British Columbians would be lost. The communities of Kitimat and Terrace would cease to exist as we know them. The whole Northwest, already in severe economic decline, would lose much of its remaining employment base.
>
> To give some magnitude of scale of the money we are dealing with, a new smelter as envisaged in the 1997 Agreement would cost in the order of $1.3 to $3 Billion. The value of the water rights in gross revenue terms is about $5 billion, much more at the new price for power. If Alcan is successful in its pursuits, it will avoid having to invest billions in B.C. (District of Kitimat 2002: 4–5)

As noted elsewhere, BC Hydro's cost of generation from its hydro dams built in the 1962–1984 period is about $5 per MWh. Alcan's costs are almost certainly even lower, given that it built its facilities in the 1950s. While there are varying estimates of Alcan's per-unit energy costs — the company is not disclosing them — it is reasonable to assume that they are probably in the range of $3 to $4 per MWh. (Kitimat's consultant, Roslyn Kunin has a slightly broader range of between $2 and $6 [Kunin 2003].) Adding the $5.147 per MWh water-rental fee the province currently collects, it is likely that Alcan's total cost is in the range of $8 to $9 per MWh. Because Alcan's hydro generated energy is rich in capacity as well as energy, it can be marketed in the United States as firm energy.[10]

Not surprisingly, then, with the explosion of prices in the California market at the turn of the century and the confident predictions that energy prices that will remain higher than they were during the 1990s, the District of Kitimat concluded that Alcan was attempting to re-orient its business from one of being almost exclusively an aluminum producer to also being an energy supplier and exporter. Even at $50 MWh, Alcan can make far more money selling electricity than producing aluminum.

The District of Kitimat has noted that while Alcan's plans for its revamped B.C. smelter appear to be designed to use considerably less electricity than the capacity of its power plant, the company is simultaneously planning a $2.5 billion smelter in South Africa, where cheap coal is readily available. Subsequently, Alcan has released many more details about its South Africa Project (*Vancouver Sun* 2005; Grant 2006). While producing aluminum at Kitimat is likely much cheaper than producing it in South Africa, selling Kitimat-generated electricity is far more profitable than producing aluminum in Kitimat. The business logic appears persuasive: maximize profits by producing aluminum elsewhere — even though it costs more — in order to capitalize on energy sales from its Kemano power plant. Additionally, the company has also announced a $2 billion investment in a new smelter in Québec as part of a deal with the provincial government and Hydro Québec. And, in the spring of 2007, it announced a $7 billion deal to produce aluminum in Saudi Arabia (Marowits 2007).

The estimated profit margins on Alcan's electricity sales are truly astounding. Most retail stores assume that a 1 to 2 percent return on sales provides a good rate of profit. Fortune 500 data on profits as a share of revenues show that, on average, the companies it lists achieve a 3 to 4 percent profit level. High profit sectors such as the pharmaceutical industry — which consistently leads the Fortune 500 in profits as a share of sales — have a profits-to-sales ratio of about 17 percent. But Alcan's profit margin on sales from Kemano is far, far higher. At $50 per MWh with an embedded cost of about $8 to $9 per MWh, over 80 percent of revenue is clear profit. At $71 per MWh, it could approach 90 percent clear profit, depending on embedded costs. This is an astounding rate of return. It also explains why Alcan has such an incentive to ratchet down its use of electricity by opting for the "half-sized" smelter — to use the District of Kitimat's term — while simultaneously announcing major increases in aluminum smelting capacity in other jurisdictions.

What is most disturbing about this situation is the government's apparent complacency — or complicity — in the loss of public control over Alcan's energy. Unlike Québec, where the government vigilantly maintains control of Alcan's water licence, requiring the corporation to use the energy it produces exclusively for aluminum production — and imposing the condition that Alcan must keep its head office in the province — the B.C. government has moved in exactly the opposite direction. It has been willing to accommodate — indeed support — the company's position that W.A.C. Bennett did not link access to the water resource to a commitment to use the resulting electricity to produce aluminum.

As noted, the District of Kitimat took both the Province and Alcan to the B.C. Supreme Court to force the company to use its electricity for aluminum smelting. During the hearings, the government stunned Kitimat by submitting a statement to the court claiming that the original purpose of the 1950 deal with Alcan was not to use the water resource to promote the economic development of the region through aluminum production. Instead, in what Kitimat saw as in contradiction to the position of earlier governments going all the way back to Bennett, it claimed that the reason Alcan was allowed to build the original Kemano power plant was to enable the company to generate electricity for any use the company chose to make of it!

Chief Justice Brenner in his decision dated March 28, 2007, agreed with the interpretation of the Province and Alcan. He ruled against the District of Kitimat's assertion that the 1950 agreement between the Province and the company linked electricity production to smelting aluminum. In his words:

> I conclude that neither the Industrial Development Act nor the 1950 Agreement contain language that would restrict Alcan in the decisions it chooses to make with respect to the sale of hydro-electric power generated at Kemano. Specifically, there is nothing in either instrument that would require Alcan to maintain any specific production level at the Kitimat smelter. Alcan is not restricted by either instrument from selling its Kemano power or using it for the Kitimat smelter as it considers appropriate. (Supreme Court of B.C. 2007)[11]

We noted, earlier, that Alcan initially marketed its surplus energy in 1990 to BC Hydro under a long-term energy purchase agreement until the (now cancelled) Kemano Completion Project was finished. However, this contract had provisions for the company to terminate it with five years' notice, and Alcan has given this notice to BC Hydro. In its August 31, 2006, submission to the BCUC, BC Hydro explains:

> BC Hydro and Alcan Inc. are party to a Long-Term Electricity Purchase Agreement dated 27 February 1990, as amended (the "LTEPA") under which Alcan Inc. sells to BC Hydro electrical energy generated at Alcan Inc.'s Kitimat generating station ("LTEPA Energy"). Alcan Inc. gave BC Hydro a notice on 1 January 2005 in which Alcan Inc. states that it is recalling its obligation to sell all LTEPA Energy under the LTEPA, effective 1 January 2010. Notwithstanding the initial Mandatory Requirements or any other provisions of this CFT (Call for Tender), recalled LTEPA Energy is not eligible to be tendered in this Call.

BC Hydro's earlier 2006 REAP submission to the BCUC reveals the amount of energy involved in this recall:

> Future of agreements with Alcan. Alcan has recalled its long-term energy purchase agreement. Due to the recall, the current supply forecast excludes 1,225 GWh/year of energy starting in F2011. This amount of energy from Alcan was previously included as part of the supply forecast used for the 2004 REAP.[12]

Inexplicably — although perhaps because of government pressure — BC Hydro failed to challenge Alcan's recall notice, even though there were very strict conditions limiting Alcan's right to make such a recall. Alcan might have been successfully challenged under the terms of the long-term EPA, which, arguably, based the right of recall on Alcan's ability to demonstrate that the energy was needed for production of aluminum. This is particularly puzzling, given that the price of the energy being recalled — roughly $35 MWh — was far below what BC Hydro knew it would end up paying to replace it. And, as we saw, the cost of this replacement energy in the 2006 tender call was $87.50 MWh, more than two-and-a-half times the price it was paying Alcan under the terms of the 1990 agreement. Consequently, the early recall would result in an increase in rates for BC Hydro customers.

Alcan's decision appears to reflect the government's policy change — which the company had advocated — to provide "open access" to the grid for private energy generators. Once Alcan stops delivering this energy in 2010, Alcan may be able to sell it directly to American customers regardless of B.C.'s requirements. Alternatively, it would be able to demand that BC Hydro pay American prices to keep it in the province.[13] As the quote above illustrates, by 2006 BC Hydro was already assuming that the 1,225 GWh per year of energy it is currently purchasing from Alcan will no longer be available. The pending energy gap resulting from Alcan's decision provided one of the arguments for the dramatic increase in BC Hydro electricity purchases from private energy interests in its 2006 energy call.

Shortly after the results of the 2006 tender call were announced, BC Hydro indicated that it had negotiated, with the help of the provincial government, another twenty-year long-term energy purchase agreement (commonly referred to as "LTEPA Plus") with Alcan, effectively replacing part of the much cheaper energy that Alcan had recalled. One of the conditions the province inexplicably imposed on BC Hydro in this process was that it had to make an agreement based on "commercial" principles, meaning, presumably, that BC Hydro should pay Alcan a rate that reflected what it was paying other energy suppliers in the province.

One reason BC Hydro has been so interested in acquiring Alcan's energy is that it is high-quality, firm energy that can offset a portion of the non-firm energy it is now committed to purchasing from wind-farm and small hydro projects. Despite the low embedded cost of Alcan's energy, BC Hydro used the prices it paid in the very expensive 2006 call as the basis for determining what it would now pay to Alcan. As a result, BC Hydro committed to purchase the Alcan energy at a price of $71.30 per MWh, with a 3 percent inflation adjustment factor built in. (This deal upset some of the 2006 tender call private power producers, whose inflation adjustment was lower.) As well, it provided a one-time payment of $111 million to Alcan to cement the twenty-year deal — a payment that some critics saw as a way of repaying the $100 million that Alcan had been directed by the courts to pay BC Hydro as a result of Enron's earlier noted failure to deliver energy to BC Hydro.[14] The total potential cost to ratepayers over the period to 2029 would be $1.84 billion in actual dollars (not adjusted for inflation).[15]

So generous was the new contract in the eyes of its critics that the BCUC was deluged with interveners objecting to what they saw as a deeply flawed deal. The District of Kitimat argued strongly against approval of the deal on the grounds that it provided no guarantee that Alcan would actually make the investment required to build a new full sized smelter and that it opened the door to further lucrative energy sales by Alcan.

One intervener, Richard McLaren, a retired Alcan manager with more than twenty years of service with the company, was particularly concerned about the impact on the economy and employment in Kitimat. He had seen how earlier deals had not resulted in the investments that had been promised (McLaren 2006b). He was particularly upset because the text of the deal was secret. Without being able to read the "fine print" it would be impossible to know whether it accomplished what BC Hydro and the government claimed. The secrecy was even more puzzling because the government chose to make the initialing of the deal a high profile media event. The Premier had actually interrupted his vacation to participate in a press conference promoting the benefits of the new long-term EPA. Normally, such an announcement would be accompanied by the details that analysts would need to see to evaluate its merits. But this was not the case. BC Hydro provided only a sixteen-page summary of the contract to the public. At the same time it submitted a 266-page legal brief to the BCUC arguing that the actual text of the contract should remain secret, an action that further heightened McLaren's concerns about the costs and benefits to Kitimat (McLaren 2006a, 2006b, 2007).

Fortunately, the BCUC decided that the details should be made public. And, when McLaren finally had the opportunity to analyze the text of the seventy-one-page contract, he concluded that the deal was very one-sided, with Alcan getting major benefits while the province got only promises that might — or might not — be kept by Alcan. In a Feb. 7, 2007, speech to an audience in Kitimat he outlined his concerns in detail:

> First of all, I stated (to the BCUC) that this new LTEPA Plus contract only guarantees power sales. Alcan guarantees to supply BC Hydro with certain fixed amounts of Tier 1 power. BC Hydro agrees to take and pay for this power. This is the 170 MW declining to 55 MW that Alcan is so fond of talking about.
>
> Because Alcan guarantees this power, if it does not deliver it on time it has to make up the shortfall sometime in the future. However, BC Hydro also guarantees to take and pay for any Tier 2 power which Alcan wishes to sell it over and above the Tier 1 amounts and up to the limit of BC Hydro's take-away transmission facilities (380 MW). Alcan never talks about this.
>
> The difference between Tier 1 and Tier 2 power is that the Tier 1 amounts are guaranteed by Alcan and the Tier 2 amounts are not. For this lack of guarantee, Tier 2 power is paid at $8/MWh less than Tier 1 after 2014.
>
> However, BC Hydro guarantees to take and pay regardless of whether it is Tier 1 power or Tier 2 power up to the delivery limit of 380 MW.
>
> This guarantee to take and pay continues even if Alcan doesn't start construction of the modernized smelter, or even if it doesn't complete it, or even if it doesn't run the smelter at full capacity. It doesn't matter: power sales continue, no matter what....
>
> What is missing is any commitment to a minimum smelter load coupled to a minimum operating rate for the smelter. As it stands now, the smelter load can be anything Alcan wants it to be, from zero up to the maximum.
>
> If Alcan wanted to shut down half the smelter and sell the power, then it would have a guaranteed buyer in BC Hydro for 380 MW. (McLaren 2006a)

McLaren went on to note that the key constraint on power sales was the existing transmission line and the agreement included provisions that could open the door to even larger power sales if the capacity of this line were expanded (McLaren 2006b).

Trafford Hall, City Manager for the District of Kitimat, was also extremely concerned about the issue of power sales and the huge financial incentive the long-term purchase agreement would give the company to cut back on aluminum production in favour of the much more lucrative activity of selling energy. His comparison of the rate of return from power sales with the rate from producing aluminum is summarized in Table 13. Hall further calculated that if Alcan were to sell the full 380 MW of energy that the transmission line was capable of delivering, its annual profit would

Table 13: Value Comparison: Aluminum vs. Power Sales

Sale Price of Energy	\$71 MWh
Deduct Provincial Water Rentals	- \$5 MWh
Deduct Production Costs	- \$5 MWh
Net Profit on Energy Sales	\$61 MWh
Percent Profit on Energy Sales	1,320%
Profit on Aluminum Production (Range)	20%–40%
Profit Advantage Selling Energy	1,280%–1,300%

Source: Presentation by Trafford Hall to a Public Meeting in Vancouver, Jan 17, 2007

be \$203 million. The net present value of this annual profit, at a 6 percent discount rate, was \$3.1 billion (Hall 2007).

The District of Kitimat also asked well respected energy analyst Dr. Marvin Shaffer to examine the details of the proposed agreement. Shaffer was the principal negotiator on behalf of the Province when the 1997 energy purchase agreement with Alcan was signed. Thus he had considerable knowledge of the background to the 2006 draft agreement between BC Hydro and Alcan. He concluded that BC Hydro was paying far too much to Alcan for the energy it planned to purchase from the company. Instead of using the 2006 tender award with its average price of \$87.50 as a benchmark, he argued that BC Hydro could have compared it with the cost of energy from a re-powered Burrard Thermal Station. This would result in a much lower price comparator, even assuming fairly high gas prices. Alternatively, BC Hydro could have examined what Alcan could get in the American energy market and offered a similar price. Using this comparator, BC Hydro was still paying far more than it ought to for Alcan's energy. In his words:

> The price BC Hydro has offered to Alcan is far in excess of this opportunity cost. The export value to Alcan would be the border price less transmission and marketing charges. Given BC Hydro's forecast export prices and B.C. Transmission Corporation's open access transmission tariffs, the net value of Alcan electricity export sales over the same time frame as LTEPA+ would be some \$45/MWh or less (in 2006\$), markedly less if it had to incur transmission upgrade costs. BC Hydro has offered a premium of \$30/MWh or more than the export value (Alcan's opportunity cost) in LTEPA+. (Shaffer 2006)

Shaffer also noted that BC Hydro's argument that signing this deal would reduce ratepayers' risk of future price escalation was deeply flawed. Risk was a two way street. By paying far more for the energy than it would have if it had chosen any one of a number of other reasonable options, in reality BC Hydro was forcing its ratepayers to take on a substantial price risk.

To the surprise of the government, BC Hydro, and Alcan, on December 29, 2006, the BCUC actually ruled against the deal (BCUC 2006). It determined that it was inappropriate for BC Hydro to pay Alcan a price based on what it had paid for new energy under the 2006 energy call, given that the contract did not trigger the construction of any new energy generation within B.C., and given that Alcan's energy was being produced from an old facility whose cost of production was much lower. In the words of BCUC Secretary Robert J. Pellatt:

> The Commission Panel concludes that BC Hydro should not have agreed to the pricing provisions of LTEPA Plus, and in particular should not have agreed to pricing provisions based on the F2006 call. Prices from the F2006 call were obtained through a competitive process for a specific product with pre-determined terms and conditions. The LTEPA Plus was negotiated in a trilateral environment with no pre-determined terms and conditions, and the pricing should have reflected both Alcan's opportunity cost and the specific risks to both Alcan and BC Hydro arising from the recall notice. (BCUC 2006)

As Pellatt indicates, the fact that this deal was the result of three-party negotiations rather than a tender process was of particular concern to the BCUC. In its subsequent reasons for the decision released a month later, the BCUC also determined that it was inappropriate for the government to have BC Hydro ratepayers give Alcan an incentive payment to build its new smelter. If the province wanted to provide a subsidy or incentive to Alcan, the BCUC felt it should do it directly. It should not expect BC Hydro ratepayers to fund it through their electricity bills.

BC Hydro made several shocking revelations in the BCUC hearings. The Crown utility admitted that it did not have anyone on its negotiating team familiar with the specific economics of the aluminum industry. Even more worrisome was BC Hydro's response to questions concerning whether it knew, or had good estimates of, the production cost of Alcan's energy. It indicated that it had no idea how much it would cost Alcan to produce the energy it was going to sell to BC Hydro. And it further indicated that it had no idea of the estimated production costs of energy from the various private power developers that had been given contracts under the 2006 tender award.[16]

At the time of writing, BC Hydro has indicated it will appeal this decision. It may opt to have the BCUC reverse its decision entirely or try to amend the contract in such a way as to make it acceptable to the BCUC. It is not clear what Alcan will do if the BCUC does not approve a re-negotiated contract, although there has been speculation that the company may choose to reconsider whether to go ahead with the construction of its new "half-sized" smelter at Kitimat in retaliation for the cancellation of the deal. At the time of writing, Alcan has just announced that it will go ahead with rebuilding the smelter, but the details of the project have not been fully released, so it is not clear how large the new smelter will be. For its part, BC Hydro has indicated it may try to renegotiate the deal.

Regardless of the outcome of this process, it is clear that, in failing to take measures to limit Alcan's ability to sell energy to the United States after the 1990 long-term EPA with BC Hydro expired, and in not aggressively pushing to have the original terms of the 1950 contract interpreted in a way that would link Alcan's energy to smelting aluminum, the province has effectively abandoned the public's interest in the water resource. With water rentals set at $5.147 per MWh — roughly 7.5 percent of the value of the water resource (depending on the sale price of the energy) — the public will end up receiving only a tiny fraction of the enormous profits the resource generates. At the same time, the public will be paying Alcan premium prices for energy generated from the public water resource.

The public, both locally and provincially, will also pay in other ways. If Kitimat's population continues to decline as a result of lower employment levels, the province's investment in public infrastructure in the District will be squandered. Of course, the residents of the area will suffer not only through job losses, but also through diminishing property values, store closures, and reduced economic opportunities (Kunin 2003).

We shall now turn to examine, more briefly, the experience with B.C.'s other major private sector electricity generator: Teck Cominco. Like Alcan's Kitimat facility, Teck Cominco's original hydro generating plants were built to provide the energy needed by its smelter, as well as related mining activities. Teck Cominco's predecessor company, West Kootenay Power and Light, was incorporated in 1897 and began building small hydro power plants in the early decades of the twentieth century. However, Teck Cominco's principal source of energy is now the Waneta Dam. Like Alcan's power plant, it was built in the 1950s, and so the cost of generating electricity is extremely low — perhaps comparable to Alcan's cost structure.

The energy from the facility has been used primarily to power the Trail smelter. The Waneta Dam and power plant has over 400 MW of capacity and generates about 2,700 GWh of energy, annually. According to the company's website, under normal operations Teck Cominco is able to sell — or export — about 900 GWh of "surplus" energy annually, although this number has varied in recent years, depending on the price of electricity on the American market. Unlike Alcan's facility located far up the B.C. coast, the Waneta Dam is very close to the border and the company has been a

Table 14: Teck-Cominco Power Sales and Revenues

Year	Surplus Power Sold (GWh)	Power Price $ MWh (US)	Revenue From Sales $ Million (US)
2001	1,159	174	$202
2002	683	23	$16
2003	769	39	$30
2004	957	44	$42
2005	1,278	58	$74
2006	891	44	$39
Total 2001–06	5,737	N/A	$403

Source: Teck Cominco SEDAR filings <http://www.sedar.com/homepage_en.htm>

regular exporter of energy through a short transmission line to the United States. Thus, it is not restricted by having to wheel its energy through the BC Hydro system.

During the California energy crisis, when prices spiked dramatically, Cominco was able to halt its production of metals at the Trail smelter in favour of exporting energy to the United States. The price was so favourable that it was able to put its workforce on lay-off at full pay for the period during which it calculated that it would make more money selling energy than metals. While California prices have dropped from their 2001 peak, the company has still made significant profits from power sales in subsequent years, as Table 14, taken from the firm's Canadian Securities Administrators (SEDAR) filings illustrates.

During a 2005 dispute with the Trail local of the United Steelworkers' of America, the company was able to use its ability to sell energy at a profit to minimize the impact of the closure of its smelter. According to Rory Carrol, even at prices much lower than those prevailing during the peak of the California energy crisis, Teck Cominco was able to deal with the loss of production resulting from the union's job action by selling the energy not being used at the smelter — and did so at a profit:

> Striking workers at Teck Cominco Ltd.'s Trail operations are demanding that the company return to the bargaining table, but there's reason to believe the Vancouver, British Columbia-based mining giant isn't in any rush. According to Canadian brokerage firm Desjardins Securities Inc., Teck Cominco could actually make more money selling its electrical power to companies in the Northwest than it could through metal sales. The brokerage firm said that if Teck Cominco sells its entire 2,700 gigawatt hours (GWh)

> of electrical power, it could make C$39 million ($32.2 million) in revenue and show an operating profit of C$24 million ($19.8 million), more than offsetting the C$17 million ($14 million) lost from selling metals. (Carrol 2005)

The windfall profits from energy sales enjoyed by both Alcan and Teck Cominco also illustrate the future problems that the government is now creating through its Energy Plan and related policies. Other private energy developers are quite likely to adopt similar approaches. They will push to transform the public's water resource into a private entitlement in which they are free to maximize their profits, regardless of the impact on both ratepayers and B.C.'s future energy security. Pandora's Box, once opened, will be very difficult for future governments to close.

The ability to sell to the American market is important in another way: it provides a guarantee that private producers will not be required to sell to BC Hydro — except at prices they find acceptable — and thus ensures that they will be able to maximize the value of their investments. While this is a wonderful arrangement for energy investors, it provides neither security of supply to B.C. customers nor any protection from future price increases driven by the demands of customers south of the border.

One of B.C.'s key comparative advantages has been its supply of low-cost electricity. The loss of this advantage will have significant — and damaging — consequences for the provincial economy, and will impose higher prices on B.C. ratepayers. And, it cannot be forgotten that B.C. is considerably colder than the United States. It may be possible to not use air conditioning in California's summer heat, but it is not possible to do without electricity during the winter in Prince George or Dawson Creek. While high energy prices may be a major inconvenience to residents of Los Angeles, they will create serious hardship in B.C.'s much colder climate.

One further point is relevant. All public policy changes in B.C. are now affected by Canada's obligations under NAFTA. While existing "non-conforming" laws and practices can remain because they are "grandparented," the provincial government is constrained not to impose new regulations or other impediments to investor rights. NAFTA's "liberalization" requirements are a one-way street. Consequently, while the government can further "liberalize" its policies, it cannot go back once it has eliminated more restrictive ones. If a company has among its shareholders investors that are from the United States or Mexico, it has the full protection of NAFTA, including its Chapter Eleven investor rights' provisions.

At the urging of private power developers, B.C. has granted "non-discriminatory" access to private interests who wish to market their energy either within or outside B.C. In opening the grid to private energy exports from companies such as Alcan, Cominco, and the numerous private power developers now acquiring power plants in B.C., the government is moving down this one-way street. It has embarked on a policy that can only be seen as reckless, given that future government action either to provide greater energy security for the province or to obtain a fairer share of the province's water resource revenues would likely expose B.C. to an investor rights challenge — a dispute that B.C. would, in all probability, lose. In sum, the government is abandoning very the policy tools that will be needed in future to ensure that the public gets a fair deal for B.C.'s bountiful water resources.

NOTES

1. Alcan employs 73,000 people worldwide, according to its 2005 TSX filing, and has operating facilities in fifty-six countries. Virtually from the day the original 1950 agreement was proposed, Alcan's role in Kitimat has been controversial. There have been numerous accounts of the contractual relationship between Alcan, the province, and the District of Kitimat — and of the conflicts around these contracts. One of the most useful is the historical summary by the District itself (District of Kitimat 2002). See also Yakabuski 2006.
2. Government of British Columbia 1949, 1950. *Industrial Development Act, 1949*. c. 31, s. 1. and Government of British Columbia. *Agreement Between the Government of British Columbia and Aluminium Company of Canada*, dated December 29, 1950. Both documents are available on the District of Kitimat's website <http://www.city.kitimat.bc.ca>.
3. Girard (2005) also provides a brief account of the tragic impact of this project on the Cheslatta First Nation.
4. One reason the government believed construction of the dam to divert the river was acceptable from an environmental perspective at the time was that the Nechako River did not have salmon spawning beds, due to its steep waterfalls and rapids. Consequently, the project was not seen as a threat to wild salmon stocks.
5. In BC Hydro's response to information requests at the BCUC on November 17, 2006, it stated that Alcan's facility now has an installed capacity of 896 MW and peak capacity of 890 MW (BC Hydro 2006f).
6. I should note my debt to Trafford Hall, City Manager of Kitimat, who provided me with a great deal of background information on the history and financial implications of Alcan's operations in Kitimat.
7. Alcan's account of this arrangement focusses on how it was assisting the province by providing BC Hydro with needed additional energy. See Alcan 2001.
8. In December of 2006 Alcan announced it would invest over $2 billion in a new smelter in Québec. One of the reasons the Québec government has been able to leverage such a major investment is that, unlike B.C., it has retained control over the water licences provided to Alcan, using them as a bargaining chip to leverage commitments.
9. Interestingly, this was almost exactly the same amount as was agreed by BC Hydro in its revised long-term EPA with Alcan in the fall of 2006 (which was

subsequently rejected by the BCUC). See BC Hydro 2006f.

10. Alcan may also be able to take advantage of its capacity-rich hydro facility to sell capacity to wind and run-of-the-river facilities, which are low in capacity, so that they can obtain better prices for their energy on international markets.
11. At the time of writing, Kitimat has indicated that it will appeal this decision.
12. BC Hydro, 2005 REAP, Section 2, page 46 (BC Hydro 2005a).
13. As we will see, it did even better than what it would likely have gotten in the American market at the time.
14. The proposed contract was to run from January 1, 2010 (i.e., the expiry date of the previous contract) to December 31, 2024, with provisions for an extension of five years.
15. BC Hydro's adjusted figure for the period from 2007 to 2029 (which includes the last three years of the current long-term EPA) is $827.8 million using a net present value adjustment factor of 5.88 percent. Arguably, this adjustment factor is high, leading to a lower net present value figure (BC Hydro 2006g).
16. This information came out during the BCUC hearings on the Alcan-BC Hydro contract. See the transcripts of the hearing for more details <http://www.bcuc.com/>.

Chapter Six

Water Resource Giveaway

Water is one of B.C.'s most valuable resources. Indeed, some would argue that it is the most valuable resource B.C. has in the context of a continent whose useable supplies of fresh water are reaching their limits, especially in California and elsewhere in the American southwest. Water is a renewable resource whose value will remain for generations to come. Water is also a resource Canadians cherish, as evidenced by the concerns they have articulated in opposition to the commercialization of water and their hostility to proposals to export water in bulk to the United States. For First Nations, water also has special cultural and religious significance.

The people of B.C. use the public water resource for a variety of purposes. However, any significant use of water is currently regulated through the province's water-licensing system. The granting of a water licence gives the recipient the ability to make use of public water for a variety of specified purposes, including agriculture, municipal drinking water, mining, oil-and-gas extraction, and hydroelectric production.

There are a wide variety of different types of provincial water licences (Calvert 2006a; Caldicott 2007). Many are for agricultural uses such as irrigation, some are for municipal water and wastewater systems, while others are granted to industrial and commercial firms that use water in their production processes. At last count, the government has issued many thousands of licences of all types. However, the water licences relevant to our study are those granted specifically for generating electricity. The government categorizes this type of licence under the heading "Water Power — General."

The awarding and administration of water licences is governed by a number of specific pieces of legislation. Arguably the most critical is the 1988 *Water Act*, passed by the Social Credit government and left largely unchanged by the NDP (except for a small adjustment in the fee system in 1994 and a consolidation in 1996). The current Liberal government has made a number of regulatory amendments to the *Act*, but it continues to use this statutory instrument as the basis of its approach to the granting of water licences and the establishment of water-rental fees.

In addition to the *Water Act*, two other pieces of 1996 legislation are also worth noting: the *Water Utility Act* and the *Utilities Commission Act*, along with subsequent amendments. The *Utilities Commission Act* regulates both public and private electricity generating facilities (designated as "utilities") and related transmission and distribution infrastructure. A final amendment, the *Miscellaneous Statutes Amendment Act* of 2006, enables private power projects to be designated as "public utilities" regulated by the BCUC and effectively outside the control of local governments' planning and zoning regulations.

Given the value of water and public concerns about its use, it would seem prudent for the government to exercise its stewardship over this resource in a very cautious manner, to ensure both that the public gets full value when it is used for private or commercial purposes and that the public never loses its future ability to reconsider and, where necessary, change the terms under which water licences are granted in response to evolving economic, social, and environmental concerns.

Properly managed, the use of water to generate electricity provides a renewable and cost-efficient method of meeting our energy needs. It is also a commercially valuable resource, whether used by the public through BC Hydro or by private energy developers. Rivers and streams with suitable sites for hydroelectric development are important public assets that have the ability to generate revenue to whoever is permitted to use the water resource.

As we shall discuss in more detail later, BC Hydro and the government have considerable data about the energy potential of small hydro developments in the province based on two major studies it commissioned from Sigma Engineering to inventory water power options, one in 2000 and the other in 2002 (BC Hydro 2000, 2002a). These studies provide site-specific and detailed estimates of the potential annual energy output — and corresponding revenues — from hundreds of small hydro sites across the province.

Given the commercial value of these sites, it would make sense for the government to treat them as productive assets and value them on the basis of their ability to generate energy revenues. Even if this process only generated a range of values dependent on electricity prices, it would still provide an indication of the long-term revenue potential of the sites. It would also ensure that if the government allowed private use of the water at these locations, it would be in a position to estimate the worth of this private use and charge a user fee that reflected the revenue potential.[1]

What is profoundly worrisome about the government's approach to the valuation of B.C.'s water-power assets is that it gives them no asset value at all. Instead, it treats them as if they have virtually no economic potential until a private developer builds a power plant on them. Water-power sites are essentially treated as a "free good" to be given away at minimal charge to whoever lines up to apply for a water licence — and a surprising number of Liberal government supporters, former BC Hydro executives, and Howe Street financers have managed to be near the front of the line. But if a future government were to try to buy back the water licences, it would quickly find that water-power assets given away for virtually nothing are now valued by their owners as gold-plated investments of enormous value to shareholders, worth tens, or in some cases, hundreds of millions of dollars.

Not surprisingly, the government's failure to even attempt to capture the asset value of B.C.'s water-power resources has triggered a new "gold rush," as private power developers stake out claims to the most promising sites across the province. As of November 2006 the province listed a total of 495 private water licences or applications under review (see Appendix).[2]

A quick review of the 495 private licences — or applications — shows that they capture virtually all the small hydro sites that can be economically developed, at least in the foreseeable future, within the province. The number of prime sites for small hydro (and for wind) is limited due to geography, energy capacity, transmission access, environmental suitability, and potential alternate uses of the location or water resource. A developer who acquires one — or in some cases dozens — of these prime sites will potentially benefit from its energy output for generations, if not centuries, into the future. The fact that these sites are currently "undeveloped"' does not mean that they have no future value. They should not be given away for the minimal cost of a permit and water-licence fees. Yet this is precisely what the government has been doing.

Along with its failure to estimate the asset value of these sites, the government has put in place a revenue structure for B.C.'s water-power resources that effectively denies the public virtually all the economic benefits arising from the energy that they can generate. To understand how poorly the public is served by the government's licensing arrangements, it is necessary to review the various kinds of payments the government receives in compensation for awarding water rights and Crown land to private energy developers.

There are three significant charges the province requires private power developers to pay for the water resource: the water-licence fee, the capacity charge — based on the facility's potential power output — and the water-rental charge, based on the amount of energy the water resource generates.

By using a standard template that ignores both the future revenue that can be produced from the water resource and the alternative uses that might be made of affected river systems, the government is allowing private energy interests to "lock in" effective ownership of the most promising hydro sites across the province for a relative pittance.

The cost of a water licence varies according to the size of the project. According to the province's 2006 fee schedule, projects with less than 20 MW generating capacity are required to pay a one-time $5,000 application fee for a water licence. The fee for hydro projects above this capacity is $10,000. In addition there is a $3,500 "Alternative Energy Project Fee" that covers the cost to the government of processing the proponent's application. Once a licence is granted, its annual renewal fee is a minimal $200.

The capacity charge is based on the rated output of the facility. This is currently $3,620 per MW.[3] For a 20-MW project — a typical small hydro project — the capacity charge works out to about $72,400, considerably less than 2 percent of the revenue a power plant this size would generate. Even for a larger one of, say 50 MW, the capacity charge would be only $181,000 annually, far less than 2 percent of anticipated revenues for the developers.

The third charge is the water rental. Significantly, B.C.'s water-rental fees are still based on an amendment to the regulations of the 1988 *Water Act* put in place back in 1994. The regulations tie future increases in rental fees to electricity rate increases granted to BC Hydro by the BCUC. The relevant legislation reads as follows:

> Indexing Factor For Fees and Rentals Under "Power Purpose" in Schedule A:
>
> Calculation of the indexing factor, with respect to rentals indicated as being indexed under the heading "Power Purpose" in Schedule A, must be done in accordance with the following steps:
>
> (a) the indexing factor for the calendar year ending December 31, 1994 is 1;
> (b) for each subsequent year, the indexing factor will be equal to the result of multiplying the indexing factor for the previous year by (1 + the percentage of approved average general increases in the British Columbia Hydro and Power Authority Electric Tariff Rate Schedule made in the preceding calendar year, excepting any rate increases resulting from the application of this regulation and passed through to ratepayers pursuant to section 61 (4) of the Utilities Commission Act).[4]

The NDP froze BC Hydro rates for eight years in a row, and so water rentals were also frozen during this period. Recently, the Crown utility has asked the BCUC to award it modest rate increases, but the cumulative total since 1994 has been extremely small (from $1.00 MWh to $1.103 MWh in the thirteen years to 2007).

There is nothing in the 1994 regulations that links the water-rental fee structure to the value of the energy produced from the water resource. While this arrangement may have been problematic even when it was first introduced, the financial consequences for the public from continuing to use this approach are now huge, given the recent large increases in energy prices that are reflected in the 2006 tender call.

The government has deliberately kept the water-rental fee at a very low rate to provide an "incentive" for private investors to build small hydro

Table 15: Provincial vs. Developer Income from a Typical Small Hydro Project

Provincial Revenue Source	Total Payment
Alternative Energy Project Fee	$3,300
Initial Water Licence Fee	$5,000
Water-Rental Charge (160,000 MWh)	$173,760
Capacity Charge (50 MW capacity)	$181,000
Land Occupancy	$500
Total Provincial Income	$363,560
BC Hydro Payments to Developer (F2006 average rate $74 MWh)	$11,840,000
Developer Income	$11,476,440

Note: Calculation based on a typical small hydro plant of 50 MW capacity generating 160,000 MWh of energy in its first year of operation. Table does not include small transmission right-of-way fees.

projects. It charges the owners of hydro facilities generating less than 160,000 MWh annually a water-rental fee of only $1.103 per MWh. Large projects, such as Alcan or Cominco, pay the same rate as BC Hydro, which is $5.147 per MWh for energy above the 160,000-MWh threshold and the lower rate on energy below it (Mattison 2006).

To put this in perspective, if a private power developer were able to produce exactly the maximum amount of energy (160,000 MWh) at the lower rate of $1.103 per MWh, it would pay the province a total of $176,480. In its 2006 tender call, BC Hydro paid an average of $74 per MWh at the plant gate for the energy it purchased from private power developers. At this price, BC Hydro would end up paying almost $12 million for 160,000 MWh of energy. So the water rental would amount to less than 1.5 percent of the value of the energy. Table 15 shows the payments a developer would have to make to the government for the use of public water and the payment BC Hydro would pay to the developer for the energy generated from this water.

There are a number of other small fees and charges private power developers still have to pay, but they are exceedingly modest. Developers pay fees for occupying Crown land, either in the form of a short- or long-term licence of occupation or as a payment to obtain fee-simple ownership. Fees for a licence of occupation of Crown land are $100 for a half-hectare or less, $500 for between a half-hectare and fifty hectares, and $2,000 for fifty hectares or more (Government of B.C. 2007a). If developers choose to acquire ownership of Crown land, the price they pay is based on comparable Crown land in the area, whose value — especially in remote locations — is almost nothing.

Where projects are located within the boundary of a municipality or regional district, power developers also have to obtain zoning approvals and pay for municipal building permits. They may also have to pay small fees for municipal services, either directly in the form of user charges or in their property tax bills. But these items are not major costs, amounting in most cases to a few thousands or tens of thousands of dollars.[5] There are separate, but relatively small, fees for transmission-line right-of-ways. In fact, the major costs faced by private power developers are not the fees charged by governments, but rather their own internal administrative expenses in acquiring the various permits, licences, and approvals.

Power producers also need a "Certificate of Public Convenience and Necessity" from the BCUC in order to construct a facility and transmit their energy (BCUC 2004). And, finally, like other property owners, energy developers have to pay taxes on the property they occupy. These vary depending on the type of tenure, but if it is fee-simple then the rate is based on comparable industrial uses.

When these various licence fees, water-use charges, and land-occupancy permits are added together, the province might receive, optimistically, only 4 to 5 percent of the gross revenue from small hydro projects, and perhaps 7 or 8 percent from the few large-scale projects now in place. Contrast this with oil-and-gas royalties, which are based on a sliding scale that reflects the market price of the resource. If the price of the commodity doubles, royalties to the government double. But water rentals are not connected to the market value of the energy they produce. Consequently, the province receives no additional revenue beyond the small incremental increases awarded to BC Hydro, even if the market price of energy doubles or triples.

On top of this, the province's ability to obtain a greater share of the revenue from these sites in future is likely to be constrained by the highly favourable terms of the contractual, licensing, and land-tenure agreements that have been awarded to energy developers. The actual terms of BC Hydro's EPAs are confidential, so it is not clear whether they have included provisions that would compensate developers if the province chose to increase water rentals significantly. But, given that this is a commercial risk the developers are aware of, it is likely that they have negotiated provisions in their contracts to ensure that BC Hydro pays the cost of any increase in water-licence renewal fees, water rentals, or capacity charges, and so there will be no way future governments can collect a larger portion of the developers' windfall profits.

While water licences are initially granted for forty years, they are renewable, which in practice means they may have no sunset clause. In retrospect, the government's decision in 1997 to grant a water licence "in perpetuity" to Alcan may have set a precedent that other private power developers anticipate they will be able to follow.

Where developers obtain fee-simple ownership of the sites of their power projects, they will have a permanent claim on power generation from that location. Given that the initial site for the powerhouse and related facilities will normally have been selected because it is the best location on a river, it is highly unlikely that any other future developer could make use of the water, because he or she would not have access to the site. And so, granting fee-simple title effectively ensures that the current water-licence holder will be able to claim the water itself in perpetuity. And, our NAFTA and WTO obligations will leave future governments no room to reverse course or significantly increase revenues in the public interest.

Similarly, efforts to restructure the terms of water licences to require the owners to sell the energy only within B.C. or only to BC Hydro may be challenged, successfully, as both violations of the original contracts and as "unreasonable interference" in the commercial freedom of firms to sell to the customers of their choosing. Amendments to water licences to keep energy in B.C. — an option future governments may want to explore — may no longer be possible, especially given that the province is already committed both to open access to the transmission grid for private companies and to their full right to export energy to the American market.

Turning to the question of who currently owns water-for-power licences, what we see is a rapid increase in the number awarded to private interests in recent years. True, BC Hydro itself has a considerable number of water licences, most of which were either inherited from predecessor companies or acquired while developing hydro projects on the Peace and Columbia rivers. But it has not been applying for many new ones in recent years. Historically, the government also awarded a significant number of licences to the private sector for mining, pulp-and-paper production, or other industrial purposes, or for Alcan's Kemano project. And a few others were issued for private power projects built before BC Hydro came into existence, or as part of what is now Fortis (formerly West Kootenay Power) and its hydro operations.

However, starting in 1987, when the Social Credit government began its efforts to privatize parts of BC Hydro, the province began issuing new licences for small hydro projects to private energy developers. It awarded these licences to introduce private capital into the province's electricity system. As we noted earlier, BC Hydro awarded a total of thirteen EPAs in the 1988 to1990 period, before the Social Credit government lost office in 1991. While private power developers did acquire a small number of water licences during the next decade, the fact that the NDP government of the day did not share the policy agenda of the previous administration made acquiring water licences much less attractive, especially as BC Hydro was not particularly interested in buying energy from small private hydro projects.

Thing changed, however, in the run-up to the 2001 election. Private-sec-

Table 16: Companies with More than Ten B.C. Waterpower Licences/ Applications for Licences

Company	Number of Licences/Applications
Hydromax Energy	38
Alpine Power	36
Cloudworks Energy	27
Plutonic Hydro	21
Canadian Hydro Developers	15
KMC Energy	14
Ledcor	14
Northwest Cascade	11
Alice Arm	10
Summit Power	10
Top Ten Licence Holders	196
Total Private Water Licences	495

Source: Land and Water B.C. Website, November 10, 2006. (Statistics compiled by author.)

tor interest in acquiring water licences revived, encouraged by the widespread assumption that the NDP would lose the election — an assumption borne out when it won only two of seventy-nine seats. Private power developers had close ties with the soon-to-be elected Liberal government, and they believed the new government would reinstate the policy of purchasing energy from small private hydro and wind-farm developers. So, they needed to begin identifying promising sites and acquiring the water rights that were a precondition of building new power plants.

A review of application dates and the dates on which licences were approved confirms that the majority of licences have been granted in 2001 or later. A quick examination of these applications reveals, not surprisingly, that a high percentage of these sites were noted in a 1983 Ministry of Energy inventory and in the subsequent Sigma Engineering updates of 2000 and 2002 funded by BC Hydro, which as noted, also ranked the sites in terms of anticipated costs per MWh of energy, and thus identified their profit potential.

While it might be assumed that the government has allocated most of the 495 private power licences and applications under review as of November of 2006 to small, independent firms or entrepreneurial individuals, this is not the case. A select number of private power developers applied for — and obtained — multiple water licences once they realized that these would be tickets to lucrative energy supply contracts with BC Hydro. (See the Appendix for a full list of licences and applications.) An analysis of these 495 licences and applications reveals that ten developers own (or have applied for) 40 percent of them. Table 16 illustrates the degree of concentration of ownership of these licences and applications.

This table may understate the degree of concentration, because it does not include a significant number of licences held by subsidiary or separate companies owned by the same parent holding company. Fully twenty-four water licences or applications have been acquired by numbered companies (either B.C. or Canadian registered), a practice that makes it difficult to identify the real owners of projects. A review of the licences also reveals that only a handful are owned by First Nations, even though virtually all of the projects are on Crown land involved in First Nations land claims.

While the government requires that BC Hydro purchase its new energy from power plants located within the province, it has made no attempt to ensure that ownership of water licences also remain within the province. The requirement that water licences can only be acquired by B.C. residents or B.C.-registered companies may appear to keep licences within the province, but it does nothing to preclude foreign investors from acquiring a water licence simply by registering as a B.C. company and paying the registration fee of just over $350. Nor does government policy preclude foreign companies from acquiring water licences by buying out B.C. licence holders or acquiring B.C.-registered companies.

Another disturbing aspect of the water licence policy is that the government has permitted water licences to be "flipped" by their original owners. This normally happens once a developer has obtained an EPA with BC Hydro. This immediately enhances the value of the water licence and allows its owner to capitalize by selling it to another power company for a very tidy profit. A $10,000 water licence may end up being worth millions — or even tens of millions — once an EPA with BC Hydro is in place. For Howe Street financiers, speculators on the Vancouver Stock Exchange, friends of the government, and some retired BC Hydro executives, this is a very sweet windfall indeed, particularly for those who plan to cash out their capital gains in the short term.

To summarize, the government has been virtually giving away water rights and related land tenure to what is, arguably, B.C.'s most valuable renewable resource. The size of this giveaway literally boggles the imagination. Assets assuring future revenue streams involving tens of billions of dollars over the coming decades are being sold for a few thousand to those who have managed to place themselves at the front of the purchasing line. The future ability of the public to share in some of the huge revenues these sites will generate is being compromised by legal contracts and licensing commitments that will enable private owners to successfully challenge any efforts to recover the unjustified windfalls they have received from the current government.

Because most of the water licences and resulting power plants are in the near future likely to be owned in whole or in part by foreign investors, Canada's international trade obligations will provide even more protection for these new private power developers.

And the public will end up paying for it all, whether in the form of significantly higher electricity bills, loss of energy security, or the erosion of BC Hydro's contribution to provincial finances.

NOTES

1. Of course, the government could choose to use the water itself by having BC Hydro develop these sites, which I feel is a much better choice. But even if we were to accept the government's questionable policy of transferring these assets to private interests, it would still be important to be able to assess the extent to which its water licensing and water rental policy is fair to the public, which owns the resource.
2. The 495 total includes only privately owned licences and does not include those licences awarded to BC Hydro. It also excludes a handful of water-power licences issued to other public entities such as the Columbia Basin Trust. Arthur Caldicott has done a detailed analysis of water licences and points out that there have been 365 new applications for water-power licences since 2000 (Caldicott 2007).
3. The current government did increase the water licence fee for small projects from $2,000 to $5,000, hardly a major increase, given the value of the sites.
4. *Water Act*, 1988. B.C. Reg. 154/94, s. 6 (Section 21).
5. Land and Water B.C., "Land Policy Pricing" July 23, 2004. Of course, private power companies also have to finance their costs associated with engineering studies, environmental reviews, consultations with local communities and First Nations, and dealings with various arms of government. None of these latter expenses generate revenue for government, but they are deductible from taxes on future profits.

Chapter Seven

Wind Energy Sell-Off

GLOBAL WARMING HAS HIGHLIGHTED the need to develop new energy sources that do not release additional greenhouse gases. For many environmentalists, a major part of the answer to addressing B.C.'s future energy needs is clear: tap into the enormous amount of wind energy available along B.C.'s coast and in the high mountain ranges of the interior. Non-polluting, renewable wind energy avoids the serious drawbacks of conventional alternatives. Unlike burning fossil fuels, it does not release greenhouse gases. And, unlike nuclear power, it avoids the worrisome — and as yet unresolved — problems of decommissioning reactors and disposing of spent radioactive fuel.

This is not to ignore the fact that there can also be significant drawbacks associated with the impact of wind-farm developments — and related roads and transmission corridors — on wildlife, First Nations traditional hunting and ceremonial grounds, tourism, and community use of the land base. Some locations that could generate considerable wind energy should not be developed because the negative environmental and social impacts outweigh the benefits of the energy they can produce. Interestingly, well-known American environmentalist Robert Kennedy Jr. — who is generally supportive of wind energy — has also been a vocal critic of constructing wind farms in areas noted for other community or scenic values. In his words:

> As an environmentalist, I support wind power, including wind power on the high seas. I am also involved in siting wind farms in appropriate landscapes, of which there are many. But I do believe that some places should be off limits to any sort of industrial development. I wouldn't build a wind farm in Yosemite National Park. Nor would I build one on Nantucket Sound, which is exactly what the company Energy Management is trying to do with its Cape Wind project. (Kennedy 2005)

While some locations should be ruled out because they impose a heavy burden on the environment, on wildlife, or on other economic activities such as tourism, others are not as intrusive. As Kennedy notes, under the right regulatory and environmental framework, wind farms may be developed in a way that ensures that benefits outweigh costs.

Energy from wind farms, like energy from run-of-the-river hydro projects, can be certified as "green," which means it can command a higher price in jurisdictions — such as certain American states — where customers want this form of energy for ethical reasons or where state governments have mandated that a specific percentage of energy sold within their jurisdictions must be "green."[1]

B.C. is blessed with some of the best sites for wind farms in the world. And there is no question that, properly located and prudently managed, wind farms can provide an important source of new electrical energy for the province (Greenpeace 2002). According to Sea Breeze Power Corporation, one of B.C.'s most prominent advocates of wind energy:

> There are many factors that make B.C. an ideal location for utility-scale wind farms, and include the following:
> - A high quality wind resource;
> - Close proximity to U.S. grids;
> - A strong demand for electricity in the local market;
> - An impending decrease in the supply of electricity;
> - An abundance of under-employed skilled labour;
> - An environmentally aware population. (Sea Breeze 2005)

However, like the government's policy toward the development of small hydro projects, its policy toward wind power has been formulated primarily with the goal of providing investment opportunities for wind-farm developers. In contrast to Saskatchewan, for example, where SaskPower, the province's Crown utility, is the owner and operator of the largest wind farms in the province, B.C. has opted to have wind energy developed exclusively by private interests.[2]

In crafting public policy on the introduction of wind energy to B.C., a number of characteristics of wind generation have to be kept in mind. On one hand, wind-farm projects are less subject to wide seasonal variations in energy production than small hydro projects. On the other hand, wind energy is more susceptible to daily or weekly variations in wind speed. To balance the lack of reliable capacity of wind generation, it is necessary to match it with another source of capacity or, ideally, a source that has storage, such as a major hydro reservoir.[3]

The fact that wind energy can be quite erratic creates significant challenges in integrating it with the transmission grid. Sudden changes in output of wind-power facilities must be balanced by corresponding adjustments in other parts of the system to prevent blackouts (Adams 2006). A company named E.ON, which operates roughly one-third of Germany's electricity grid, notes that it has experienced enormous fluctuations in monthly wind generation. Energy production in some months is more than four times that of other months (E.ON 2006a). A large part of Germany also experienced a major blackout in November of 2006 as a result of an unusually calm period during which the overall system did not have the capacity to keep the lights on. Closer to home, Alberta's grid operator has indicated that the system cannot handle more than about 900 MW of wind power if it is to avoid outages. While new technologies and better weather forecasting techniques may address the problem of daily and monthly fluctuations more effectively in future, the current rule of thumb is that the maximum share of a system's total wind generation must be kept below 10 percent: otherwise it is vulnerable to unpredictable outages.

In other jurisdictions, and especially in Europe, where energy prices are far higher than in B.C., wind farms have expanded significantly over the past decade. For example, Germany had 18,286 MW of installed capacity by the end of 2005 (E.ON 2006a). Its *Renewable Energy Act* has a renewable target of 20 percent of all Germany's energy by 2020, much of which will be from wind farms. The pace has been slower in Canada, but is now accelerating. By the end of 2005, Canadian wind-farm developers had installed 239 MW of new wind energy capacity, according to the Canadian Wind Energy Association, but none was in B.C.[4] Several contracts were included in previous BC Hydro tender calls, but the projects were never built. In fact, at the time of writing, the province still does not have a single wind farm in full operation. One reason may be that the North American market for wind turbines and related generating equipment is booming to the point of being "overheated." As one observer from the magazine *Windpower Weekly* put it:

> "The problems the industry faces at this juncture centre around capital cost. Capital cost has gone through the roof, whether it is turbine costs, transportation costs or balance of plant costs, and it is making it increasingly difficult to make the economics work on wind projects," says Jan Paulin, CEO of Padoma Wind Power, a wind project developer based in California. He is also concerned about much weaker warranties on wind turbines being sold today. "What we are seeing in this market today is very close to what I would call insanity." (*Windpower Weekly* 2007)

But, despite concerns over costs, B.C. is still pushing ahead with private wind-farm developments. A total of six projects are now in the final stages of operational testing in the province and another seventeen are in various stages of development. BC Hydro awarded three new contracts as part of its 2006 tender call and these appear to be proceeding.

Given that wind energy remains much more expensive than most other options at this point, why is it being pushed forward? One reason is the hope that B.C. could become a "leader" in wind energy. A jurisdiction in which new and innovative technology is being developed has a strong appeal to those who see wind farms as having the potential to anchor a major new industry in the province (Bisetty 2006).

According to NaiKun Wind Developers, its proposed 1,750 MW wind-farm project off the coast of the Queen Charlotte Islands in northern B.C. will:

- Feed a growing British Columbia energy market;
- Establish British Columbia and Canada among the world's leaders in renewable energy development;
- Substantially contribute to national greenhouse gas emission objectives;
- Provide clean, renewable, made-in-B.C. electricity for generations to come. (NaiKun Wind Developers 2007)

Improvements in technology and increases in energy prices in the Pacific Northwest may enable wind to become a more significant source of B.C.'s energy, particularly given the existence of large hydro storage reservoirs in the province. However, for the foreseeable future wind power can only be utilized if governments — or ratepayers — are willing to accept a very significant cost premium. Indeed, even in Europe, wind energy still relies significantly on government subsidies, despite the fact that energy prices are generally higher (E.ON 2006b).

Given this economic context, it is not surprising that private power developers have been energetically lobbying the province to provide them with a variety of different subsidies, including virtually free access to the best sites in B.C., generous energy supply contracts from BC Hydro (including tenders specifically targeted at wind energy independent of its cost), assistance with obtaining environmental and other land-use approvals, subsidized access to the transmission grid, exemptions from provincial sales taxes on their equipment and from local property taxes, and access to energy storage in BC Hydro's reservoirs. Some have even wanted to make their land tenure into a mortgageable asset. They have got most of what they have lobbied for and are pushing energetically for the rest.

Significantly, Robert Hornung, the President of the Canadian Wind Energy Association, wrote to both provincial Energy, Mines, and Petroleum Minister Richard Neufeld and Larry Bell, CEO of BC Hydro, on August 4, 2006, praising BC Hydro's decision to give EPAs to three wind-farm projects. The letter was sent only a week after BC Hydro announced the outcome of its 2006 tender call (Hornung 2006).

Perhaps the most significant government policy has been the ban on BC Hydro developing, owning, and operating its own wind farms. The Energy Plan has effectively cleared the field of any potential public ownership in this area, ensuring that all future development will be carried out by private power developers. In addition, the government has directed BC Hydro to turn over much of its earlier research on wind power to private developers. It is worth noting in this regard that BC Hydro's evaluation of wind energy prospects in B.C. started back in 1981, so it had accumulated a considerable amount of information on the issue (BC Hydro Power Pioneers 1998).

More recently, BC Hydro has been working with various firms interested in wind projects to determine more precisely the estimated capital costs and potential revenues from promising sites. BC Hydro's Green and Alternative Energy Division has commissioned a number of studies to assess the potential of new wind farms. Two studies in particular merit attention. One examined wind potential on Vancouver Island, and the other looked at opportunities for wind-farm generation on the mainland (BC Hydro 2001, 2002b). In its report on wind potential on Vancouver Island, BC Hydro noted that:

> Many areas on VI (Vancouver Island) have a good wind resource potential, with a predicted annual average wind speed of 6 to 8 meters per second (m/s). Generally, in North America a site with an annual average of 7 m/s is considered economically viable. Candidate sites were identified utilizing a screening exercise consisting of model-predicted wind speeds, topographic map (1:50,000 scale) reviews and helicopter flyovers. Areas identified have a total installed capacity potential of over 650 MW. (BC Hydro 2001: 2)

The report went on to indicate that by 2009–10 it might be possible to develop 483 MW of capacity and 1,154 GWh of energy annually from wind resources on the island.

BC Hydro's study on the potential for wind farms on the mainland included a list of the ten most promising sites, noted the absence of any current major wind-farm projects, and indicated that there was significant potential, although it was characterized by low capacity factors and relatively high costs at the time the study was carried out:

> Wind energy has not yet been developed at a large scale in B.C., and BC Hydro has focussed much effort in the last few years on exploring and enabling this resource. The wind projects identified in this study have an energy potential of approximately 730 MW (1,600 GWh/year) with capacity factors between 18 and 38 percent. The production costs range between six and twelve cents per kWh. (BC Hydro 2002b: 26)

The location of wind farms is not only determined by the availability of wind. Wind-farm developers also need access to the transmission system:

otherwise, the costs of new transmission lines can make it prohibitive to develop a project. Not surprisingly, much of the current wind-farm activity is in the Peace River area, because it is relatively easy to locate wind farms near BC Hydro's high-voltage transmission system, built to move energy from the major hydro dams to the lower Mainland. This fact was noted in a recent study by Pollution Probe and the Pembina Institute that noted: "With large-scale wind development, BC Hydro can use its hydro reservoirs to support short-term wind output variations, and in turn use wind to support long-term variations in hydro levels" (Pollution Probe/Pembina Institute 2006).

Consistent with the current government's privatization agenda, BC Hydro has been transferring various components of its monitoring system and related research activities to private interests as they begin developing sites for which they have obtained permits.[5] And, BC Hydro continues to finance research that, presumably, will be of considerable value to private wind-farm developers. In 2005 it commissioned Gerrard Hassan to conduct a study assessing the overall potential of wind in B.C. He identified a total of approximately 5,000 MW of potential, with slightly over two-thirds of this being in the interior and the remainder along the coast or on offshore islands (Hassan 2005; Pollution Probe/Pembina Institute 2006).

More recently, the B.C. Transmission Corporation has funded a detailed study of the costs and viability of new transmission connections for potential wind-farm developments in various areas of the province. Interestingly, while the details of this study have been made available to private energy developers, unlike most BC Hydro studies it is not publicly available on the B.C. Transmission Corporation's website, which notes that access is restricted to the industry.

A problem faced by almost all wind-farm developments is that wind power is still far more expensive than alternatives. According to a Canaccord Capital study quoted in the *Globe and Mail*, the cost of wind energy varies between $67 and $105 per MWh, figures consistent with the estimates made in the BC Hydro-funded studies cited earlier (Robinson 2005). This is largely due to the fact that, even at the best sites, wind speed is not adequate to fully utilize the generators, so the best wind farms can only operate at between 30 and 40 percent of their installed capacity. And many will end up operating even less efficiently.

The problems of wind-farm development in B.C. are underscored by the province's recent experience with the proposed $100 million Holberg Wind Energy project. Announced with great fanfare in 2004, the project was to construct between thirty-seven and forty-five wind turbines at the northern end of Vancouver Island, sixty kilometres west of Port Hardy (Government of B.C. 2004). Owned jointly by B.C.'s Stothert Power Corporation and Global Renewal Energy Partners Inc. of Denmark, it was to be operational in 2006. BC Hydro committed to purchasing its energy — enough for 17,000 households — through a twenty-year energy supply contract (Lavoie 2004).

Energy, Mines, and Petroleum Resources Minister Richard Neufeld was forced to admit that the government's initial attempts at promoting privately developed wind farms had run into significant teething troubles. But rather disingenuously, he insisted on blaming the problems on BC Hydro and indicated that he still believed that it would be possible to stimulate the development of this industry, pointing to the likely success of more recent efforts, such as the Holberg initiative: "B.C. Hydro doesn't have experience with wind power and it's new for B.C. folks.... They've all worked together very hard to make it work and we're pretty proud this is taking place," he said (Lavoie 2004).

Despite these encouraging homilies, the Holberg project was mothballed, presumably due to the relatively high cost of its energy — a cost that even a long-term contract with BC Hydro apparently could not address satisfactorily at the price level BC Hydro negotiated with the company (Warkentin 2005). But this apparent setback should not be viewed as evidence that there will be no further developments in this area. Quite the contrary, that experience appears to have convinced the government that it will have to do more, both through the price it gets BC Hydro to pay for wind energy and through direct subsidies for its development, such as paying for new transmission lines and sub-stations rather than requiring developers to cover these costs.

Wind farms share another important characteristic with run-of-the-river hydro generation: they are very capital intensive. For this reason, the economic spin-offs to the province's economy are marginal. The proposed Holberg wind-farm investment of $100 million would have created only six permanent jobs in the region (Lavoie 2004). This works out to over $16 million per job. Windmills were to be manufactured out of province, so there would be no jobs triggered in this part of the production process. Even the construction stage would create only 100 person-years of employment during its year-to-eighteen-month start-up phase.

The benefits of such projects to local communities are even less when their owners live elsewhere (as they normally do). And the sixty-to-eighty-metre-tall windmills, along with their transmission lines, impose significant limitations on alternative uses of land on, or around, the large sites on where they are located. Depending on the technology used, some projects may generate considerable noise pollution affecting wildlife as well as local residents, hikers, and campers. And, unless B.C. becomes a major manufacturer of wind-farm technology, it is not clear how much capital-intensive wind farms will contribute to B.C.'s future economic development.

Wind farms require access to Crown land — large amounts of land — to be viable.

As noted earlier, at the time of writing BC Hydro has only awarded a handful of contracts to wind-farm developers (including some that have been mothballed, such as the Holberg proposal). However, according to Natural Resources Canada, wind-farm developers have applied for federal environmental approvals for a significant number of other projects. If approved, these would effectively "lock in" private control of many of the best wind energy sites in the province. Table 17, taken from the National Resources Canada website, lists project applications for B.C.

The provincial government, which is responsible for awarding land tenures, also has an extensive database on wind-farm proposals. According to the Ministry of Land and Water, it has received applications from private energy developers for the rights to investigate, or occupy, more than 340,000 hectares of Crown land for new wind farms. The Ministry has three main categories in its database: investigative permits, active development approvals, and operational wind farms. As of May 2007, 133 investigative permits had been issued. An additional seventeen projects were in the development phase, and another six were considered operational, although some may still have been in the final testing stage. Table 18 shows the major applicants, ranked according to the number of sites they are seeking or have approval to develop. There is already a high degree of concentration in wind-farm ownership, with the top ten companies owning 116, or approximately 75 percent, of the total applications and approvals. Arguably, these applications and approvals are for the most promising sites in the province. Like small hydro, the number of suitable wind-farm sites is not unlimited. The best sites have already been identified, and these are the ones private interests are now busy acquiring. Once this "low-hanging fruit" is picked, other sites may be considered, but they are likely to be more expensive or more intrusive on other environmental, recreational, or community uses.

Like run-of-the-river sites, the province has been treating Crown lands suitable for wind farms as virtually a "free good." The government's position is that private investment is the key to the development of the province's wind resources. And so it provides investors with access to — and ownership of — the best sites in the province.

As with small hydro sites, the only ownership restrictions are that the prospective investor must be a Canadian citizen, a permanent resident in B.C. over nineteen years of age, a registered cooperative, or a B.C.-registered company. Given that any Canadian or foreign company willing to pay the $350 fee can obtain registration as a B.C. company, there is no effective restriction on foreign ownership of wind farms. As with small hydro projects, applications are on a first-come, first-served basis. Initially, a proponent gets an investigative permit for two years, but it is renewable, and once the firm has invested a small amount in evaluating the site, it can apply for a full "Licence

Table 17: Natural Resources Canada, List of Wind Farm Proposed Projects for B.C. (2006)

Name of Proponent	Registration Date m/d/yr	Registration Number	Capacity MW	Expected Date of Commissioning
AXOR Group Inc.	6/20/2002	5902-A1-2	10	Dec. 2009
AXOR Group Inc.	6/20/2002	5902-A1-3	40	Sept. 2006
AXOR Group Inc.	6/20/2002	5902-A1-4	20	Nov. 2008
AXOR Group Inc.	6/20/2002	5902-A1-5	15	Nov. 2009
AXOR Group Inc.	6/20/2002	5902-A1-6	70	Nov. 2008
AXOR Group Inc.	6/20/2002	5902-A1-7	95	Sept. 2006
Sea Breeze Energy Inc.	8/21/2002	5902-S3-1	175	Oct. 2008
Sea Breeze Energy Inc.	8/21/2002	5902-S3-2	175	Oct. 2008
Holberg Wind Energy Inc	11/27/2002	5902-S6-1	64.5	June 2009
Holberg Wind Energy Inc	11/27/2002	5902-S6-2	75	June 2009
NaiKun Wind Ltd. Part II	12/16/2002	5902-N3-2	180	Oct. 2006
Earth First Energy Inc.	3/18/2003	5902-E3-1	50	Dec. 2007
Dokie Wind Energy Inc.	10/15/2003	5902-D2-2	100	Sept. 2007
Skypower Corp.	1/6/2004	5902-S10-5	200	Dec. 2009
Aeolis Wind Power Corp.	4/27/2004	5902-A6-2	200	Sept. 2006
Aeolis Wind Power Corp.	4/27/2004	5902-A6-3	200	Sept. 2007
Aeolis Wind Power Corp.	4/27/2004	5902-A6-4	200	Mar. 2007
Aeolis Wind Power Corp.	4/27/2004	5902-A6-5	125	Jan. 2007
Chinook Power Corporation	2/2/2005	5902-C8-1	75	Nov. 2006
Chinook Power Corporation	2/17/2005	5902-C8-2	240	Mar. 2007
Nomis Power Corp.	2/28/2005	5902-N6-1	50	Mar. 2007
Katabatic Power Inc.	6/20/2005	5902-K4-1	36	Oct. 2007
Dokie Wind Energy	6/30/2005	5902-D2-1	150	Sept. 2007
Dokie Wind Energy	6/30/2005	5902-D2-3	150	Sept. 2007
Bear Mountain Wind LP	1/26/2006	5902-B8-1	123	June 2008
Total Estimated Capacity of Wind Farms (MW)			2,818.50	

Table 18: Crown Land Applications by Private B.C. Wind-Farm Developers

Company	Investigative & Monitoring	Development & Operational	Total
Chinook Power Corp.	15	7	22
Earth First Energy Inc	16	1	17
Finavera Energy Canada Inc.	16		16
Sea Breeze Energy Inc	15	1	16
0737440 B.C. Ltd.	13	2	15
Willow Ridge Energy Inc	8		8
Aspen Wind Energy Inc	3	4	7
Aeolis Wind Power Corp	6		6
Harvey, Simon	5		5
0733546 B.C. Ltd.	3	1	4
3422534 Canada Inc.	4		4
Dokie Wind Energy Inc	1	3	4
0733554 B.C. Ltd.	2	1	3
0742880 B.C. Ltd.	3		3
G.W. Energy Ltd.	3		3
Katabatic Power Corp.	2	1	3
B.C. Wind Corporation	2		2
B.C. Wind Power Corp	2		2
English Bay Energy Ltd	2		2
Rupert Peace Power Corporation	2		2
Treaty 8 Dev Corp	2		2
0733547 B.C. Ltd.	1		1
0733551 B.C. Ltd.		1	1
Banks Island Wind Farm Ltd.	1		1
Crying Girl Energy Ltd.	1		1
GreenWing Energy Management Ltd	1		1
Kwoiek Creek Resources Ltd Part	1		1
Peace Energy Renew Energy Coop	1		1
Rengen Power Corp.	1		1
Robson Valley Power Corporation		1	1
Windlab Systems Pty Ltd	1		1
Totals	133	23	156

Note: Data downloaded from the Ministry of Land and Water website, May 2007. Table compiled by the author with the help of Craig Williams.

of Occupation." The government awards these licences for an initial thirty-year period. These give the proponent virtually all the rights of ownership, including exclusive use of the land. The developer may also negotiate with the government to acquire fee-simple acquisition of the land during the term of the Licence of Occupation. The fee for investigating potential sites is $500, while the fee for setting up each meteorological monitoring tower is an additional $500 annually. A permit to build a road to the site is $500 and is valid for up to ten years (Government of B.C. 2005a).

Because wind energy is more expensive than other sources, the province believes that it has to keep developers' costs down if it is going to be able to stimulate the growth of this sector. This means charging very low land-occupancy fees and other related development charges. On October 14, 2005, Richard Neufeld, Minister of Energy, Mines, and Petroleum Resources, announced that the government had worked out a successful deal with the wind-farm industry that would stimulate further private investment in wind power. Its key feature was to provide a stable, long-term rental arrangement for the use of Crown land by wind-farm owners. According to the Ministry's press release announcing the deal:

> "In partnership with the wind power industry, we have come up with an innovative solution to ease the financial risk for wind power producers, which will ensure we can move forward in developing alternative energy opportunities," said Neufeld. "New participation pricing features will allow the industry to develop and mature over the first 10 years," (Government of B.C. 2005b)

Under the new policy, the government will not charge any "participation rents" (that is, rents for use of Crown land), for the first ten years a wind farm is in commercial operation. After that point, the rental will be variable, ranging from 1 to 3 percent of the gross annual revenues of wind farms. Where a wind farm's production averages less than 25 percent of its rated capacity, the government will charge a rental of 1 percent of revenues. Between 25 percent and 40 percent, it will charge 2 percent, while all production over 40 percent of capacity will be charged a maximum of 3 percent of gross revenues (Government of B.C. 2005b).

While this rental arrangement for the most promising wind-farm locations may suit their private developers, it is not clear how it squares with the public interest. Although wind-farm energy is still expensive, its price relative to other energy sources may eventually drop, giving owners of these highly subsidized wind farms significant windfall profits — profits the government intends to keep in the hands of private developers.

To further encourage the development of wind farms, the government has also encouraged BC Hydro to adopt a "diversified" energy portfolio.

This means that even if wind energy is more expensive than other alternatives, BC Hydro will try to reserve a block of energy in its future tender calls specifically for wind farms. Like run-of-the-river projects, financing for additional wind-farm projects is likely to continue to be provided through BC Hydro's long-term supply contracts at prices that make wind investments attractive.

In its 2006 tender call, BC Hydro awarded two large and one relatively small wind contracts. In total, wind-farm contracts accounted for approximately 979 GWh of energy, annually, roughly 14 percent of the total energy in the call.

One contract went to Dokie Wind Energy Inc. on a site near Chetwynd. It is to produce 536 GWh annually and has a capacity of 180 MW. Dokie Wind Energy was established in 2004 to develop wind farms in B.C. It is a joint venture of Earth First Energy of Victoria and Toronto-based Creststreet Capital Corporation. The Dokie project has cleared the environmental assessment process, but some environmentalists remain concerned about its impact on wildlife, especially migratory birds (Pynn 2006).[6]

A second contract went to Bear Mountain Wind Limited Partnership. It is to supply 371 GWh annually and provide capacity of 120 MW. Bear Mountain is a joint venture of AltaGas Income Trust, Aeolis Wind Power Corporation, and a local cooperative. It signed a twenty-five year EPA with BC Hydro for Bear Mountain Wind Park, located near Dawson Creek. The company plans to have sixty wind turbines in operation by 2009 (Bear Mountain Wind Limited Partnership 2006).

The third wind-energy contract was with Mount Hays Wind Farm Limited Partnership. It has a 731-hectare site just south of Prince Rupert. The project will have an installed capacity of 25.2 MW and is expected to produce 72 GW of energy annually from its seventeen wind turbines (Katabatic Power 2006). Its contract with BC Hydro will run for twenty-five years. Mount Hays Wind Farm is owned by Katabatic Power, a private company which, according to its website, is owned by investors from Richmond, B.C., and San Francisco, California. Katabatic indicates that it will invest $50 million in this development. On November 22, 2006, the company announced that it had placed an order for $35 million in new wind turbines from a Montréal firm, AAER. But the company was not starting from scratch. According to Jonathan Raymond, Chief Operating Officer of Katabatic Power, "BC Hydro has had the investigative meteorological test masts in the Hays site for a number of years, so the company already has data showing the site's potential" (*Prince Rupert Daily News* 2006a). Katabatic CEO Tony Duggleby explained the background to the additional wind monitoring his company was doing on the project during the spring of 2006, acknowledging BC Hydro's previous work on the site: "We have three years of BC Hydro data, so with this test tower we're not actually after whether or not it's a good wind site" (*Prince Rupert Daily News* 2006b). In its description of the Mount Hays project, Katabatic notes that the site was one of the ten most promising sites earlier identified by BC Hydro on the B.C. mainland.

Katabatic is also in the process of developing another project in B.C., the Banks Island Wind Farm, a much larger project rated at 3,000 MW with development rights on a 40,000-hectare site (Katabatic Power 2007). It will be one of the biggest in the world if it goes ahead in 2009, as the company anticipates.

Katabatic's CEO has previously been involved with another major B.C. wind-energy company, Sea Breeze Power Corporation. According to an article about the company posted on Katabatic's website: "Duggleby is no stranger to B.C.'s developing wind-farm industry. He was the former Chief Operating Officer for Sea Breeze Power, which is developing the Knob Hill Wind Farm north of Port Hardy, on Vancouver Island" (*Prince Rupert Daily News* 2006a).

Dokie, Bear Mountain, and Katabatic are but three of the emerging players in B.C.'s private wind industry. While it is not possible to provide a detailed overview of all the companies now acquiring Crown land for the purpose of future wind-farm developments, a brief look at another of the most active firms will provide insight into how B.C.'s wind industry is evolving. Sea Breeze Power is owned by a group of British Columbian and American investors, according to information posted on its website and in its filings with the U.S. Securities and Exchange Commission. While Sea Breeze manages a number of its projects directly, it also owns several other subsidiary companies registered in B.C.[7] Sea Breeze is involved in three major areas of energy development: run-of-the-river hydro (which we will examine in a subsequent chapter), proposals to construct major transmission lines, and wind-farm development.[8]

On the transmission side, the company has an equal partnership with Boundless Energy LLC of York Harbor, Maine, "to explore merchant possibilities in the transmission of power." The partnership is incorporated in B.C. as Sea Breeze Pacific Regional Transmission System Inc. Boundless Energy has considerable expertise in other jurisdictions in the construction and operation of high-voltage, direct-current transmission systems. This partnership is focussed on three transmission initiatives involving participation by several other companies.

The first is a proposed 1,100 MW high-voltage cable across the Strait of Juan de Fuca. Its proponents filed an application with the National Energy Board for approval to build this high-voltage, direct-current transmission line from the southern end of Vancouver Island to a site near Port Angeles, Washington. This would provide a new transmission link between B.C. and the American Northwest, facilitating the movement of energy between these two jurisdictions. If completed, it might also provide a transmission point for B.C. renewable energy to wider markets in the United States (Sea Breeze 2007).[9]

The second transmission project would involve constructing a 1,600-MW transmission line between the Columbia River and San Francisco, referred to as the West Coast Cable. It is currently being reviewed by the California ISO and the West Coast Electricity Coordinating Council. It is also being examined, according to Sea Breeze, by the Pacific Gas and Electric Company (PG&E). According to Sea Breeze:

> Such a cable would enable PG&E and other California utilities to access inexpensive hydroelectric energy from the Pacific Northwest, and, through the new Juan de Fuca corridor, also provide access to the vast renewable energy resources of western Canada.... The two transmission projects described above, along with an under-utilized segment of grid controlled by Bonneville Power Administration, would form a new transmission pathway between energy-rich Canada, and the constrained, highly populated energy load centers of California. (Sea Breeze 2007)

Turning to its wind farm activities, Sea Breeze has identified a number of promising locations across the province for future development. According to a November 2005 company management analysis, by that time it had applied for investigative permits on sites with a total land area of just over 216,000 hectares. Eight of the firm's potential sites are located on Vancouver Island, while most of the remaining sites are in the Thompson-Okanogan region. Table 19 shows the sites the company listed in its 2005 U.S. Securities and Exchange Commission filings. In its Securities and Exchange Commission filing for the fiscal year ending 2004, Sea Breeze noted that it "is presently holding 52 Investigative Use Permits issued by the British Columbia Ministry of Sustainable Resource Management."[10] At the time of writing, Sea Breeze's Knob Hill site was the first wind farm to complete the formal environmental assessment process in B.C., having been approved in September 2004. The 450 MW facility is now proceeding to the construction stage.

While Sea Breeze may be exceptional due to the number and size of the parcels of land it has applied to investigate, a number of other developers have been equally aggressive in obtaining rights to explore future wind-farm sites. A brief review of the websites of the most prominent wind-farm developers now active in B.C. (as well as Ministry data cited earlier in this chapter) reveals that many of these companies already have long lists of potential sites under investigation or development. Presumably they will end up building on the most promising of these sites in the near future, once they obtain EPAs from BC Hydro.

Table 19: Sea Breeze B.C. Wind Farm Investigative Permits on B.C. Crown Land

Site Name	General Location	Area (Ha)
Ashnola Forest	Okanagan	4,579
Barton Hill	Okanagan	1,090
Bouleau Mountain	Okanagan	3,184
Dome Rock	Okanagan	2,120
Fly Hill	Okanagan	1,090
Mount Chapperon	Okanagan	4,555
Pattison Lake	Okanagan	4,880
Simem Creek	Okanagan	4,961
Tahaetkun Mountain	Okanagan	4,050
Trepanage Plateau	Okanagan	4,803
Goodspeed	northern Vancouver Island	4,781
Great Bear	northern Vancouver Island	4,232
Pemberton Hills	northern Vancouver Island	3,945
Wolverine	northern Vancouver Island	4,598
Franklin Range	northern Vancouver Island	3,927
God's Pocket	northern Vancouver Island	3,687
Hushamu 1-4	northern Vancouver Island	995
Nimpkish Block 1	northern Vancouver Island	3,427
Nimpkish Block 2	northern Vancouver Island	1,964
Shushartie North	northern Vancouver Island	4,735
Shushartie South	northern Vancouver Island	5,000
Windy Ridge	northern Vancouver Island	731
Knob Hill	northern Vancouver Island	4,509
Tatnall Reefs	northern Vancouver Island	1,765
Banks 1	Mid Coast	4,974
Banks 2	Mid Coast	4,977
Banks 3	Mid Coast	4,994
Aristazabel 1-11	Mid Coast	52,322
Price 1-4	Mid Coast	16,721
Cape Caution 1	Mid Coast	5,300
Cape Caution 2	Mid Coast	4,900
Cape Caution 3	Mid Coast	5,000
Cape Caution 4	Mid Coast	4,900
Cape Caution 5	Mid Coast	4,900
Calvert 1	Mid Coast	4,927
Calvert 2	Mid Coast	5,000
Calvert 3	Mid Coast	4,900
Roberts Bank	Georgia Strait	9,237
Total Hectares		216,660

Source: Sea Breeze 2006a

However, some of the companies may also be speculating. By spending a relatively small sum now, they can obtain the right to build in the future. Thus, if BC Hydro continues to award new contracts in its coming tender calls or if the province mandates that it must purchase more wind energy, developers will be well positioned to take advantage of such opportunities. In other cases, developers may simply be planning to stake a claim and then sell to the highest bidder. Given the low investment required to acquire these locations, such acquisitions are not a bad bet for the developers involved.

There is also another threat to B.C.'s public power system from the privatization of its wind energy. As noted earlier, wind energy has an uneven energy profile. Output fluctuates unpredictability on a daily, weekly, or seasonal basis, and it lacks capacity. However, if the energy can be stored and if it can be matched with suitable capacity, it is much more valuable. Like investors in run-of-the-river projects, proponents of wind-farm development have been lobbying the province for access to BC Hydro's storage reservoirs. The ability to store their energy in BC Hydro's reservoirs would enable them to secure more lucrative contracts with foreign customers because they could guarantee a reliable supply of firm, "green" energy on a year-round basis.

Access to storage — either for small hydro or wind power — has thus become an increasingly important issue for private power developers. They have been pushing the government to consider ways in which BC Hydro might be required to provide such access. This point was made by Guy Heywood of Renaissance Power in a 2006 paper promoting the benefits of private power projects:

> the "greenest" of the new energy sources that can be developed in the province — wind and run-of-river hydro — are not "firm" or constant energy sources, as they rely on natural resources (rain and wind) that are variable on a daily and seasonal basis. Electricity generated from these sources needs to be combined with the storage capacity from the large BC Hydro dams in order to become dispatchable as a firm and reliable source of power to the grid and ultimately to the end consumers. With the bias in government policy and BC Hydro towards the use of the storage capacity of the hydroelectric dams to support energy trading activities, this storage capacity is not available to support new, non-firm energy from independent power producers that might be otherwise more economic to develop. (Heywood 2006)

Of course, the use of BC Hydro's storage for this purpose would reduce the utility's ability to use the same storage for engaging in opportunistic energy trading with the United States and Alberta — trading that generates significant revenues for BC Hydro and enables it to limit the negative

Table 20: Structure of the Wind Power Production Incentive Program

Commissioning Date	Amount of Financial Incentive for the Ten-year Period
April 1, 2002 to March 31, 2003 inclusive	1.2 cents per kilowatt-hour (¢/kWh)
After March 31, 2003 and on or before March 31, 2006	1.0 ¢/kWh
After March 31, 2006 and on or before March 31, 2007	0.8 ¢/kWh

Source: Natural Resources Canada website downloaded November 4, 2006

impact on rates of energy market purchases from out-of-province suppliers. To put this more directly, giving storage to wind-farm operators would have a direct — and negative — impact on BC Hydro's own revenues. It would entail a further subsidy to wind-farm investors at the expense of BC Hydro ratepayers and/or government dividends from BC Hydro.

A discussion of private wind farms would not be complete without a brief examination of the lobbying achievements of the industry at the national level. The flow of subsidies and tax breaks is not limited to B.C. Under the mantra of supporting "green" energy, private power developers have succeeded in persuading the federal government to implement generous tax breaks for their capital investments as well as major subsidies for the production costs of wind energy itself.

In the December 2001 federal budget, the government introduced the Wind Power Production Incentive program. According to Natural Resources Canada, since the five-year program began, it has provided subsidies supporting the installation of 1,000 MW of new capacity. At the time, Natural Resources Canada claimed that "the incentive will cover approximately half of the current cost of the premium for wind energy in Canada compared to conventional sources. Once approved, qualifying private power producers will continue to receive this subsidy for the first ten years of a project."[11] The structure of the incentive program is set out in Table 20.

Ottawa gave every province a proportionate share of the funds. Wind-farms developers with projects in B.C. are entitled to qualify for this federal subsidy, in addition to the assistance provided by the province. While the Harper Conservative government initially appeared to want to back away from renewing these subsidies, more recently it has indicated that it, too, will be providing funds to encourage the development of wind energy. At the time of writing, it appears this will take the form of a one-cent-per-kWh subsidy (equivalent to $10 per MWh). When this is added to the price BC Hydro is paying under the 2006 tender call, it results in a cost to the public of $97.50

per MWh — a rich price indeed.

One final point regarding the provincial government's private wind-farm strategy merits attention. It is the question of the future asset value of the wind resource. Like small hydro projects, wind energy is renewable. And while the components of wind turbines will wear out after their estimated twenty-five-year operational life, they can be replaced. The key asset is the land base, and the key question is: how valuable will this resource be in the future? The government has given no indication that this issue — and the legacy we will leave to future generations — is of any concern to it. It has been handing out development permits as if Crown land effectively has no real value and therefore the public has no reason to continue to control its development.

Awarding long-term land tenure arrangements that effectively amount to fee-simple ownership of Crown land to private and, in many cases, foreign wind-farm developers raises issues similar to those associated with granting fee-simple ownership to run-of-the-river developers. While the energy costs of wind farms may not be economical at today's prices — and as far as this author is aware, none of the companies is yet using its access to the transmission grid to sell to the United States because BC Hydro currently pays much more for their energy than they can get south of the border — in future this situation may change as a result of technological advances or new green-energy requirements by American states. And so the best sites may end up becoming very valuable assets. How valuable they will be is still unclear. But by giving rights of occupancy — or fee-simple ownership — to B.C.'s best sites to private interests, the province may be handing developers huge financial windfalls amounting to literally billions of dollars of energy assets. And, in the process, it may also be precluding other public options for land use down the road.

Like small hydro projects, many wind farms are being acquired by investors who are not from B.C. Both national and international companies are very active in acquiring investigative permits and Licences of Occupation to build projects in B.C. In choosing to promote private development of this energy resource, the government has effectively given national and multinational energy developers control of B.C.'s renewable energy.

Foreign ownership of wind farms — and particularly ownership, because of NAFTA, by American or Mexican investors — raises important public policy issues that have not been widely discussed in B.C. Aside from the public's loss of the future asset value of the sites, which is arguably quite substantial, the government's policy is also prejudicing B.C.'s ability to ensure that this energy is available for customers within the province in the future. As with small hydro projects, NAFTA will make imposing restrictions on energy exports very difficult, regardless of provincial need. Instead of securing B.C.'s future energy supplies, government policy does the opposite. And, in the context of an open border with the United States and Alberta, it will force B.C. customers to pay market prices for access to energy produced within the province, in spite of the enormous subsidies the public is providing this industry.

That this is not simply a theoretical argument is underlined by a recent decision by the California Public Utilities Commission to authorize the payment of up to $14 million to PG&E to study the feasibility of acquiring wind and other renewable energy from B.C. and the related costs of a new transmission system for the purpose of moving it to California (California Public Utilities Commission 2007).

In awarding funding for this study, the Commission asserted as a "finding of fact" that: "There are potentially viable British Columbia renewable resources that may be available for PG&E to develop or acquire."

The relevant section of the decision reads as follows:

> PG&E is authorized to spend up to $14 million for external consultants to prepare a renewable study, as modified, to evaluate the feasibility of obtaining wind generated and other renewable electric power from various regions in British Columbia, Canada... PG&E shall ensure that the B.C. Renewable Study:
>
> a. addresses transmission costs and hurdles to the development of alternative routes which allow delivery of energy into California;
> b. considers the costs and benefits of various ownership alternatives and regulatory arrangements;
> c. does not include or repeat generic resource studies of British Columbian renewable energy potential or possible British Columbia-California transmission paths;
> d. develops a standard firming service;
> e. addresses potential mutual benefits for British Columbia and California. (California Public Utilities Commission 2007)

Far from seizing an opportunity for British Columbians to take advantage of the long-term possibilities of wind energy to ensure future energy supplies and maintain prices based on the cost of production, the government is squandering another of B.C.'s most valuable renewable resources. Given its commitment to private ownership and open export markets, and given the interest by American energy companies in B.C.'s renewable energy, we may see a situation where most of B.C.'s wind energy potential is captured by American investors for export to the American market, with virtually no benefit to the province, despite the extensive provincial and federal subsidies in place to support the development of this resource.

As we hinted near the beginning of this chapter, the government had another, much better, alternative. It could have adopted an approach similar to that of Saskatchewan by using its Crown corporation to develop its wind-power resource. Using this model, B.C. could have ensured that the future development of the province's wind resources remained owned and controlled by the people of B.C. and the energy generated remained available to meet the future needs of B.C. customers. It could also have used the public-ownership model to promote locally based suppliers, manufacturers, and construction firms. Yet these options have been recklessly abandoned in the government's rush to privatize B.C.'s electricity system.

NOTES

1. Interestingly, large hydro projects are not normally considered "green." Certainly, the flooding of large areas, particularly in provinces such as B.C., Québec, and Manitoba, resulted in considerable environmental damage. But another factor is that virtually all large hydro is public, and the "green" certification process is effectively controlled by private energy interests anxious to increase the value of their run-of-the-river and wind-farm energy. They do not want competition from publicly owned large hydro facilities.
2. SaskPower's Centennial Wind Farm, located twenty-five kilometres southeast of Swift Current, is the largest of three wind farms in the province. It supplies 150 MW of power to the province's electricity grid, representing about 5 percent of Saskatchewan's energy requirements. When it was completed at the beginning of 2005, it was the largest wind farm in Canada. One of the province's other two older wind projects is also wholly owned by SaskPower, while the third is a joint venture with the private sector. The combined power from these smaller projects is 22 MW. Saskatchewan has aggressively pursued a strategy of using its wind-farm investments to stimulate local economic development and employment.
3. During the 2005–06 IEP process (in which this author participated), when the option of including a significant amount of wind energy was reviewed, it became clear that this could only be done by having BC Hydro add additional capacity to its major dams by putting in new turbines. This would enable the Crown corporation to compensate for the lack of reliable capacity and unpredictable characteristics of wind energy. Without this hydro-based capacity, the viability of additional wind-farm energy was quite problematic.
4. There are different estimates of the amount of installed capacity. Another for 2004 was 439 MW by the Canadian Clean Air Renewable Energy Coalition (Tampier 2004). The confusion may be related to whether the start-up and testing phase after construction is considered operational or not. Nevertheless, growth in installed capacity is clear.
5. BC Hydro stopped releasing data on wind measurements to the public in August 2004.
6. Pynn also noted that a number of scientists have raised concerns about the quality of the information accepted by the government as part of the environmental

assessment process.

7. Sea Breeze Power subsidiaries, according to its Consolidated Financial Statement of 2005 and 2006, are: Powerhouse Developments Inc., Sea Breeze Energy Inc., Powerhouse Electric Corporation, Sea Breeze Management Inc., Sea Breeze Power Projects Inc., Harrison Lake Hydro Inc., and Sea Breeze Pacific Regional Transmission System, Inc.
8. Curiously, like many of the other new private energy companies starting up in B.C., Sea Breeze had virtually no revenues for the five years up to its 2004 U.S. Securities and Exchange Commission filing in which it stated: "The Registrant has a limited history of operations. The Registrant currently has not generated any revenues from operations. Each of the Registrant's proposed hydroelectric, wind energy, and transmission projects is in either the planning or permitting phases of development. The Registrant does not expect to receive any revenues from operations until the required approvals are received and the projects begin operations in a commercially profitable manner. There can be no assurance that any approvals will be obtained for the proposed projects or that the Registrant will obtain the required financing." The company trades on the Toronto Stock Exchange's Venture Exchange.
9. Sea Breeze also applied to build a transmission cable from Vancouver to Victoria. However, it subsequently withdrew this application due to issues related to the B.C. Transmission Corporation's competing bid. Sea Breeze requested the BCUC to pay its costs and received $251,725.
10. According to Sea Breeze, "The Investigative Use Permits are issued for a term of two years and allow the Registrant to enter the land, which is owned by the government of British Columbia. Sixteen of the Registrant's fifty-two prospective sites are located on northern Vancouver Island, twenty-six are located on the mid-coast between the south tip of the Queen Charlotte Islands and the northern tip of Vancouver Island (of which five are offshore), and ten are located in the Okanogan region (south-central British Columbia in the region of the Thompson Plateau)."
11. Natural Resources Canada website, downloaded November 4, 2006.

Chapter Eight

Economic and Social Impacts

The government's support for private power projects has profound implications for local communities and First Nations across B.C., particularly in those regions where there are significant opportunities for the development of new small hydro or wind-farm facilities. These projects impose major costs on local residents, but provide few benefits. In the language of economists, they are characterized by major "externalities" — that is, negative impacts borne by others. But, unlike publicly owned power projects, where at least the people of the province gain from the energy produced, private projects only enrich their investors while usually providing few jobs, little in local tax revenue, and minimal ongoing economic activity for the communities where they are built.

Aside from the temporary construction jobs and the short-term stimulus to the local economy during brief building periods, the capital-intensive nature of power projects means that, once completed, they provide very few permanent jobs and minimal local economic benefits, despite the very large revenues they generate for their investor owners, who — almost invariably — live outside affected communities. Once in place, private power projects restrict other community recreational uses of rivers for local people, such as hiking, fishing, kayaking, and horseback riding, as well as for locally based tourism operations such as fishing lodges, outdoor sports facilities, bed-and-breakfast operations, and the like. Across B.C., local governments are increasingly aware of this problematic standoff between costs and benefits and, understandably, are much less enthusiastic about supporting power developments than the provincial government and its developer friends.

Even the construction phase — arguably the only significant benefit most communities can expect from these projects — is now creating problems in many regions. A combination of factors, including the Alberta tar-sands boom, the government's Olympic spending spree, the rapid expansion of new mining projects, and a growing economy have led to shortages of skilled workers across the province. The construction squeeze has also resulted in escalating prices for key building materials such as steel and cement. Yet the government's Energy Plan is triggering a flood of new, private power projects at precisely the time these other construction activities are placing major strains on B.C.'s economy. The timing could not be worse.

Despite this, the Energy Plan encourages prospective investors to push as hard as possible to get construction started, regardless of the interests — or wishes — of local communities. Developers want their power plants up and running so they can tap into the cash flow from their rich BC Hydro contracts. Given the very high profits involved, developers have a huge financial incentive to push aside any local objections to their projects. This pressure is generating conflicts in communities across the province. (Later in this study we will examine two specific conflicts between private energy developers and local communities: Squamish-Lillooet and Kettle River-Christina Lake.)

There are a number of reasons why local communities are largely excluded from the economic benefits of private power developments. The design and engineering components of these capital-intensive projects are normally carried out in the developer's head office in Vancouver, Calgary, or any one of a number of other major urban centres. The actual construction work is normally sub-contracted to outside construction and engineering firms not based in the community. And, given that special skill sets are required for many of the jobs on these projects, few, if any, local residents may be qualified to do the work. At the same time, communities are affected by the influx of temporary construction workers making short-term demands on local housing and services even though they do not contribute significantly to the local tax base and may not even pay B.C. income taxes.

Similarly, the work required by project developers to meet the — limited — environmental assessment requirements and to handle the various steps in the overall permitting and approvals process is normally carried out by outside consultants specializing in engineering, environmental testing, stakeholder relations, or land-use and project-planning issues. Financing, accounting, energy marketing, and other functions are also managed from head offices. Senior company executives — many of whom receive quite generous salaries, share options, and other perks for their roles — are also very unlikely to be from the local community.

Construction is normally tendered to companies located outside the region, and so local residents often find that very few of these relatively well-paid jobs are available to them. Unlike Columbia Hydro Constructors Ltd. — the construction arm of BC Hydro — which has a negotiated framework agreement for ensuring that local residents, First Nations, and members of equity groups receive employment and training when it embarks on major construction projects, private energy investors are not constrained by policies that require local employment.

Similarly, local businesses and suppliers may not get opportunities to bid on many of the contracts associated with construction because developers and contractors have their own supply arrangements with firms located outside the region. And, major pieces of capital equipment — turbines, electrical components, control-centre technology, and the like — are almost always manufactured elsewhere. In its submission to the Squamish-Lillooet Regional

District, for example, Ledcor indicated that it would spend $10 million of its estimated $75 to $80 million capital budget on local goods and services (Squamish-Lillooet Regional District 2006a). In the end, communities only receive a small portion of the capital spent on project construction.

Once a facility is in place, the owner requires only a skeleton staff to operate and maintain it. In our chapter on wind farms, we noted that few permanent jobs were likely to be created by the very large capital expenditure of the proposed Holberg project. The same is broadly true of small hydro developments. The Cascade Heritage Power Park proposed for the Kettle River near Christina Lake by Powerhouse Energy Corporation (a Sea Breeze subsidiary), is a typical example. In its application for project approval, Powerhouse indicated that the $35-million capital project would result in three permanent jobs and possibly three part-time summer jobs. Some small hydro developments, such as Synex's Mears Creek development on Vancouver Island, have implemented remote satellite-monitoring systems (BC Hydro 2004c). Remote monitoring systems allow developers to control various aspects of a project's operations from offices in Vancouver — or, theoretically, anywhere in the world with the right satellite connections — thus reducing the need for on-site local employees to monitor or make changes in equipment settings.

The lack of benefits for local communities was summed up by the Squamish-Lillooet Regional District in the following words:

> In the Regional District's experience, small hydroelectric projects have not generated significant local benefits, particularly in the areas of employment and local purchasing. During construction, much of the expertise and equipment has been brought in from outside the region, as it is often very specialized and not available locally. Once operational, the plants are usually fully automated and provide only limited local employment. (Squamish-Lillooet Regional District 2003)

Some small hydro projects can actually cost jobs by squeezing out other economic activities, giving them a negative net employment impact. While this impact obviously varies from project to project, it points to the need to consider the small increase in employment from power plants in the context of the potential loss of jobs in other sectors of the local economy.

In a staff review, Squamish-Lillooet Regional District indicated that its policies regarding approvals of new power plants, such as the one proposed by Ledcor on the Ashlu River, had to consider the large number of jobs in the local tourism industry that might be affected:

> Considerable objections (by local residents) were based on the high

> tourism values of the Ashlu and several submissions were provided from the tourism industry indicating the high economic value of outdoor recreation businesses. One submission from a group of 14 local outdoor recreation businesses estimated their revenues were $3 million annually, with over 400 employees. (Squamish-Lillooet Regional District 2006a)

Another issue of concern to local communities has been the relatively low tax revenues municipalities and regional districts receive from private power projects.[1] While municipalities are able to levy higher rates of taxation than unincorporated areas, in both cases tax revenues are still only a tiny fraction of the revenues energy developers receive. And, a significant proportion of the money collected by local governments goes to pay, not for services to the community, but for services developers require, such as fire and emergency protection, policing, road maintenance, and the like. These costs to local government must be deducted to get an accurate indication of the true value of developers' tax contributions to the local community. Finally, there are unaccounted lost commercial and tax opportunities associated with the negative impact of power projects on local tourism, agriculture, and recreation.

When we add up all the ongoing local spending by private energy developers, the returns to local communities are minimal. For example, in its original application for approval of the above-mentioned project near Christina Lake on the Kettle River, Powerhouse Energy indicated that its total projected spending in the region, once the project was up and running, would be $425,000, annually (Powerhouse Energy Corporation 1999). But the 97-GWh annual revenue stream would produce an estimated cash flow of about $4.7 million at energy prices prevailing at the time of application. Thus, local spending would amount to only about one-tenth of the annual return on the water resource. And some in the local community believe this estimate of local spending may overstate the eventual local employment benefits. A review of the number of permanent jobs created by the various projects to which BC Hydro has awarded long-term EPAs shows that this example is typical of the gap between the high financial returns to outside investors and the minimal returns to the community.

From the perspective of local communities and First Nations, another key weakness of the government's approach is that it ignores the need for comprehensive regional planning that allows full input from the affected communities and takes into account "big-picture" impacts in a comprehensive and integrated manner. Sound planning should incorporate a variety of relevant factors, including the cumulative impacts on the region of numerous power projects, other uses for the land and river systems, community values, environmental concerns, maintenance of pristine valleys for future generations, and alternative economic development possibilities such as kayaking, horseback riding, fishing lodges, water sports, and tourism.[2]

Many of these sites are valuable for reasons quite independent of their ability to generate energy. They may have special significance for First Nations as burial grounds, places of religious significance, or as traditional hunting or fishing grounds. Many river systems host rare species of fish, insects, plants, and wildlife. Their scenic beauty may be a major tourist attraction.

The fact that they may have these other attributes does not automatically rule them out as sites for energy generation, but it does mean that the planning and permitting process must be managed in a way that takes full account of all potential benefits and uses of the sites. And, where a small hydro or wind-farm facility is introduced, it should be done in a manner that minimizes adverse impacts on local communities, while providing reasonable benefits to the community in exchange for the opportunities lost for alternative land and water uses.

But this is not the approach the government follows. Instead, it has turned the planning process on its head. Public resources are being allocated to make it as easy as possible for private interests to obtain the approvals they need to develop the sites on which they have staked a claim. The focus is on how to get individual projects up and running, rather than developing a comprehensive regional land- and water-use plan that evaluates all relevant issues and takes into account the concerns of all those who might be negatively affected by the projects.

Private investors are not responsible for regional planning. They have no reason to be concerned about the order in which projects should be developed (or not, as the case may be). The relationship between the impact of their individual projects and others in the region is of no matter to them, nor is the cumulative effect of having literally dozens of projects in a river system. It is up to governments to do this sort of planning, but the provincial government has failed to do so. And, it has also deliberately removed the ability of local governments to do it through Bill 30. Instead it is allowing — indeed encouraging — private, largely unregulated development based almost entirely on the interests of investors.

The independent construction of a number of individual projects in the same area can have significant cumulative or "add-on" effects. One or two run-of-the-river projects may not have a major regional impact, but if all the major water systems in an area are built on, the basic character of the area may be significantly and profoundly altered, particularly if there are numerous new power lines and access roads accompanying the power plants. As the government pushes through more and more private power projects, communities across the province have become increasingly concerned about these negative impacts and have started to "push back" against the government's policies in their efforts to bring some semblance of rational planning to the development process.

Another local concern — particularly by those in the environmental community — is that many of the small hydro projects are not nearly as "green" or benign as their proponents claim. In fact, the term "run-of-the-river," widely used by power developers to describe their projects, is arguably inaccurate in many instances. It misleadingly implies that power generation is actually being carried out in the river, when in fact it is normally done by diverting the water into a pipe or tunnel where it then flows down into a power plant. To do this, it is necessary to build a dam to create a head pond. This is needed to allow the silt to settle, ensuring that the water diverted to the power plant is relatively free of debris. Dams are often major concrete structures accompanied by inflatable weirs to enable the developer to control the height of the water in the head pond. In some cases, the dam will provide water storage as well.

Many head ponds are a kilometre or more in length, transforming fast flowing rivers into small reservoirs. The head pond is the starting point for a penstock, which can be a large-diameter pipe or, quite often, a tunnel drilled through rock to carry the stream's water to the power plant below. Some of these penstocks are quite lengthy. The Ashlu project, for example, will have a six-kilometre tunnel, while Chekamus has one eleven kilometres long. Diverting water from the stream can have a significant effect on the water left flowing in the streambed, often resulting in an increase in water temperature, especially during periods of low flow in late summer. This, of course, can have negative impacts on fish and other aquatic life.

In his thoughtful and detailed examination of a number of recent small hydro projects, Arthur Caldicott has documented a variety of significant environmental issues. He writes:

> All small hydro projects require a dam. It is more often called a weir, but the words are synonymous. Intake weirs are frequently a combination of a concrete dam and retaining walls, topped with an inflatable rubber barrier which allows more precise water supply management. Plutonic is proposing weirs six metres high, fully inflated, on the East Toba and Montrose sites. These are modest. At the McGregor/Herrick project, a dam 77 metres high is being proposed on the McGregor River, about 120 km northeast of Prince George. That's a pretty big dam. (Caldicott 2007)

In addition to the direct impact of the dam, head pond, penstock, and power plant, new power plants' transmission requirements may also add to their "footprint" in significant ways. Developers often need a transmission sub-station to facilitate shaping the energy that will be fed into BC Hydro's grid, and they need new high-voltage lines to connect to it. Where existing BC Hydro lines are not adequate to handle the new energy from these projects, the Crown corporation may have to upgrade its own lines and/or install new sub-stations. To this must be added the access roads and various buildings to enable plant operators to service and repair their equipment. New roads can inflict significant environmental damage and may also open up pristine areas in ways that may be inconsistent with sound land-use planning.

Plutonic Power, for example, is planning to build a 148-kilometre long line from Saltry Bay south of Powell River to the East Toba River through largely untouched forests and along mountain hillsides. The right of way will be 120-metres wide and will have to be cleared of brush continuously to ensure that trees do not fall on the lines. Caldicott calculates that this will involve clear-cutting a total of 1,780 hectares (Caldicott 2007). However, we are not dealing with just one or two new transmission lines in a given area. In the Squamish-Lillooet region alone developers have taken out water licences for seventy potential projects and roughly a dozen are now in place, with more under construction or on the drawing board. Seven projects have been proposed on the Pit River system east of Vancouver. And on and on it goes, across the province.

Aside from their direct impact on the land base, new transmission lines can also have a negative visual impact on otherwise pristine river valleys and mountains. This can adversely affect the tourism and recreation industries. And it can reduce property values along the line, an issue of particular concern to residents of the Whistler area, according to the Squamish-Lillooet Regional District:

> This is an issue of particular concern in the Sea to Sky portion of the SLRD due to the high visual impact of power lines and the region's dependence on tourism for 25 percent of its economic activity. The large number of lines already in the corridor has been an issue of ongoing concern and discussion.... To protect the area's natural beauty and recognize the economic value of the area, there is a need to formally recognize scenic value zones on local official community plans and to establish visual quality guidelines. (Squamish-Lillooet Regional District 2003)

Major transmission upgrades require a "Certificate of Public Necessity and Convenience" from the BCUC. While this approval process may provide an opportunity for local residents to raise concerns, the mandate of the BCUC is not sufficiently broad to encompass many of them. The BCUC is unlikely to refuse to grant access to a developer if the project has already received the other required provincial approvals. The problem is that the most "economic" routes for new power lines may not be the most desirable from a variety of other perspectives — perspectives the BCUC is not mandated to incorporate into its decisions.

All of this is to underline the fact that the cumulative environmental impact of all this construction is neither as minor nor as benign as private power advocates claim. There is a major disconnect between the public-relations descriptions of these projects as "green" and the reality of their footprints on land and water systems.

The government's narrow, project-by-project approval process is not well suited to developing regional plans that minimize environmental and other damage to entire valleys. Pressure from individual developers who have a good site — that is, a profitable one — can result in construction of lines that would not be built if a broader planning process were in place. But developers are interested in cashing in on the value of their water licences, and so they have no incentive to postpone development until such planning is in place. And, private power developers have a clear financial interest in building the most direct — and cheapest — tie-in to the grid, even though this may result in far more damage to other parties than a less direct but more costly route.

The government is exacerbating this problem through the direction it has given to the new B.C. Transmission Corporation (BCTC) to organize its operations in a way that supports the growth of the private energy sector. According to its most recent "Service Plan," the Corporation identifies the following as part of its mandate:

> BCTC goals are strongly aligned with the province's Energy Plan released in 2002. The creation of BCTC advances an important Energy Plan commitment to improve transmission access and planning, and to provide a more focussed approach to the operation and management of British Columbia's publicly owned electric transmission assets. A key commitment of the Energy Plan is to encourage increased private sector participation in meeting British Columbia's growing electricity needs. BCTC has a key role in facilitating the interconnection of new generation facilities being developed by the private sector. BCTC's proposals for new rate designs, "open season" and "clustering" processes, and new approaches to interconnections, approved by the BCUC as part of the Open Access Transmission Tariff, will enhance the ability of the independent power sector to contribute to the province's electricity needs in a cost-effective way. (B.C. Transmission Corporation 2005: 20)

This statement underlines the inherent conflict between meeting developers' needs to have transmission access built on the basis of minimizing costs and the broader need for rational planning of all regional transmission lines. Transmission lines should be built, not only on the basis of the lowest cost to energy developers, but also to avoid "spaghetti-junction" scenarios in which other community, tourism, and environmental values are treated simply as "externalities" subordinate to the financial concerns of private power interests.

Local residents quickly realize that the attractive plans and drawings provided by architects and engineers working for private power developers are nothing like the reality they end up dealing with when construction starts. As one irate community resident commented, "The only thing 'green' about these projects is the cash flow."

There is a fundamental disconnect between the high profits investors receive from private power projects and the minimal benefits and significant costs experienced by local communities. Local opposition to such projects is frequently portrayed as simply a self-interested, knee-jerk, not-in-my-backyard reaction. But communities have sound reasons for opposing many of these projects. The resulting conflicts between communities on the one hand and private power developers and the provincial government on the other are clearly illustrated in two regional disputes between developers and local communities. The next two chapters will examine some of the major economic, environmental, and planning issues raised by the government's privatization policies. The purpose is to not only to show what is happening in these two areas but, more broadly, to highlight what is happening across the province as more and more lucrative BC Hydro EPAs are given out to private developers. The conflicts highlighted in these two examples are likely to be replicated in numerous other areas across the province as the construction of power plants funded by the 2006 and subsequent tender calls proceeds. They also underline the perversity of a policy that pursues the interests of developers, regardless of the consequences for local communities.

NOTES

1. This discussion does not take into account the fact that BC Hydro is now committed to paying the property taxes for capital investments made by private energy developers when they enter into a new EPA. Of course, for those few projects that do not depend on such agreements, municipal tax would be paid by the developers.
2. See, for example, the numerous articles and letters from the tourism and kayaking community submitted to the *Whistler-Squamish Chief*, as well as the extensive discussions recorded in the minutes of the SLRD and various other local papers across B.C.

Chapter Nine

Conflict on the Ashlu

THE $87-MILLION PROPOSAL BY Ledcor to develop the Ashlu Creek run-of-the-river project in the Squamish-Lillooet Regional District (SLRD) illustrates many of the issues outlined in the previous chapter. It has triggered a major controversy in the region — a controversy that has taken on provincial proportions and generated significant friction between municipal governments and the province. Ledcor's application for planning permission from the SLRD for its new power plant mobilized a wide variety of different community interests who joined together in a lengthy struggle to try to stop it. This broadly based community opposition resulted in the SLRD turning down the company's application for planning permission for the project for almost four years, until the government passed legislation to push through its approval.[1]

While, in the end, the government was able to force the SLRD into acquiescing to the construction of Ledcor's Ashlu power plant, the conflict highlights a number of challenges now facing local communities across the province when they try to delay or stop construction of new private power facilities. First, it shows the extremes to which the government will go to get its power privatization agenda implemented. Throughout the dispute between the company and the SLRD, it was clear that the government supported the company and viewed the elected local government as simply an obstruction to be overcome. Far from attempting to objectively evaluate community concerns, the government used a variety of different strategies to cajole and eventually bludgeon the SLRD into accepting its agenda. When one piece of legislation (Bill 75) proved insufficient, the government moved to pass another (Bill 30) to override opposition to Ledcor's proposed power plant.

This dispute also illustrates how the award of a BC Hydro EPA provides an enormous financial incentive for private power developers to get their projects up and running. While Ledcor may have wanted to pursue the project in any case — and, at the time of writing, this is simply not something that is easy to confirm — it can be argued that the deal BC Hydro offered Ledcor was significant in encouraging it to go forward with the project in the face of considerable opposition from various local community groups. Encouraged by the government, Ledcor used a number of different approaches to persuade the community to agree to its proposal, including negotiating a financial partnership with the local First Nations band in which it apparently committed to sharing in the revenue stream and eventually in ownership of the facility.

The conflict also exposed the failure of the province's environmental assessment process to effectively address fundamental environmental concerns associated both with the direct impact of this specific project and, more broadly, with the construction of a very large number of power projects in a sensitive river system. Indeed, not a single private power project has been rejected as a result of failure to meet the requirements of the government's environmental assessment process, despite the arguments and evidence presented by environmentalist and citizen groups regarding a wide range of projects across the province (Caldicott 2007).

The Ledcor-SLRD dispute underscores the conflicting economic interests between a company determined to turn its water licence into a valuable revenue stream and a community that saw the project as likely to result in major losses to its tourism, hiking, kayaking, and recreation industries — losses attributable both to the new restrictions on public access and river use resulting from the construction of the power plant and from the broader effects of new power lines, access roads, and the facility itself on the area's scenic values, so critical to its key industry, tourism.

Before examining the project itself, it is worthwhile profiling the company that has generated so much controversy. Ledcor is Canada's second-largest construction company and a major player in B.C.'s economy. According to its website, it is a private company and has 4,500 employees. Its head office is located in Vancouver and its American head office is in San Diego. It is involved in building numerous projects in other parts of B.C. and in other Canadian provinces. It is a prime contractor for various oil-and-gas developments in Alberta and a major builder of small hydro plants commissioned by other energy investors.[2] Its activities are not limited to Canada: it is also a major international company with projects across the United States, in the U.K., Russia, and in various other jurisdictions.

The Ashlu project is not the only power development the company has sought to build in the Squamish-Lillooet region. Ledcor holds seven other water licences (or applications for licences) in the Ashlu drainage area, including one on Sigurd Creek. It is an owner, or part owner, of developments in Fitzsimmons Creek, the Britannia Beach Remediation Project, and a Squamish wind farm. Ledcor originally applied for its Ashlu water licence in 1989, and it submitted a proposal to supply energy to BC Hydro under a 1994 tender call. However, BC Hydro did not select its proposal, even though, according to the company, it ranked as one of the top ten submitted to the Crown utility. In 2002 it again submitted a proposal to supply energy to BC Hydro, and on September 29, 2003, BC Hydro announced that it would enter into a twenty-year EPA with Ledcor.

Ledcor's proposal is typical of many run-of-the-river applications across the province. It requested permission to divert much of the flow of the Ashlu River through a six-kilometre tunnel to a new generating facility. The water

Table 21: Sea-to-Sky Energy Projects in Operation, Nov. 1, 2005

No.	Stream	Diversion Amt Cubic Metres/Second	Project Size Megawatts
1	Brandywine	4.0	7.6
2	Britannia	0.3	
3	Cheakamus	65.0	158.0
4	Furry (Upper)	4.0	11.0
5	Henriette	0.3	
6	Mamquam (Lower)	23.5	50.0
7	Mamquam (Upper)	27.0	25.0
8	Mineral Creek		0.1
9	Miller	5.5	32.0
10	Miller (South)	0.6	
11	Phyllis	0.4	
12	Rutherford	18.4	46.0
13	Soo	16.5	12.0
14	Woodfibre	0.3	
Totals	Operational Projects	166	342

Source: Whitewater Kayaking Association of British Columbia 2006

would then be returned downstream, leaving an area of the river between the intake and return pipes with reduced water flow. To generate energy, Ledcor proposed building a new powerhouse and installing three turbines with capacity to produce 230 GWh of electricity annually.[3] At prices of about $50 per MWh, this would result in an annual cash flow of about $11.5 million. At $75 per MWh, it would generate about $17.25 million.[4] It is not clear what Ledcor is actually receiving in its contract with BC Hydro, but in the spring of 2007 BC Hydro applied to the BCUC to amend the EPA. The BCUC agreed to this, but has refused to release the revised terms (BCUC 2007). According to BC Hydro, the Ashlu Creek project would cost an estimated $87 million to build (BC Hydro 2002a).

Ledcor's application was controversial for two reasons. The first was that it represented yet another power project in a region that already had a significant number in operation, as well as applications for many more. The second was the direct impact the project would have on the Ashlu River itself. A number of individuals and organizations were already becoming alarmed at the proliferation of private power projects in the region. According to the Whitewater Kayaking Association of B.C. (WKABC), by 2005 there were already a total of fourteen operational projects with a capacity of 342 MW

Table 22: Potential Sea-to-Sky Energy Projects, Nov. 1, 2005

No	Stream	Diversion Amt. Cubic Metres/Sec	Project Size Megawatts
1	Ashlu	29.0	49.0
2	Billy Goat	11.5	9.9
3	Birkenhead	15.0	6.7
4	Callaghan	13.7	9.9
5	Cheakamus (gorge)	25.0	30.0
6	Cheakamus (US Daisy)	14.0	9.3
7	Conroy	6.0	4.9
8	Crawford	3.2	4.9
9	Culliton (Lower)	6.0	4.9
10	Culliton (Upper)	6.0	12.0
11	Douglas	11.0	35.0
12	Fire	10.0	25.0
13	Fire Lake	2.5	8.2
14	Fitzsimmons	4.0	8.0
15	Fries	3.5	12.0
16	Fries (trib)	3.5	12.0
17	Furry (Lower)	4.8	6.6
18	Gowan	9.0	18.2
19	Haylmore	6.2	15.0
20	High Falls (Lower)	3.9	7.0
21	High Falls (Upper)	3.9	4.0
22	Joffre	5.7	19.0
23	Kakila	4.1	6.7
24	Lillooet (Lower)	30.0	19.0
25	Lillooet (Keyhole Falls)	62.0	61.0
26	Lizzie	4.0	7.2
27	Livingstone	9.0	18.2
28	Lovelywater	1.1	0.6
29	Mill	8.0	14.1
30	Mkw'alts	17.0	49.0
31	North	4.5	8.7
32	Owl	3.0	19.0
33	Pebble	7.1	10.0
34	Raffuse	2.4	8.0

35	Ring	3.0	6.4
36	Rogers	2.6	2.5
37	Rogers	10.0	21.0
38	Rubble	0.0	9.0
39	Ryan	25.0	49.0
40	Skookum	6.5	8.5
41	Sloquet	13.7	4.9
42	Sloquet - N	2.5	4.2
43	Sloquet - S	2.5	3.7
44	Snowcap	14.0	19.0
45	South	6.6	19.9
46	Stawamus	2.8	4.9
47	Tantalus	1.1	4.9
48	Tuwasus	10.3	8.8
49	Twenty One Mile	2.5	2.3
50	Twin One	3.2	9.3
51	Twin Two	1.0	7.1
52	Wedge	2.6	4.3
53	Squamish Spit Wind		
54	Meager Geothermal		192.0
Totals	Potential New Projects	460	915

Source: Whitewater Kayaking Association of British Columbia 2006

in the Squamish area's twelve river systems. Table 21 lists these.

These operations were in addition to older BC Hydro projects that already were generating 696 MW of power in the area. The alarming issue for many citizens in the area was the number of new power projects that might go forward in the coming years. Table 22, again compiled by WKABC, lists these. All but two of these are small hydro projects.

When the potential projects were added to the existing ones, the region could have as many as sixty-six small hydro projects, as well as a wind operation and a thermal plant. And there is no guarantee that developers might not make further applications for other possible sites.[5] If most of these were to be built, they would create a "spaghetti junction" of transmission wires and access roads through some of the most pristine parts of the region. Ledcor's application would add to a development process that many in the community feel has already gone too far in disturbing the scenic and recreational values that have been such an important factor in sustaining the local economy. And, while Ledcor's original application to build the power plant pre-dated the government's decision to hold the 2010 Olympic Games at Whistler, its construction would add to a local economy already over-heated with road construction and the development of numerous Games facilities.

Ledcor's proposal quickly cleared provincial regulatory hurdles, while the government actively supported the company's application by assigning staff from various ministries to assist Ledcor in its efforts to obtain the required provincial and federal approvals. However, the government did even more than this. It also directed staff to work with the company to overcome community opposition. Ledcor required planning permission from the SLRD, but the SLRD was not an arm of the provincial government and its decision-making process reflected the views and interests of people in the community. And so the SLRD became the focal point of conflict between the provincial government and the company on one side, and the local community on the other.

The SLRD devoted an inordinate amount of its time and resources to evaluating the potential impacts of the proposal, hearing numerous submissions from the company, various government ministries, local businesses, environmental groups, and individual residents. It also directed staff to carry out extensive research, both on Ledcor's specific proposal and on the larger question of the approval of more private power plants within its jurisdiction. All of this was to provide the SLRD with the information it needed to decide whether it should approve the project. The various staff reports — and particularly the 2003 SLRD study, "Independent Power Project Development in the Squamish-Lillooet Regional District" — constitute one of the most thorough assessments of the impacts of small hydro projects on communities carried out to date in B.C.

To understand why the SLRD was prepared to challenge the government, it is helpful to review some of the issues raised by community members. One of the most vocal and articulate criticisms of the Ledcor proposal came from what initially might seem an unlikely source — the local kayaking community. The Ashlu River is one of the premier kayaking rivers in North America. Kayakers from across the continent — and from around the world — regularly come to the area to enjoy the challenge of its raging currents. This is a major component of the local tourism industry, and those in the kayaking business saw the project as a major threat to their livelihoods. The potential negative impact of the Ledcor proposal and the many other small hydro facilities already in place or planned for the area was outlined by Stuart Smith of WKABC:

> They have cumulative impacts beyond each individual project. Add the headpond length for all those projects, the volume of water stored in each headpond, the kilometres of transmission lines each project contributes, the clearing of the diversion corridors, the sub-stations,

> the road building. Each is nowhere near as large as the impacts of Daisy Lake, but sum them all up and the perspective changes. Miller Creek was a harbinger of concern with these projects, including issues with fisheries, community, power lines, process, project design, and more. The Soo project demonstrates the issue of de-watering, and the parallel power lines on the Mamquam projects illustrate the lack of cooperation and planning. These are a few examples of issues. The long-term impacts of widespread stream-flow reduction and wildlife disturbance remain unknown. Add to this the concerns over the long-term implications of privatization of power, and of the export issue, implications of which are clearly not well-defined or understood. These projects are not simply all good for us, without costs or impacts. It is widely known that some projects carry more issues than others. The developers on the Ashlu project chose to move ahead knowing there were large issues; this was their choice. It is unfortunate, but avoidable, that controversial projects are put forward while more appropriate ones are not. Let us not confuse opposition to one project with opposition to any projects, or to the best projects, properly integrated with community values. The clearly missing element is a process for filtering out the good projects. Recognize that the industry is highly unlikely to call each other's projects for what they are — some good, some not so good. Yet certainly no one wants to go through another Ashlu review process — not the proponents, not the investors, not the local governments, not the opponents, and not the Province. (S. Smith 2005a)

Smith's comments reflect a range of concerns, but they also acknowledge that, properly planned, some projects do make sense. His opposition was not a knee-jerk, not-in-my-backyard response, but rather one that recognized that, done properly, there could be significant benefits from some of these developments. At the same time, he believed that the proponent-driven approach to approval of small hydro projects without an overall plan for development of small hydro in the region was already resulting in unnecessary damage to the local environment and economy.

Smith also highlighted the basic failure of the government's environmental assessment process to address the overall impact of locating so many hydro facilities in the area:

> The current environmental review process focusses on a limited stretch of the rivers in question and no work has been done in terms of cumulative impact.... I really think that the provincial government is lacking a larger perspective and is evaluating these projects on an individual basis. (S. Smith 2005b)

In an interview with Lisa Richardson of the online journal *The Tyee*, Smith further underlined the cumulative impact of unregulated, run-of-the-river developments in the Squamish-Lillooet area:

> "The raw fact is that one run-of-the-river is way more environmentally friendly than a big dam," says Stuart. "But are 100 IPPs, or twenty of them, more environmentally friendly than one Daisy Lake dam? It's just not a clear question. There are a lot of unknowns and the pace we are moving at doesn't allow us to monitor the impacts. This thing is happening way too fast." (Richardson 2004)

Smith also noted another weakness in the process: the basic imbalance in resources between a provincial government that was using considerable amounts of its staff time and other resources to push through the project and the volunteer-based opposition groups operating on a shoestring budget: "We are small group of volunteers against the money of corporations.... I feel like we are making zero progress with the amount of work we are required to put in to compete with million-dollar corporations" (S. Smith 2005b).

The SLRD tried to use its planning and zoning authority to bring some semblance of order and rationality to this otherwise anarchic process. Its first major step was to commission its staff in 2002 to do a major review. It was released to the public on April 28, 2003 (SLRD 2003).

The conflict between the province and the SLRD can be more readily understood in the context of the concerns the latter raised over the anarchic planning process the province has unleashed. It outlined these as follows:

- incremental development;
- approval processes — including timelines, lack of clear criteria for project, selection and handling of post-approval changes;
- power line and BC Hydro system implications of development;
- public input/public consultation;
- community benefits;
- enforcement and accountability (SLRD 2003: 8).

The SLRD was particularly worried about the absence of a suitable planning framework that took into account the overall impact of projects on the region, its values, and priorities. It argued that the province's policy toward independent power producers resulted in a "limited ability to evaluate or address cumulative impacts," that it was characterized by a "lack of good information on which to properly evaluate proposed projects," and that the first-come, first-right-of-approval process "favours early projects rather than the best projects" (SLRD 2003: 9).

The SLRD further analyzed a number of issues it confronted in dealing with the approvals process. It noted problems arising from the fact that three levels of government (federal, provincial, and municipal) were involved, along with First Nations. Each had its own legislation or bylaws and corresponding agencies and processes for project approval, based on a variety of different considerations. As well, the timelines for each of the separate approval processes were often different and there was little coordination in the overall process among the various governments and agencies. Yet, ironically, and despite the complexity of the process and the large number of agencies involved, the approval system did not provide the capacity for rational, long-term regional planning of project development.

The complexity of the overlapping approval processes resulted in other types of problems. To meet approval requirements of one agency, modifications in the design of a project might be required. However, approval from another agency may be predicated on the original, rather than the modified, proposal.

In its 2003 review, the SLRD made clear that it did not oppose small hydro projects being developed in the region. But it also cautioned that the conditions under which such reviews should be handled should be clearly stated:

> The SLRD endorses a goal of regional sustainability and supports the development of green energy projects in the region when those facilities:
>
> - have been properly evaluated and are shown to be technically sound, environmentally sensitive and socially responsible;
> - are located, designed, constructed, and operated in a manner that is consistent with the overall vision for the region and do not negatively impact on its primary economic activities (e.g., tourism in the Sea-to-Sky corridor);
> - can be connected into the existing transmission and distribution infrastructure with minimal impact and do not require the development of any new major transmission corridors; and
> - provide tangible community benefits comparable to projects constructed since 2001.

The 2003 SLRD review also outlined fifteen specific policy concerns that it believed should inform the evaluation of future private power projects in the region. And, it set out a series of twelve specific actions that it intended to adopt to oversee future development of such projects within its jurisdiction. These included, among others, scenic value zones to protect the scenic and tourism values in the region; working with BC Hydro to incorporate regional values and priorities into future electricity planning; clarifying the roles and relationships of the various levels of government regarding private power planning and approvals; ensuring adequate opportunities for public consultation, including consultation with First Nations; establishing mechanisms to ensure commitments by developers are properly enforced; legislative amendments to make BCUC oversight of projects more effective; and, working with other local governments across the province to share research and information about local government policies.

The SLRD was concerned that without proper regional planning, approving projects on a "one off" basis would lead both to more transmission lines being built and to their inappropriate placement, with negative impacts on scenic values in the region. In the words of the SLRD's 2003 review: "One of the implications of moving to a policy favouring small-scale power plants is the potential for a proliferation of power lines. Instead of requiring one major line to connect a large generating station to the BC Hydro grid, numerous smaller lines will be required."

The SLRD was also very concerned about enforcement of regulatory requirements and commitments made by developers during the approvals process. Enforcement of the terms and conditions of approvals was fragmented among a number of different government bodies and enforcement powers were often inadequate. This meant that proponents could avoid, or minimize, earlier commitments to local communities — and the communities would not have legal authority to address such avoidance. The province also lacked a clear plan for documenting and following up on such commitments, or for ensuring that standards and requirements that were conditions of the approvals were properly monitored after projects began operating. The SLRD was concerned that, due to the involvement of a number of different agencies in the approvals process, changes made in the design, location, and other features of projects were being made after earlier approvals had been granted based on previously submitted plans. This concern also applied to post-approval changes, where the province appeared not to be properly monitoring whether such changes were consistent with the original basis of the approval:

> The issue of tracking and enforcement of commitments is also a key issue and a primary concern of many local residents and community interest groups. During public consultation, commitments are often made by proponents in an effort to resolve community concerns. However, there is no formal process for these commitments to be tracked and enforced. (SLRD 2003: 10)

This issue has been exacerbated by the "flipping" of projects from their original proponents to new investors who did not participate in the original consultative process and may not even have been aware of some of the verbal commitments made by the previous developer. As a consequence, new owners might take a very narrow, legalistic approach to honouring obligations the original owners made, restricting their actions only to those items that were part of a legally binding commitment. And so, once the firms that make them sell their interests in the project, verbal assurances to the community about specific proposals for providing local benefits or ameliorating various irritants associated with these projects may not end up being honoured.

The SLRD was also concerned that project approval criteria were unduly vague and, in some cases, contradictory. And, proponents were not always required to provide the relevant information community members needed to understand and analyze the implications of a proposal.

The 2003 SLRD review also noted the marginal economic development benefits of a number of previous private hydro projects in the region. It noted that they "have not generated significant local benefits, particularly in the areas of employment and local purchasing." It went on to indicate that, "during construction, much of the expertise and equipment has been brought in from outside the region, as it is often very specialized and not available locally. Once operational, the plants are usually fully automated and provide only limited local employment." Consequently, the SLRD review felt that various levels of government should focus more attention on ensuring that the local community received a fairer share of the economic benefits of new power projects.

During the period the SLRD was developing its 2003 review and policy framework, another consultative process was also addressing some of the same issues. The Sea-to-Sky Land and Resource Management Plan Committee (commonly known as the LRMP) began to meet in September 2002. It included representatives of twelve organizations, including the Ministry of Energy and people in the area with an interest in tourism, forestry, recreation, labour, agriculture, fish and wildlife, or conservation. Its focus was to clarify how to manage private power projects in the region. On October18, 2004, members of the LRMP, with the notable exception of the Ministry of Energy, signed onto a number of recommendations for a regional energy infrastructure development strategy for the LRMP area. The report included a recommendation to exclude the Ashlu, along with a number of other rivers, from private power development (Sea-to-Sky LRMP 2004).

Shortly thereafter, on January 21, 2005, the SLRD Council, based on its own assessment of the costs and benefits of the proposed Ashlu project and on the views of the local community, voted eight to one against approving it. This decision was not arrived at lightly. It followed an extensive two-year consultation process involving presentations by Ledcor, various government ministries, and a wide range of local citizen groups, as well as considerable public debate within the community (SLRD 2005).

When it became clear, in the days preceding the SLRD vote, that Council would not approve the project, the Minister of Sustainable Resource Management, George Abbott, tried to intervene to delay a decision so that Ledcor could have additional time to advance its case. But the Council felt it knew enough about the project to make a decision and went ahead with the vote.

After municipal elections in November 2005, the province again intervened in an effort to get the SLRD to overturn its previous decision. In a letter to Council, Greg Reimer, Deputy Minister of Energy, Mines, and Petroleum Resources, offered to put in place a regional planning strategy for ten of the twelve river systems in the area, excepting only the Callaghan and Ashlu systems. The Deputy Minister's carrot was that the Ministry would put on hold the granting of new water licences for development in ten of the area's river systems — at least until a comprehensive review process was concluded. This, Reimer argued, would address the earlier concerns raised by the SLRD regarding the anarchic development process in the region. The *quid pro quo* was that the Council would revisit the decision on the Ashlu.

Reimer's letter reveals the extent of the government's involvement in supporting Ledcor's application. It reads, in part, as follows:

> In summary, the Ministry is prepared to make a recommendation to Government that water reserves be placed on 10 of the 12 streams identified as a high priority for analysis by the SLRD Board. This is in response to the SLRD Board's resolution of January, 31, 2005, and with a view to advancing Ledcor's Ashlu project. It is my understanding that Ledcor will be submitting a rezoning application in the near future. Should the re-zoning not be approved, our recommendation regarding the water reserves will not proceed. (Reimer 2005)

Members of the community immediately noted that there was nothing in the government's offer — the carrot — that would provide permanent protection against further development in these ten river systems after the Ashlu project was approved. They felt that, far from ending the flow of new development applications, approval of the Ashlu project would, over time, be interpreted by the province as simply one more step on the road to approval of projects on the other rivers.

The "stick" at this stage in the dispute was Bill 75, *The Significant Projects Streamlining Act* (Government of B.C. 2003).[6] This legislation gave Cabinet the power to designate as "in the public interest" any new "provincially significant project." This controversial power, passed by the Liberal government in its first term in office, allowed the Minister, using an Order-in-Council, to overturn a local government zoning decision if the project involved was deemed of major economic importance to the province. It gave the government the ability to push through significant capital projects such as public-private partnerships, which was how it was originally viewed by many of its critics.

But Bill 75 was worded more broadly and, arguably, it could be used to approve private power projects as well. While Reimer's letter to the SLRD did not specifically threaten the use of Bill 75, both the government and the SLRD knew that this power might be available to the Minister if he decided he wanted to override the SLRD's continued opposition to the Ledcor project. At the same time, use of this power would have clearly provoked a considerable backlash, especially as it did not entail any process by which the government might justify its decision.

The government's threat placed the SLRD in a very difficult position. It could accept the limited offer of a temporary moratorium on the issuance of water licences on the other ten river systems in exchange for approval of the Ledcor proposal. Or, it could turn down the offer and risk having its previous zoning decision overturned anyway by Order-in-Council under Bill 75. In this latter case, it would get nothing. There would be no moratorium on development in the other river systems.

Despite this pressure from Ledcor and the provincial government, the SLRD voted in January 2006 to table Ledcor's re-application for its zoning permit for a minimum of six months so that it could determine what, precisely, the government was prepared to do with respect to developing a regional plan for energy development.

But the government had yet another card to play. Frustrated with local opposition to private power projects and aware that a number of other communities were beginning to challenge its Energy Plan, it decided to pass a new piece of legislation, Bill 30, *The Miscellaneous Statutes Amendment Act*. This gave "utility status" to private power projects and so transferred the final say over approvals to the BCUC. This provided a broader approach to circumventing municipal planning and zoning approvals than did Bill 75, and it also placed some distance between the government and the decision-making process. Instead of Cabinet having to deal with projects on a case-by-case basis — a practice that had clear political drawbacks — the BCUC would be handed the job.

Given the BCUC's narrow mandate, which focusses primarily on the impact of power projects on ratepayers, and its lack of expertise in areas such as environmental assessment and municipal planning, its decisions would be determined by criteria that simply did not take into account issues being raised by local communities. In effect, the BCUC would have virtually no option but to approve applications from private power developers.

The fact that the province included within the scope of Bill 30 legal authority to enable the BCUC to override the opposition of local governments to private power projects indicates how determined it has been to push through its private-sector energy development agenda. The point is clarified in a letter dated September 29, 2006, from Energy, Mines, and Petroleum Resources Minister Richard Neufeld to SLRD Chair John Turner. Neufeld wrote:

> Section 121 of the UC (Utilities Commission) Act provided that nothing in or done under the Local Government Act or the Community Charter supersedes or impairs a power conferred on a public utility. This section, which dates from 1957, established the respective roles of the Province and local governments in regard to public utilities, which include independent power producers (IPPs). For example, local government land use decisions cannot prevent a public utility which has been conferred a power via a Certificate of Public Convenience and Necessity (CPCN) from constructing a facility. The amendment that clarifies that Section 121 continues to apply to public utilities which have obtained a CPCN, or have been exempted from the requirement to obtain a CPCN under existing Sections 88 or 22 of the UC Act. (Neufeld 2006)

Neufeld goes on to indicate that to qualify under Section 121, projects have to be on Crown land, have a BC Hydro EPA, and have the appropriate federal and provincial authorizations.

But Bill 30 has not been a cake-walk for the government. The SLRD saw itself as the likely target of the Bill due to its refusal to approve Ledcor's application (Thompson 2006). It responded with a strong Council motion right after the first reading of the Bill that was reflected in a press release it issued on May 2, 2006. It read, in part:

> Whereas the amendments to the Utilities Commission Act proposed by Bill 30 will serve to: eliminate local government involvement and engagement in IPP review and approval processes, remove jurisdiction of local government over IPPs on Crown Land, remove local government from the responsible development of clean, renewable energy sources, impair co-operative inter-governmental relations, and Whereas these amendments will have significant impacts for local governments throughout the province when the full scope and potential of IPPs are considered (e.g., wind, geo-thermal, coal-bed methane and run-of-river projects);
>
> Therefore be it resolved that the Province of British Columbia be requested to immediately set Bill 30 aside and return to working with Union of British Columbia Municipalities to complete the commitments of the Memorandum of Understanding in Independent Power Projects as quickly as possible. (SLRD 2006b)

The SLRD contacted other municipalities across the province to organize opposition to Bill 30. It sent letters to other local governments outlining its concerns and began building alliances at the municipal level to oppose the legislation. On October 25, 2006, at the annual meeting of the Union of British Columbia Municipalities (UBCM), delegates voted overwhelmingly in support of a motion demanding the repeal of Bill 30. Of the estimated 800 delegates present from across the province, representing both urban and rural municipalities, only two opposed the resolution.

Of course, such resolutions have no binding force and are, at best, simply a signal of discontent. The government understood it was under no obligation to heed the UBCM's appeal. In fact, given its substantial commitment to the private power industry, its recent re-election with a comfortable majority, and the predominant position it holds in numerous other delicate relationships with municipal governments, the likelihood of a reversal in provincial policy was always remote. Shortly after the vote, the Minister of Energy, Mines, and Petroleum Resources made it clear he had no intention of following the UBCM's advice. But the struggle over Bill 30 did mean that, for the first time, the government was beginning to pay a political price for its energy policy from a group that has, historically, been one of its key supporters on many other issues.

In the end, the province and Ledcor got their way. With the backing of Bill 30, the company was able to begin construction on its new power plant despite the concerns of the community and the opposition of the local government. But the conflict has resulted in raising the profile of the issue of private power projects at the provincial level and alerting other municipalities and regional districts across the province about the adverse impacts of such projects. The stand taken by the SLRD has also triggered opposition to the current Liberal government's policies from other local governments — and this despite the fact that these governments have traditionally been among its strongest allies.

NOTES

1. Another project in the same watershed was also rejected: the Cayoosh Creek Project, which First Nations in the area opposed.
2. Ledcor is also a major donor to the B.C. Liberal Party, contributing $25,000 in 2000, $2,990 in 2004, and another $5,000 in 2005, according to Elections B.C. (Elections B.C. 2001–2005).
3. Ledcor's Ashlu Creek website <http://www.ashlucreek.com> accessed Jan. 6, 2006. This 230 GWh estimate is a bit higher than the Sigma Engineering estimate in its 2002 study of small hydro (BC Hydro 2002a).
4. Ledcor already has a 6.6 MW project in operation at Fitzsimmons Creek in the same area.
5. The most significant of these, listed by project and proponent in the area near the

Ashlu are as follows: Stoke Creek (Cloudworks Energy); Fire Creek (Cloudworks Energy); Douglas Creek (Cloudworks Energy) Mkw'alts Creek (Cloudworks Energy) Lillooet River (Cloudworks Energy) Rafusse Creek (Rockford Energy) Yahoo Creek (Dick Stainsby) Texas Creek (Enerserv); Culliton Creek (Panawed Energy); Fitzsimmons Creek (Ledcor) Callaghan Creek (Ledcor).

6. Bill 75 was widely criticized in the environmental community because it would allow the government to override environmental concerns about matters such as mining in parks and pollution from new industrial projects (West Coast Environmental Law Association 2003).

Chapter Ten

The Cascade Heritage Project

The controversy in the Squamish-Lillooet Regional District has parallels in other regions of the province. The fallout from the 2006 BC Hydro tender awards (and the prospect of a 2007 and subsequent tender calls) is spurring developers to push ahead with dozens of new projects across the province. However, it is worth examining one other major project to further illustrate the ways private power projects are now impacting local communities.

One of the most well known of these controversies has arisen over the proposal to build a 25 MW run-of-the-river hydro project in the Cascade Falls Canyon on the Kettle River about one mile from Christina Lake in the Regional District of Kootenay-Boundary. The four-hectare riverfront site was originally developed in 1898 by the Cascade Power and Light Company, which had had a 5 MW power plant in operation there. However, as other power projects emerged in the region providing cheaper energy, this plant was eventually closed down, allowing the canyon to revert to its pre-development status.

The land was purchased by Powerhouse Developments, now a wholly owned subsidiary of Sea Breeze Power Corporation, the current applicant.[1] Encouraged by the then Social Credit government's interest in purchasing energy from private power developers, Powerhouse drew up its initial plans in 1990 to take advantage of the government's policy of requiring BC Hydro to purchase energy from private power interests (Powerhouse Developments 1999). In 1991, the company applied for approval to develop the site for energy production under the Small Hydro Projects program.[2] In December 1993, it made application for a water licence to build a new run-of-the-river generating station on the site. However, the application did not proceed as the company anticipated, largely "because of the project justification requirements" (Powerhouse Developments 1999).[3] The company then tried unsuccessfully to be included in BC Hydro's 1995 private energy tender call.

The company's proposal to redevelop the power plant was unwelcome to many residents of the area. They raised a wide range of concerns about its impact on the community's tourism, kayaking, agriculture, and other economic activities, as well as concerns about the local use of the canyon and its water resource.

In the following years, Powerhouse continued to work on the development of the project, carrying out environmental studies and engaging in community consultations, with the expectation that the project would eventually be approved.[4] This work culminated in 1999 when Powerhouse submitted a detailed, 188-page application for a "Project Approval Certificate" (Powerhouse Developments).

This application proposed constructing a new power plant at the site of the demolished generating facility, erecting a 4.5-metre-high weir and sluice gate, building a 610-metre canal, drilling a 140-metre tunnel, and putting in a 140-metre penstock to feed two turbines at the powerhouse. The estimated cost of the project at the time of application was $24 million, half of which the company asserted would be spent in the region. To make the project more attractive to the local community, Powerhouse indicated it would also build a new $900,000 scenic park with on-site tourism amenities.

The company anticipated construction would take twenty months and create forty temporary jobs. Once finished, it anticipated spending $375,000 on annual operational expenses — half of it in the region — and $50,000 on park operations, for an annual total of $425,000. Powerhouse said that, on completion, it would also contribute $260,000 in water rentals and $38,000 in corporate capital taxes — which have since been abolished — to the provincial government. As well, it estimated that the project would provide $350,000 in property and school taxes to the local community (Powerhouse Developments 1999).

In its 1999 submission, the company noted that deregulation was sweeping across North America and that, in this new environment, it could anticipate sales to West Kootenay Power, BC Hydro, or some of the small regional public utilities in B.C., such as Kelowna, Summerland, Penticton, Grand Forks, or Nelson. Or it might sell directly to customers in the United States or through the international spot market (Powerhouse Developments 1999). Power sales were important, because a condition of approval at the time was the ability to show that a power sales agreement had been — or soon would be — negotiated.

The company tried to enlist the support of the provincial government for its project. On June 1, 1999, company President William L. Lang wrote to then Minister of Employment and Investment Mike Farnsworth outlining the benefits of the project to B.C. and indicating that he was looking forward to a satisfactory outcome to the application process. In his words: "We are looking forward to the review of our Cascade Heritage Power Park Project, which is in process now, and hopefully a favourable news release from your office at the appropriate time." Farnsworth's reply of July 28, 1999, was generally supportive, but made no specific commitment on behalf of the government.

The company's application ran into problems: the various approval agencies felt it did not contain sufficient information about certain critical areas. A letter dated August 6, 1999, from Sherri McPherson, Project Review Coordinator of the Environmental Assessment Unit of the Ministry of Environment, Lands, and Parks, to Derek Griffin, Project Assessment Director, Environmental Assessment Office, outlined a number of Ministry concerns about the proposal and concluded that:

> Following review of the above application for a Project Approval Certificate under the province's Environmental Assessment Act, the Ministry of Environment, Lands, and Parks/Ministry of Fisheries (the Ministry) has concluded that the application contains insufficient information regarding the potential for environmental effects and mitigation measures. The Ministry does not support a recommendation for a project approval at this time, and recommends that the project proceed to the project review stage (Stage II). (McPherson 1999)

The letter was accompanied by a detailed analysis of a number of issues, including impacts on water flows and temperatures through the canyon and consequences for fish and aquatic habitat. The attachment also noted the special significance of the canyon itself:

> The Kettle is one of only 18 "Heritage Rivers" accepted by the B.C. Heritage Rivers Board. While not a legal designation this still shows the high value of the Kettle in the province as the competition for heritage status was quite fierce and only a limited number of rivers will achieve this status (maximum about 20). The former Environment Minister stated that "each of these rivers stands out on its own" and "Heritage River status will draw more attention to the exceptional value of these rivers."
>
> These special physical features make this site unique in terms of biodiversity, particularly fish habitat availability and fish utilization, compared to other reaches and tributaries of the Kettle River. The application does not give recognition to these unique environmental conditions available for fish species, and as a result potential adverse impacts are inadequately acknowledged. Specific comments and concerns relating to this are outlined in the sections which follow. (McPherson 1999)

In November 1999, the Cascade Heritage Power Park Project Committee, which had been mandated by the government to manage the consultative process with the community, released a fifty-seven-page advisory report. The report's fifty-one specific recommendations outlined what the company needed to do to meet the legal requirements of the federal and provincial environmental assessment acts, as well as the requirements of other Canadian and provincial legislation. The recommendations also addressed potential cross-border issues, due to the fact that the Kettle River entered the United States five miles downstream from the proposed project and it could potentially affect American interests).[5] One of the reasons for such extensive documentation being requested was the fact that many members of the local community were deeply concerned about the impact of the project (Cascade Heritage Power Park Project Committee 1999).

To ensure that all aspects of the project were fully evaluated, a local citizens' group contracted an environmental consultant, Patrick Yarnell, to do a socio-economic impact study, both for their own information and to meet the requirements of the province's Environmental Assessment Office (EAO), which was continuing to review the project. In his report, released in September 2001, Yarnell questioned many of the company's assertions about the economic benefits of the project to the region:

> The economic impacts of this project are largely construction related, benefiting local motels and restaurants while hampering other tourism operations. No significant long-term economic benefits are expected for the community from the power plant. The proposal includes a museum and park, although a park is already being considered by both the province and the regional district. The project would severely compromise the natural value of the free-flowing river and the falls, which is inconsistent with existing local economic development based on scenic beauty and adventure tourism. Several local business operators would have significant portions of their businesses damaged or destroyed by the impoundment of the river. (Yarnell 2001: ii)

Yarnell also surveyed local businesses to gauge their support for the project. He found that the four local contractors included in his business survey were very pessimistic about their prospects of obtaining work on the project. They felt that the lion's share of contracts would go to firms outside the area, including firms from Alberta (Yarnell 2001). Their scepticism was based on the experience of the B.C. Gas Southern Crossing pipeline project in 2000, in which they believed that only two people in the Christina Lake area got jobs, while the bulk of the work was done by Alberta residents. Similarly, local hoteliers felt that the benefits of additional room occupancy and other expenditures by non-resident construction workers would not compensate for the likely loss in long-term tourism resulting from the negative impact of the project on the scenic beauty of the canyon (Yarnell 2001).

Many in the community also felt that, once completed, the project would restrict the region's opportunity to take full advantage in future of the agricultural, tourism, and recreational potential of the river system — an economic potential that, arguably, would contribute far more to job creation and regional development than would the capital-intensive use of the water system associated with this project. The proposed tail pond would flood the most attractive white-water stretch on this section of the Kettle River. Some opponents from the American side of the river were concerned that, during the summer, water flow over the falls would be reduced to a trickle and its interest as a tourism attraction would be largely eliminated (Heflick 2004). They were also concerned about the possibility that solar heating of the head pond would damage the trout population downstream:

> John Kinney, biologist with the United States Fish and Wildlife Service, indicated that "native trout such as bull trout and cutthroat avoid warmer water. If the temperature of the Kettle rises, they may look to tributaries or even return to the Columbia in search of cooler water. If they don't find it, they won't survive, or their abundance may be reduced to unacceptable levels. A rise in temperature may preclude any type of natural or anthropogenic bull trout recovery in the Kettle River." (*North Columbian Monthly* 2000)

Upstream users of the river on the Canadian side of the border were primarily worried about the impact on future access to water, while others in the community were sceptical about the net employment effects. They contrasted the small number of permanent jobs to be created by the project with the much larger number that could result from more extensive tourism use of the canyon (Yarnell 2001).

After Yarnell's 2001 report was released, the company attempted to address some of the report's criticisms of the project, as well as some of the concerns raised in numerous letters by local residents about the possible negative impact of the proposal on the community. However, the company's proposed changes did not satisfy the Kettle River Review Committee (KRRC), a group of concerned local citizens who opposed the project. The KRRC was particularly worried about the impact on other water users and on tourism in the region (KRRC 2004). A flourishing kayak operation used the canyon and horseback-riding operations took tourists through it. These businesses had paid for recreational tenures to use the area and they were concerned that they would effectively lose the benefit of their tenures. By 2004, when public consultations were concluded, local residents had sent over 600 letters to the province raising concerns about the project, a clear indication of the extent of community opposition.

The KRRC did not take the position that the project should never be built. Rather, it wanted the province to carry out a full review of the potential impacts of the project — environmental, agricultural, economic, tourism, and so on. It was confident that such a review would clearly demonstrate that the costs of the project to the community and the province far outweighed any potential benefits. According to KRRC member Kathy O'Malley, the question they wanted answered was: "What is the highest and best use of the river, the canyon, and its land base for the community?" If all these factors were properly considered, she believed, there would be no justification for this project going forward (O'Malley 2007).

In 2003, under the framework of the Liberal government's revised *Environmental Assessment Act*, Powerhouse re-applied for a water licence and various other related approvals to build the new power plant. As noted earlier, in its 1999 application it indicated that the capital cost of the project would be about $24 million. It subsequently revised this figure upwards to $31 million, presumably to reflect inflation in construction costs over the period. Yet, despite the increase in capital costs, from the proponent's perspective the project would be still be a very good investment, generating anticipated annual revenue of just under $5 million for the 97 GWh of energy at an estimated price of $50 per MWh. Its investment would be even better if energy prices were to rise significantly in the coming years.

According to a 2004 consultant's report prepared for Powerhouse by Timo Makinen of Vizon SciTec, the province would get about $170,000 annually in water licence fees, water rentals, and capacity charges if the project were to go forward (Makinen 2004). However, this amount represents only about 3 percent of Powerhouse's anticipated $5 million annual revenue. And, it does not take into account the costs to the province of staff time and resources associated with the very extensive EAO consultations that have already taken place or the costs of subsequent project monitoring.

In an earlier evaluation of the tax benefits to the local community, the Director of Finance for the Regional District of Kootenay-Boundary calculated that Powerhouse would pay a total of $188,000 in local property taxes, of which the province would get roughly two thirds ($128,000) in school taxes. This would add perhaps another 2.5 percent of the value of its energy sales to provincial coffers in return for giving Powerhouse the water resource. (This figure is dependent on the actual property assessment of the completed project.)

But the local government would also have to provide fire protection and other services to the new power facility. According to the Director of Finance's estimate, the breakdown of municipal taxes would be as follows:

> About 26 percent, or $50,159.55 for 2001, is for Regional District of Kootenay-Boundary purposes, 55 percent of this (or $27,500 which is 14 percent of the total) is for Christina Lake specific services such as fire protection, recreation, and milfoil and mosquito control. The

balance, or approximately $22,500, would be collected for Grand Forks Area and regional services.

It is also worth noting that, as a result of recent changes in government policy designed to make investments in private energy generation more attractive, these calculations would only apply if Powerhouse sold the energy to a purchaser other than BC Hydro. As discussed earlier, BC Hydro now refunds to developers an amount equivalent to their property taxes for the additional assessments associated with the value of their new power plants (BC Hydro 2005b).

Makinen also estimated that Powerhouse would make another contribution to provincial finances through payment of annual corporate taxes, which he estimated to be about $33,000, annually. However, given that the company has spent well over $1 million on the project already but has received no revenue from energy sales, the province would not likely receive any corporate income taxes for many years to come. In the company's U.S. Securities and Exchange filings and in its more recent filings with Canadian regulators, parent company Sea Breeze indicates that it will likely have significant tax write-offs for many years into the future. And, the current Liberal government's abolition of the corporate capital tax means that this source of provincial revenue would no longer be collected either.

When the costs to various levels of government of evaluating the project, monitoring it in future, and providing it with municipal services are all taken into account, a reasonable estimate of the net revenue to all levels of government is in the range of 5 to 6 percent of the anticipated sale price of the energy the project will generate.

This very low level of benefits to government might be less worrisome if the project provided significant economic benefits to the community. However, like other run-of-the-river projects, the Cascade Heritage Power Project is very capital intensive. Powerhouse acknowledges that its $31 million investment would create only three full-time positions at the powerhouse and an estimated three seasonal positions in a proposed tourism office and museum funded by the company.

Makinen's 2004 report accepts the company's estimate that it will spend roughly $470,000 on local staffing and other operating expenditures on the facility each year, an upward revision that presumably reflects the fact that prices had increased in the years following the 1999 application. This figure includes an estimated $50,000 for the operation of the museum and park. But these are ancillary to the power plant itself and their long-term survival may not be guaranteed. Many of the project's critics believe Powerhouse's estimates of local economic benefits are overly generous (Yarnell 2001, 2005). But, even if we accept Makinen's numbers at face value, total annual operating expenditures in the community would amount to just 10 percent of the projected annual revenue stream.

Given the extensive opposition to the project, the company made a number of amendments to its proposal to provide additional benefits to the community. It also took steps to respond to community demands for additional mitigation expenditures and guarantees concerning future use of the water resource. However, on revisiting the issue in the summer of 2005, Yarnell, in a further detailed socio-economic study, continued to question the long-term benefits of the company's application, even with its additional mitigation proposals:

> Based on the concepts of community values, nature-based tourism opportunities and long-term sustainability, the proposed hydro development does not appear to be a positive project for the community of Christina Lake.
>
> Such a finding is not a case of taking a position against small hydro in general. A decision on this proposal must weigh the socio-economic effects of this specific hydro development against the long-term vision of the local community and the potential of Cascade Canyon as a natural feature and a protected area. Without the hydro development, the community and the province retain the option to conserve the cultural, spiritual, natural and scenic qualities of the canyon, while continuing to raise the profile of the Kettle River, the Spirit of 2010 (Trans-Canada) Trail, and the canyon's features and opportunities that complement existing lifestyle and tourism activities around Christina Lake. (Yarnell 2005: 5)

Yarnell's 2005 report compares the regional economic benefits of the project to the economic costs associated with reduced tourism opportunities, loss of the scenic value of the canyon, and impacts on local agriculture of its additional water licence entitlements. He concludes:

> Because changes to the proposal cannot address the substantive issue of the mere presence of generating facilities, my original conclusions stand: the presence of the impoundment, weir and other hydroelectric infrastructure, and the reduced flows through the canyon, would alter the canyon in a manner that is not consistent with community values and the region's strategy for economic development, including negative impacts on specific tourism operations and the displacement of locally unique activities and attractions. (Yarnell 2005: 45–46)

Yarnell also questioned estimates by another consultant, Cathleen Berris, who was commissioned by Powerhouse in 2003 to examine the tourism impacts of the proposal. He did not agree with her view that the powerhouse and weir would themselves be significant tourist attractions, citing the relatively modest number of tourists visiting the much more spectacular Keenlyside Dam and other hydro developments in the region. He noted that the facilities tourists are most like to visit are quite different from the assumed attraction of a new visitors' centre devoted to highlighting the project (Berris 2003, Yarnell 2005). Kathy O'Malley of the KRRC voiced similar scepticism based on the fact that there were already a number of museums in the area, all of which were finding it difficult to attract enough visitors to stay in operation. She felt it was unlikely, given this fact, that the powerhouse, proposed museum, and dam would attract many tourists.

Farmers upstream of the canyon raised another concern about water use. They felt that, once diversion of water to the plant began, their careful use of water for irrigation during the summer dry period would no longer be reflected in the volume of water remaining in the stream to preserve fish stocks. In a close-knit community, farmers realized they had an obligation to consider the impact of their irrigation on others in the community, and they had normally been willing to take less than their full entitlement in order to protect the fish. In an e-mail opposing the project sent to Garth Thurwood of the EAO on Oct. 7, 2004, local farmer Fred Marshall noted this point: many farmers in his area had deliberately taken less than their entitlement of water to ensure that the fish in the river were conserved during the summer drought of 2003. He did not want such conservation practices to end up providing more water for the power plant, at the expense of the fish that farmers wanted to protect.

Marshall's concerns reflect another issue that has a wider application in B.C.'s privatization of hydro production. The Cascade Canyon project gives Powerhouse water rights to a significant volume of water in a watershed that already has a number of other licensees upstream that require water for agricultural irrigation, municipal water supplies, and residential use by people living along the river. The Powerhouse water licence is for forty years, but it is renewable, so, in theory, the company could have access to the water flow forever. In approving the project, the government may be sowing the seeds of future conflicts over water use.

To maximize the average amount of energy provided by the facility, Powerhouse requires a minimal flow of water to its turbines through much of the year. But during late summer there may not be enough water flowing through the canyon to allow full agricultural uses, normal power production, and enough water to protect fish and the various forms of plant and animal life that depend on this water flow.[6]

While the water licence does provide for a modest water reserve — largely as a result of KRRC and other community efforts — this does not mean there will be no further tensions over the use of the water resource. Providing a licence guaranteeing the proponent access to a minimum flow of water (subject to certain conditions) may open the door to future conflicts with potential upstream users not already included in the water reserve, such as ranchers, golf-course operators, and agricultural users who might also want to use this water during the dry summer months. Parts of this area of the province are very dry during the summer — close to desert conditions prevail in some locations — so access to water may be a growing concern, especially if the region's population expands or if there is additional economic activity. In allowing construction of the power plant, the government is clearly signaling that private energy generation is a higher priority than alternative economic development options for the area.

The campaign by local residents to stop the construction of the Cascade Heritage Power Plant continued until the passing of Bill 30, after which it was clear the government would approve the project regardless of the views of local residents. What is remarkable about this battle is not that the government eventually won it, but rather that the community succeeded in delaying construction for such a long time, especially considering the limited resources available to community residents and the ability of the government to make full use of its resources in support of the project.

The KRRC managed to ensure that the water licence provided for a water reserve to protect upstream water users. Without such a reserve, there was a possibility that during periods of low water the rights of those upstream might end up in conflict with the rights given to Powerhouse. In the worst-case scenario, other users might have had to curtail the amount of water they removed from the river for municipal uses, agricultural and greenhouse operations, or recreational activities in order to ensure that enough remained in the river to produce energy at the power plant.

However, the KRRC failed to achieve one of its other main objectives: ensuring that other upstream users could have access to the water for future power production. One of the major local industries, Pope and Talbot, operated a lumber mill in Midway, and there was speculation in the community that it was considering installing a co-generation power facility. To do so, it would need access to some of the water that flowed into the canyon. And the town of Castlegar, also upstream from the canyon, at one time had its own reservoir, which had enabled it to generate a small amount of electricity for local residents. It might conceivably want to do this again at some future point. Yet the government ignored these possible future uses of the water resource and refused to set aside a water reserve specifically earmarked for potential upstream power projects.

In comments that parallel the experience of community and environmental activists in the Ashlu-Ledcor dispute, Yarnell was highly critical of the role of various government ministries involved in evaluating the costs and benefits of the proposal. Echoing concerns raised by Squamish-Lillooet Regional District, he argued that the government's involvement unduly favoured the interests of the developer at the expense of the community:

> It is a serious issue for the ministry responsible for economic development, tourism and small business... to fail to consider the substantive issue of introducing an industrial facility in an area known to be dependent on scenic beauty and nature-based tourism. In the second place, it is a problem that the ministry failed to look beyond the proponent's reports and either consult alternative analyses or initiate its own dialogue with local businesses, development organizations and regional governments in order to draw its conclusions. (Yarnell 2005: 16)

Specifically, Yarnell felt that the evaluations provided by different ministries uncritically accepted virtually all Powerhouse's claims about the benefits of the project, while ignoring — or discounting — the more sceptical assessments of members of the local community.

Yarnell was also concerned that the various ministries involved in consultations associated with the project were willing to endorse the project in principle before many steps in the EAO process had been completed, leaving the local government in the awkward position of having to attempt to override provincial approvals if it felt the project was not in the interests of the community.

As was noted by critics of the Ashlu project, there is a major imbalance in the resources and information available to members of the community compared with those of the government and the proponent. Many local residents who had concerns about the project did not have the financial or other resources to carry out detailed socio-economic or environmental studies. They were lucky in having someone like Yarnell willing to work with them. Lack of resources, the complexity of the EAO review process, and short timelines all put local residents at a clear disadvantage in dealing with the well-resourced consulting studies commissioned by investors seeking approval for new power projects, a problem exacerbated when the government is committed to pushing through projects in order to get its broader policy agenda implemented.

This points to a further weakness in the evaluation process. The one organization — the provincial government — with the capacity to balance the scales is also actively promoting privately owned "green energy" projects. It has a clear interest in not providing resources to local communities that might oppose these projects.

Turning to the question of what will happen to the energy Sea Breeze will generate, at the time of writing, it is not clear whether the company will, in the short run, sell this energy to BC Hydro, Fortis, or American customers. However, while it may begin operations with an EPA with BC Hydro — and in the short term this would be its most lucrative option — recent provincial regulatory changes (including Bill 40, noted earlier), would allow it to export energy to the United States, so there is no guarantee it will stay in the province.

In its 2004 Annual Report filed with the U.S. Securities and Exchange Commission, Sea Breeze noted that it intended, in the long term, to sell a portion of the energy from its wind and run-of-the-river projects to customers in California. It also indicated that it was continuing to explore the feasibility of negotiating energy supply agreements with American purchasers:

> The recent B.C. electricity restructuring has opened up the market to allow independent power producers to sell power to large industrial customers and certain municipalities. In addition, all new generation capacity in the province must now come from independent power producers. Access has also opened up to the U.S. market through the regional transmission system.
>
> Sea Breeze will target the U.S. energy market through Power Purchase Agreements with power brokers, marketers, and utilities. The company intends to export large blocks of power to California, which currently has a requirement that investor-owned utilities provide 20 percent of their electricity by 2010 from renewable sources, and is considering an increase of this requirement to 33 percent by 2020. (Sea Breeze 2004b)

While it is not clear whether these comments applied specifically to the Cascade Heritage Power Project, they indicate that the company is contemplating the possibility of exporting B.C.-produced energy. So, if B.C. customers want this energy the future, they will have to pay what American customers are prepared to pay. Given the very high prices BC Hydro is now paying, this may not be a problem in the short run — except to ratepayers who will have to pay the high price involved. But because Cascade may run for a century or more, the long-term implications are more worrisome. Far from providing additional energy security, the fact that the facility happens to be located in the province provides no guarantee that the energy generated will stay here.

Another issue raised by the Sea Breeze project is the question of foreign ownership, one in which there appears to be some confusion. Sea Breeze is registered as a B.C. company, but it appears to have both Canadian and

American investors among its shareholders. According to a June 26, 2006, filing with the U.S. Securities and Exchange Commission, Sea Breeze was defined at the time by the American regulator as an American-controlled corporation:

> Sea Breeze Power Corp. ("Sea Breeze") no longer qualifies as a foreign issuer, as per the 1933 Securities Act, Rule 405, and the 1934 Securities Act, Rule 3b-4. The Registrant has more than 50 percent of their outstanding voting securities owned by residents of the United States and, as of June 27, 2005, the majority of the Registrant's directors are United States citizens or residents. (Sea Breeze 2006b)

Regardless of whether more recent changes have shifted effective ownership to Canada, and regardless of whether American shareholders are now a minority, the inclusion of even some Americans as part-owners means that the project's owners would qualify for the full protection of NAFTA's Chapter Eleven investor-rights provisions. In supporting the private project, the province may be — knowingly or not — laying British Columbia open to possible international trade disputes over the use of both the water and the resulting electricity.

The government finally succeeded in overriding the thirteen-year struggle of the community to stop construction of the private power project on the Kettle River: on August 4, 2006, the company got its Environmental Assessment Certificate. With Bill 30 in place, further opposition seems futile. At the time of writing, the company has obtained all the approvals it requires under the various pieces of provincial legislation. It is now waiting for the last approval it requires from the federal government, which is likely to be given by the time this study reaches bookstores.

Like the Ledcor-Ashlu river dispute, the Cascade Heritage Power Project highlights why there has been so much community and First Nations' opposition to run-of-the-river and wind projects in other communities across the province. Despite the very high anticipated financial returns for their private, and in many cases foreign, owners, the projects provide almost no economic benefits for local residents. This is true whether we are looking at profit share, local construction spin-offs, resulting permanent jobs, or purchases from locally owned businesses.

Yet the costs in terms of disruption to tourism, lost opportunities for other recreational uses, restrictions on access to river systems, damage to fish stocks, and intrusion of new roads and transmission lines into otherwise pristine areas are all borne by the local community. Residents are expected to shoulder these costs, not for the greater public benefit — as when publicly owned BC Hydro is the proponent — but for the benefit of private investors with little or no connection to the community.

In contrast, BC Hydro's major dams and transmission lines, which also came with many costs to local communities and First Nations, provided B.C. residents with cheap and reliable energy for generations. BC Hydro was directed to provide a variety of local spin-offs from construction, purchasing, and maintenance operations.

Although the government is reluctant to admit it, the consolidation of the industry in private hands will result in large, foreign-owned conglomerates with no ties to local communities owning the bulk of B.C.'s new "green energy" projects. For local communities this is bad news, indeed. When the owner of a power project is a distant investor whose headquarters is in Houston, New York or London, England, the ability of local residents to deal with concerns about the management and operation of private power plants will be far weaker than dealing with elected representatives in Victoria. Commitments made by previous owners in order to persuade communities to accept their projects may not be honoured, as the new investors may not be aware of, or feel obligated to respect, undertakings made by previous owners. All of this underlines the public policy weaknesses of the government's policy of promoting private ownership of small hydro projects in B.C.

NOTES

1. Sea Breeze was originally incorporated on January 18, 1979, as a B.C.-registered company with the name Northern Horizon Resource Corporation. However, its name was officially changed to Sea Breeze Power Corp. on July 29, 2003, and it is registered under the *Business Corporations Act* of B.C.
2. Sea Breeze has a number of subsidiaries and jointly owned companies. In its Consolidated Financial Accounts for 2005 and 2006 it lists the following wholly owned subsidiaries: Powerhouse Developments Inc., Powerhouse Electric Corp., Sea Breeze Energy Inc., Sea Breeze Management Services Inc., Sea Breeze Power Projects Inc., and SBJF Holding Corp. The company also has proportionate interest (80 percent) in the assets of the Slollicum Joint Venture, a 50 percent interest in the assets, liabilities, and expenses of Sea Breeze Pacific Regional Transmission Systems, Inc., which itself holds a 100 percent interest in and is the general partner of two limited partnerships, Sea Breeze Pacific West Coast Cable LP and Sea Breeze High Desert Conversion LP (Sea Breeze 2007).
3. There was an Order-in-Council dated Sept 8, 1993, that specifically designated the project as a "regulated project" under legislation in place at the time.
4. It is worth noting in this context that a July 28, 1994, resolution of the Board of Directors of the Regional District of Kootenay-Boundary indicated that it could not support the project because "not all potential impacts had been determined or clarified." This may have been another contributing factor in the slow progress of the application.
5. In fact, it did generate opposition from various American groups, most notably Citizens for a Bi-National Review of the Dam, which succeeded in getting several

American legislators involved in discussions about the project (*North Columbian Monthly* 2000, Heflick 2004).

6. Under these conditions, the company may not be able to generate any power at all, a possibility that has been addressed in the water licence conditions.

Chapter Eleven

Not So Green After All

THE EVIDENCE PRESENTED THUS far in this study makes it clear that the government's Energy Plan of 2002 and its re-packaged "greener" Energy Plan of the spring of 2007 have major weaknesses from an environmental perspective. We have identified some of the problems arising from allowing the financial interests of energy developers to shape the planning and location of new wind-farm and small hydro facilities. However, the weaknesses of the government's approach go deeper. Under the Energy Plan, environmental concerns are near the bottom of the list of the government's priorities, even though they are frequently referred to as if they were the driving force of much of its policy agenda. Smoke and mirrors, rather than serious environmental objectives, are what the government is actually delivering to the people of B.C.

At the most basic level, the move to a deregulated, market-based electricity system — the government's long-term objective — effectively destroys the logic of rational demand-side management. Under the old system when BC Hydro was an integrated utility, it could take into account all the economic costs and benefits of policies to reduce growth in energy demand. The costs of energy conservation initiatives could be offset by savings resulting from not having to make major new capital investments in new generating facilities — investments that would result in borrowing large sums and hence increasing B.C. Hydro's interest and amortization costs.

During the early 1990s, BC Hydro initiated conservation programs in order to avoid such costly new investments. As an integrated utility responsible for providing energy to its B.C. customers, it could "capture the benefits" of conservation initiatives on the basis that they would cost less than would borrowing large sums for new power plant construction. As Marjorie Griffin-Cohen points out:

> There exists a powerful logic of conservation which is lost in a deregulated system. A regulated utility that is required to provide electricity to its customers faces enormous start-up costs for any new generation of power brought on line. Whether this involves new gas turbines, new "green" energy, or more turbines on dams, it is a very expensive business. Once a system is in place, it is in the interests of a regulated utility to encourage its customers to conserve energy, and it will go to considerable lengths to see that this happens through

> "demand-side management" (DSM). DSM attempts to "find" energy by encouraging all classes of customers to reduce their demand for energy. (Cohen 2006: 87)

Cohen goes on to point out how this logic, which is based on a single-supplier model with a captive customer base, is undermined by the introduction of a competitive electricity market:

> The logic of power conservation completely changes in a deregulated market, where the goal is to encourage a large number of producers to compete against each other for customers. The whole point of production in a private market-based system is not to curtail demand, but to foster it and to sell as much as possible. In this case, if competition among suppliers actually emerges, it will be in their interests to entice customers to consume as much as possible — in that way, everyone will be able to sell more at the highest possible prices. (Cohen 2006: 88)

So, the move toward a competitive energy market, where every firm attempts to expand its sales and market share, creates a dynamic in which the overall growth of energy consumption is the major driving force of energy policy. If conservation initiatives succeeded in stopping the growth of energy demand, all firms would end up with lower sales, lower profits, and no prospects of future growth. While this may make sense from the perspective of conservation, it is fundamentally in opposition to the prevailing logic of markets, where no individual firm is expected to voluntarily forgo sales — and profit — opportunities, and where no individual firm is responsible for the cumulative impact of the market. The logic of market competition is clear: expand sales and energy use. And, as more and more private energy developers become embedded in B.C.'s system, the pressure to expand energy use and create more opportunities for private energy sales, either to BC Hydro or to the export market, increases correspondingly.

Thus, by undermining the single-supplier model — the foundation of BC Hydro's earlier role in the province's electricity system — in favour of a competitive energy market, the government has simultaneously undermined the most powerful and effective approach to curtailing energy demand. While BC Hydro has been directed by the government to continue to promote "Power Smart" initiatives, it has lost the ability to capture the benefits of conservation initiatives because the growth in the market is something over which it no longer has control.

As well, as noted at the beginning of this study, the government has manufactured an energy "crisis" to create the rationale for forcing BC Hydro to purchase more and more high-priced energy from private power developers. The government has used this manufactured crisis to push through its agenda, arguing that it has no choice but to acquire an enormous amount of new private energy to meet B.C.'s future needs. This, in turn, has meant that literally dozens of streams and rivers across the province are now being developed to supply energy that, arguably, is not needed in the first place, because better options are available. And the policy, if continued, will result not in dozens, but in several hundred, sites being built on, with all the environmental damage associated with new power plants, access roads, transmission lines, and all the other impacts of small hydro developments.

By precluding other more sensible and environmentally responsible options for managing B.C.'s future energy needs, the government is wrecking havoc on pristine rivers and streams across the province to enable its friends in the private power industry to profit from lucrative BC Hydro EPAs. In an earlier chapter we mapped out what these better options are: returning the Columbia River Downstream Benefits, restricting private exports of B.C. electricity, making industrial customers pay more realistic prices for their energy to give them an incentive to conserve, maintaining capacity in the lower Mainland by re-powering Burrard, continuing to rely on BC Hydro's storage to obtain the benefits of energy trading, strengthening "Power Smart" programs, and reviewing the question of whether Site "C" might be less environmentally damaging than damming up a hundred or more rivers across the province. In sum, it is not B.C.'s need for new energy, but rather the government's policy decision to promote its private power agenda that is at the root of its highly questionable environmental polices.

Not surprisingly, a major government concern has been to persuade the environmental community that its policy of expanding private power production is compatible with conservation objectives. Keeping environmentalists "onside," or even minimally neutral, on the question of new private power developments has been an ongoing challenge, given the emerging reality of the industry's environmental practices. Nevertheless, the government — with the help of its industry friends — has succeeded to a remarkable degree.

One way in which it has done this has been to avoid discussing the negative environmental impact of the dozens of new private power plants and focus instead on the more attractive concept of developing "green" energy. Implicit in this agenda is the notion that expanding energy consumption is good as long as the new energy comes from renewable sources within the province. The government asserts that its energy policies are environmentally responsible because they promote development of energy from small hydro and wind facilities. The "green" energy designation is designed to appeal to public concern about conservation while simultaneously providing a justification for the wide range of public subsidies now being given to private power developers.

But a closer look at the government's criteria for defining the environmental status of new power projects reveals its questionable basis. According to the BC Hydro's website, in order for a power project in British Columbia to be designated "green," it must be:

1) Renewable: the energy source must be replenished naturally. For example, hydroelectric plants use water, which is renewable. Natural gas generation is not green because it relies on non-renewable fossil fuel;
2) Properly Licenced: the project must conform to relevant regulations of B.C. regulatory bodies (BCUC, B.C. Transmission Corporation, Land and Water B.C., etc.);
3) Socially Responsible: the project must take full consideration of aboriginal, community, economic, health and safety, and ethical issues;
4) Low Environmental Impact: the project must not negatively affect the environment, damage fish populations, endangered species or reduce air quality.

One major problem with this approach is that it does not address the basic question of whether we should be sourcing more energy from such power plants in the first place. Not to build at all — especially if there is a great deal of environmental damage associated with a project — is a much better alternative.

To further enhance its green image, the government has directed BC Hydro to acquire a significant proportion of its future energy requirements from sources that meet its "green" criteria. Both wind farms and run-of-the-river projects thus qualify for green designations and, therefore, have received special consideration in BC Hydro's energy tender calls. For example, the 2002–03 tender call was reserved exclusively for green energy. BC Hydro described the environmental benefits of this procurement as follows:

> BC Hydro has announced the projects that successfully bid into the 2002/03 Green Power Generation procurement process. Combined, the 16 projects… 14 hydro, one landfill gas and one wind energy, represent 1,764 gigawatt hours of new green generation, to be purchased by BC Hydro under 10- to 20-year contracts. (BC Hydro 2002/03)

As it turned out, many of these "green" projects never got built. Ironically, this may actually have been beneficial from an environmental perspective. But BC Hydro continued with this approach, including in its 2006 tender call a designated share — roughly 10 percent — of energy specifically for small "green" projects.

When we look more closely at the government's policy on acquiring new energy we find that, in reality, it constitutes a major step backward. In the 2002 Energy Plan, the government established criteria for determining the mix of energy sources BC Hydro would be directed to acquire. In addition to the 10 percent of energy that would have to be "green," the Crown utility would have to ensure that at least 50 percent met the definition of "clean," which meant sources that were no more polluting than previous alternatives.

The government's adoption of the 50 percent "clean" energy target opened the door to sourcing up to half of the province's new energy from non-renewable sources, most notably coal, but also biomass (wood waste) and other thermal options. Consistent with this policy, BC Hydro gave contracts to two major coal-fired projects. Reaction to the coal-fired plants was so significant that in the spring of 2007 it imposed new carbon sequestration requirements on them as a condition of the sale of their energy to BC Hydro.

It should also be noted that the targets the government established for "green" and "clean" energy were entirely voluntary. Thus, while it could direct BC Hydro to follow these guidelines, developers of thermal-based energy not planning to sell to BC Hydro would be free to build new power plants without facing any legally binding requirements to produce "green" or "clean" energy as part of their energy mix.

Government's assurances that all energy from run-of-the-river or wind sources is "green" requires a more detailed analysis that looks at the actual impact of projects, rather than simply assuming that these forms of generation are environmentally benign. It is certainly true that that, in the right location and with appropriate environmental safeguards, some projects can be built and operated with little negative impact on the environment. But there is always some environmental damage, even in the most carefully planned project. But other projects can be extremely detrimental to the environment. They can significantly damage fish and aquatic habitat, and destroy valuable spawning areas. During construction, power projects can alter stream flows, remove large numbers of trees, destroy natural vegetation, and open the door to erosion of hillsides and valleys. Penstocks and water diversion tunnels can permanently change natural river flows and adversely affect water temperatures.

Many of these projects also end up with reservoirs flooding significant land areas. These reservoirs are held back by what are, in reality, small dams, even though they are described, rather innocuously, as "inflatable weirs." In fact, all run-of-the-river projects require some sort of dam, whether it is made of concrete or an inflatable membrane, because they require a pond to allow sediment to settle so it does not clog pipes and turbines in the power plant (Caldicott 2007). These reservoirs expose the water to solar heating which, combined with the lower stream flows in the original streambed, can also have significant effects on fish mortality and fish spawning activities. And, as noted earlier, the necessary — and highly intrusive — roads and transmission lines, often in pristine river valleys, as well as construction of new sub-stations, all wreak their own environmental havoc. Even modest hydro projects can permanently change environments in areas that might best remain untouched to preserve their natural attributes for future generations. Clearly, some of these projects cause major damage. Calling them "green" is quite misleading, to say the least.

But the issue is not simply one of evaluating the environmental impact on the basis of an individual project. The damaging cumulative impact of a group of run-of-the-river or wind-farm facilities in a valley or watershed can also be very significant. If all the approximately seventy applications for water licences in the Squamish-Whistler area were to be approved and the power plants built, the entire character of the area would change and the impact on the environment would be very significant. This underscores a key problem with the government's focus on approving individual projects in the absence of a broader regional assessment of environmental impacts. Labeling individual projects as "green" does not adequately address the larger question of the cumulative impact of a group of green projects on an entire river system or valley. The approval of several projects in a river valley may not cause major environmental damage: but including literally several dozen, as is the case in the Whistler-Squamish area, can fundamentally alter land use and undermine important environmental attributes of the area.

Ignoring the cumulative environmental impacts, the government simply classifies all run-of-the-river or wind-farm projects individually as "green" energy, regardless of their environmental impacts. Because private energy interests do not own and are not likely to be able to construct large hydro projects, this form of renewable energy has not been designated as "green," even though some large hydro projects are no less environmentally friendly than many of the run-of-the-river projects the government is now promoting.[1] And, the designation of "green" itself has been privatized: various private consulting companies are permitted to certify projects as "green," and this designation is then accepted by BC Hydro.

While the government has justified its support for private hydro and wind-farm projects on the basis of promoting "green" energy, it has used its policy of reducing the alleged excessive regulatory burden on business to significantly weaken the environmental assessment process. In eliminating alleged "red tape," the government has compromised environmental standards and made it much more difficult for environmental advocates and community members to voice legitimate concerns — or raise substantive objections — about the damage being done by private energy developers.

For example, the government's revisions to the provincial environmental assessment process now permit small projects of less than 50 MW (which is not that small, in fact) to be approved through a truncated, fast-track assessment process carried out largely within government agencies (Caldicott 2007). This reduces developers' costs for environmental studies, public consultations, and responding to information requests. It also expedites the approvals process and gets the cash flowing more quickly. But, it also means that the environmental assessment process is no longer adequate to effectively assess the full impact of projects. And, once a project is approved, the owner can apply to have its capacity rating increased. Thus a 49-MW project that was approved on the basis of the government's truncated process might subsequently be upgraded to a 75- or 80-MW project without having to undergo a full environmental assessment.

The government's developer-driven revisions to the approvals system, its arbitrary decision to have a truncated environmental assessment process for small power plants, and its narrow focus on individual projects — as opposed to the regional impacts of multiple projects — effectively excludes communities and environmentalists from raising legitimate concerns about the cumulative environmental impact of power developments in their areas. In reality, once a private power developer has an EPA with BC Hydro, the project will invariably get approved. Not a single proposed project has been rejected on environmental grounds.

The government also downplays another important environmental issue: the fact that it has put in place new policies — such as Bill 40, which eliminated the requirement for an Energy Removal Certificate, thus facilitating out-of-province exports — that are opening the door to private energy exports. When combined with policy changes giving private power developers "non-discriminatory" access to the transmission grid for exports and the 2007 Energy Plan's commitment to a long-term objective of creating a 6 percent energy surplus to cushion the province from potential shortages in low-water years — all of which will come from private power developers — the government is deliberately creating conditions for a significant expansion of private power exports.

Building for export imposes significant additional environmental costs, both directly through the impact of new power plants and indirectly through the need to build additional transmission capacity to facilitate the flow of electrons south of the border. All power projects — even the most environmentally benign — still impose some costs. For domestically produced and consumed electricity the key is to ensure that the environmental and social costs are balanced by corresponding benefits to the public. However with private exports, the costs will be borne by B.C. while the benefits will accrue to those investors lucky enough to own power plants. Such a policy makes little sense, either environmentally or, for that matter, in terms of public policy.

Similarly, allowing firms such as Alcan and Cominco — and, down the road, many of the new run-of-the-river and wind-farm projects — the option of using the transmission grid to export energy will promote unnecessary environmental damage in B.C. Encouraging private energy exports will force BC Hydro to tender for even more new energy to compensate for the energy being exported, thus expanding the number of projects being built and increasing the corresponding environmental costs to the province.

On top of this, the government's policy of awarding water licences on a first-come, first-served basis and then giving private developers the opportunity to bid on lucrative BC Hydro EPAs further undermines its case that it is promoting sustainable energy policies. There are enormous environmental — as well as financial — implications flowing from the privatization of virtually all water licences for run-of-the-river projects across the province. The perverse incentives created by this policy framework encourage investors to do everything possible to get their power plants approved, regardless of whether they impose inappropriate environmental costs on river systems. Private ownership of vital water resources also denies communities the future ability to decide on other options for water — options that may be far more environmentally benign than their use by private power producers.

Another major environmental issue is the government's failure to adequately address the need for ongoing regulation and monitoring of small hydro projects. The dramatic growth in the number of privately owned run-of-the-river projects in B.C. raises the question of how the government will ensure they are operated in a manner that does not violate the terms of their water licences. Given the revenues involved, there are ample incentives for private power developers to "push the envelope" to maximize the benefits they obtain from their water licences.

Water-for-power licences normally specify the volume of water that must remain in the streambed, the conditions under which flows can be interrupted for maintenance and repairs, and a variety of other requirements intended to limit the negative impacts of new power plants. For example, minimum flows in the natural streambed are necessary to prevent an increase in water temperatures that may negatively affect fish stocks.

However, developers have strong economic incentives to maximize energy generation from their facilities. The marginal cost of generating additional increments of electricity is extremely low once a plant is up and running — in some cases nothing at all. But water is money. The more water that flows through a small hydro project's turbines, the more revenue the owner gets from the increased electricity generated. Even a small increase in water flowing through turbines can result in tens, or hundreds of thousands, of dollars in additional revenue. While the minimum acceptable water flows should be simply a matter of good science, the reality is that developers often try to negotiate for more by arguing that there are no fish stocks in a stream and so there is no need to maintain flow levels consistent with fish survival. Or, they might argue that the minimum flow levels Ministry staff recommend are excessively high and then provide alternative assessments that establish more profitable thresholds (Caldicott 2007).

But it is not simply in trying to establish minimum acceptable flow levels that problems can emerge. Monitoring water usage is also a major issue. If private producers are able to use more than their licences permit and avoid being caught, the financial benefits can be very large. In the absence of rigorous regulation and detailed monitoring of private power projects, some may use far more water than legally permitted.

The amount of water necessary to maintain the ecology of streambeds must be monitored by measuring actual day-to-day flow conditions. It is not enough to base the amount producers are allowed to divert on daily or weekly averages, because conditions can quickly change significantly, even in a few hours on some streams. Given that investors have a huge financial incentive to maximize the volume of water flowing through their turbines, the need for rigorous monitoring of operations is clear.

Monitoring water use will become an increasingly significant issue if, as BC Hydro President Bob Elton has recently indicated, the Crown utility restructures its future EPAs to give private developers shorter contracts and the ability to sell blocks of energy to other purchasers, presumably in the United States, where "green" energy commands a premium in some states. If this happens, it may not easy for the government to monitor how much water is being used to generate power, because BC Hydro will no longer be buying the energy and would not have data on the volume and timing of energy being produced.

In the face of these growing regulatory challenges, it would be logical for the government to beef up its regulatory staff. Instead, it has downsized staffing levels at the Environment Ministry by roughly a third in recent years. It has also implemented a fundamental regulatory policy change that incorporates the view that industry self-regulation (or "voluntary compliance") is preferable to a more traditional — and rigorous — regulatory approach. Increasingly, power developers will monitor their use of public water on their own. Allowing developers to self-regulate their operations creates a basic conflict between their economic interests and ecological imperatives. The fox is now guarding the henhouse.

Given the remote locations of many of the sites and the current skeleton-staff levels at the Environment Ministry, the question of how the public will be protected from unauthorized use of water is very significant (Caldicott 2007). Who is to know whether additional water is being siphoned into turbines during the middle of the night? Who is to know whether water temperatures have risen to the point where fish stocks are threatened? And what is the penalty when private developers are caught taking more water than their licences permit?

There is a basic conflict between the government's commitment to clearing away alleged excessive regulatory "red tape" and the need to increase its monitoring capacity by hiring additional staff and putting in place new mechanisms to oversee water use, as the Regional District of Squamish-Lillooet learned to its sorrow in its battle against Ledcor's Ashlu project:

> There is a great deal of concern regarding the issues of enforcement and accountability. These range from general concern with existing enforcement mechanisms to lack of the ability of government to enforce standards (specifically in areas where there have been significant staffing cutbacks) to the lack of clear, measurable performance criteria. (Squamish-Lillooet Regional District 2003: 14)

Even where there is no intent to take water beyond what is permitted, there can be other problems associated with controlling the operation of run-of-the-river projects. One that has already come to light is the unplanned release of large volumes of water due to operational problems with a facility. As Lisa Richardson wrote in *The Tyee*:

> Residents north of the Squamish Valley in Pemberton were irate when the Miller Creek IPP run-of-the-river micro-hydro project unexpectedly released huge rushes of water from their project, causing damage to fish life and threatening several local farms. (Richardson 2004)

The Squamish-Lillooet Regional District also noted that the concept of self-regulation is analogous to the admittedly over-used comparison of the fox guarding the chicken coop. It questioned the idea of private power developers hiring their own professionals to monitor and audit performance, a practice that appears to have a built-in conflict of interest. The question of what happens if power developers are caught violating the terms of their water licences is an important one. Ideally, penalties for violators should be tough enough to act as an effective deterrent to illegal practices. Thus far, there is little evidence that the government has either the desire, or the policy and legislative tools, to make this happen.

It might be argued that as long as BC Hydro is the primary purchaser of run-of-the-river energy it can act as an enforcer of environmental standards by monitoring the energy private power developers send to its transmission grid. But knowing how much energy is coming into the grid does not mean it knows whether the energy was generated at the expense of providing adequate streambed flow volumes. And, BC Hydro is not mandated to enforce environmental standards — and, particularly, appropriate use of water flows — on private power projects. This is the responsibility of the provincial government. Because energy from some of these projects may end up being sold to third parties in future, BC Hydro may not even be involved. To date, there has been no indication that the government has any appetite for giving the B.C. Transmission Corporation authority to monitor the energy output of private power plants to assess whether they are violating the terms of their water licences by, for example, generating extra energy at night. Without such authority, it is not clear how the government intends to acquire evidence that may point to unauthorized use of the water resource.

Another worrisome development is the fact that Bill 30 gives the BCUC a central role in the approval process for private power projects. These projects are now defined as "public utilities" and the BCUC has the power to approve them independent of any concerns or objections raised by local governments. And, the BCUC has been clear that it does not have an environmental mandate and considers environmental issues only in the context of their impact on electricity rates, as the following quotation from a letter to the B.C. Sustainable Energy Association confirms: "BCUC staff note that the Commission's jurisdiction in incorporating broad environmental policy concerns into its utility rate proceedings is limited and the Commission has generally interpreted its mandate as being one of foreseeable costs to ratepayers" (BCUC 2005).

In light of the many environmental issues arising from the number of new private power projects and the numerous challenges in regulating them, the question that logically arises is: how can we explain the considerable support they have received from parts of the environmental community? One reason is the widespread support for the goal of promoting renewable energy. Many environmentalists want to see less reliance on fossil fuel, nuclear, and other non-renewable energy sources. The government's ban on BC Hydro building any new small hydro or wind facilities effectively forces those supporting more green energy projects to look to private energy developers to achieve this objective. For some environmentalists, private green energy is preferable to no green energy, given that public options are not allowed. For others, the question of ownership and control of the system is irrelevant: for them, getting green energy projects built is all that matters.

Another reason the government has been able to gain support for its private power agenda is BC Hydro's legacy from the 1962–1984 period, when it built major dams and transmission lines in the province. To some critics, the dams themselves were an environmental disaster. In creating huge storage reservoirs, the Crown utility flooded huge tracts of land and disrupted the ecology of entire river valleys. But, even accepting that this damage was part of the cost of generating electricity for the province, BC Hydro has been criticized for failing to address environmental issues that, arguably, were within its power to resolve. Some environmentalists are still understandably wary of BC Hydro's ability to "clean up" its act.

However, given the extensive public scrutiny that its operations now face, particularly from the environmental community, BC Hydro has had to address many of its former shortcomings. It has also taken some modest steps to mitigate some of the environmental damage resulting from the construction of large dams and transmission lines. More importantly, as a publicly owned corporation, it can be made more accountable for its environmental policies than privately owned companies. Its activities are open to public scrutiny, through the Legislature, through freedom-of-information requests, and through the absence of commercial secrecy in its operations (with some exceptions). The ability to make BC Hydro accountable for its environmental performance is not in question — the real question is whether there is political will on the part of government to direct it to do so.

Ironically, this very public accountability is itself a reason for some of the ongoing criticism of BC Hydro's environmental practices. Critics can access a great deal of publicly available information about BC Hydro's operations, and this makes it much easier to document the practices — and failures — of the Crown utility than its private counterparts. Faced with an almost impenetrable wall of commercial confidentiality in the private sector, some critics have found it much easier to focus their limited resources on highlighting problems with BC Hydro's operations — problems that can be raised in public forums such as the Legislative Assembly where BC Hydro's shortcomings can be used to embarrass the government of the day. The Crown utility's environmental failings are also open to public scrutiny, both through freedom-of-information requests and by simply asking the company for the information. It is far easier to target the one organization that shares information with the public rather than embark on the much more difficult, costly, and usually less productive effort to uncover problems in the private energy industry.

Private power developers themselves have also worked hard to portray their projects as environmentally responsible sources of "green" energy. A quick overview of the press releases of proponents of many of these projects reveals that the terms "green," "environmentally responsible," "sustainable," and the like are peppered throughout their documents. Who gets the money is notably absent, except in company pitches to investors.

At the same time, private producers argue that large hydro is not environmentally friendly while small hydro and wind are. However, Professor Marjorie Griffin Cohen notes that one well-respected agency that has carefully reviewed the effects of a variety of different energy production technologies concludes that both small and large hydro can have similar ratings:

> Pace University Center for Environmental Legal Studies compares different types of electricity generation and assesses their impacts on the environment by levels of emission and damage to land and water use. Large hydro dams and "run-of-the-river" hydro projects can be "low impact," and they usually are when they are public and highly regulated to take into consideration the fish habitat, water, and land impacts of their operations. Private hydro plants tend to be less environmentally friendly than these low-impact projects but are still better than gas-fired plants and considerably better than oil, coal, or nuclear systems. Hydro systems… both large and small, that are poorly sited and managed without regard to fish and land management score worse than gas-fired generation, but are still preferable to oil, coal, and nuclear systems. (Cohen 2006: 82)

The assumption that small is always better than large hydro is not necessarily true: it very much depends on the specifics of the project itself.

Private power advocates also claim that BC Hydro, with its high overheads, unionized staff, and bureaucratic culture, is incapable of building small projects in a cost-effective manner or of addressing the needs of local communities. So, if green energy projects are to be built at all, it must be by private entrepreneurs.

The private power industry has also worked hard to build connections with sympathetic environmental groups and to give prominence to those that support its investment objectives. It invites environmentalists to look at plans, attend open houses, visit sites, participate in conferences, and learn about the technical aspects of some of its projects. It advertises in selected environmental journals and on movement websites. It supports conferences and other events organized by environmental groups. And, it extols the virtues of the small, independent, imaginative power entrepreneurs who, we are told, are leading the charge for environmentally responsible power production. These creative individuals and companies are portrayed as environmental Davids engaged in a one-sided battle with the huge "Goliath" of BC Hydro, a bureaucracy wedded to costly mega-projects rooted in the past.

The private power industry also minimizes the extensive role now being played by both Canadian and American energy conglomerates in B.C.'s renewable energy sector. Many of these are far larger than BC Hydro, as are the domestic and foreign banks, investment houses, venture capital funds, and multi-billion dollar energy traders who are big players in the private power industry in B.C. Nevertheless, the industry message is "small is beautiful." Small projects, they imply, are being built primarily by small start-up companies and local entrepreneurs. Private is small, while, in contrast, publicly owned BC Hydro is totally out of touch with current environmental thinking and the conservation needs of the province.

For their part, some environmental groups have pushed for more small hydro and wind-farm projects to be built in B.C. They have not questioned the province's privatization agenda, believing that developing green energy projects is desirable regardless of ownership or control. In their view, BC Hydro should be purchasing far more energy from renewable sources and supporting a whole range of small-scale power initiatives. Their support of much in the government's 2002 and 2007 Energy Plans has had the effect — whether intended or not — of endorsing the expansion of the private power industry in B.C.

But a critical problem with some proposals being advanced by several environmental organizations in B.C. is that that they are drawn from jurisdictions where the private sector has historically had a much greater role in electricity generation than has been the case in B.C. In such jurisdictions, governments have simply not had the kind of policy tools available to the B.C. government, by virtue of its ownership of BC Hydro. Instead of focussing on how to use public-sector resources to implement environmental policies directly through BC Hydro and government ministries, they have adopted market-based policies.

For example, the B.C. Sustainable Energy Association has advocated a variety of new policies to allow private generators to hook into the transmission grid and to have governments subsidize the purchase of their energy, as some countries in Europe do:

> To speed the adoption of these technologies, the government should legislate a Sustainable Energy Feed-in Tariff (SEFIT), similar to those that have been successfully adopted in Germany, Spain and 15 other European Union countries, and in China. Producers of wind, tidal current, wave, and other sustainable energies would be guaranteed grid access and a fixed price for 20 years, with the cost of grid extensions being shared equally between the producer and B.C. Transmission Corporation. BC Hydro would be required to purchase the electricity at a contracted price set by a technical committee that reported to the government. The BCUC would be directed to assign the costs to BC Hydro ratepayers.
>
> The price would be specific to each type of sustainable energy, with the level set to encourage the development of those projects that

> are closest to being market-ready. This suggests a tariff that offers a moderate premium over the current market value of electricity. The total premiums that producers would be paid above market rates should be capped at $25 million per year for wind and $12.5 million per year for each of wave and tidal. This would limit BC Hydro's rate increases to a maximum of about 2 percent. To distribute the benefits of the tariff as widely as possible, the SEFIT would be available for only the first 100 MW of any one development. (B.C. Sustainable Energy Association 2005)

The key weakness of this approach is that it does not acknowledge that, but for the government's Energy Plan, BC Hydro could build such projects itself. And, in the process, the Crown utility could avoid many of the problems associated with private energy development. Such recommendations also fail to take into account the reality that, in parts of Europe and other international jurisdictions, governments simply do not have public enterprises with mandates at all comparable to that of BC Hydro. So, of necessity, these governments have to develop policies that incorporate an already existing private energy industry into their conservation planning. Such policies may make perfect sense in these countries, given their existing energy systems, but it is not clear that they are superior to what the B.C. government could do through proper policy direction to BC Hydro.[2]

Another factor is the way the government has used BC Hydro to promote the environmental benefits of private power development. Far from being a proponent of public power, the Crown utility now provides extensive material on its website that extols the virtues of various private hydro and wind-farm developments. It supports and participates in various conferences sponsored by organizations such as the Independent Power Producers Association of B.C. It convenes meetings involving power developers, communities, environmentalists, and First Nations. And it defends its purchases of private energy in forums such as the BCUC. As well — and presumably at the government's direction — BC Hydro has funded very expensive ad campaigns praising government energy policies that will purportedly provide the province with energy self-sufficiency within a decade by purchasing new power from private power developers. Their projects, we are told, are essential to ensuring that B.C.'s future energy supplies will be sustainable and environmentally responsible.

Typical of BC Hydro's promotion of private "green" energy projects is the following joint press release by CEO Larry Bell and Premier Gordon Campbell announcing the results of the 2003 energy call:

> The largest purchase of green energy in B.C.'s history will pro-

> vide about $800 million in private-sector investment in 16 power projects, and an additional 1,800 gigawatt hours per year to meet the energy needs of British Columbians. The announcement was made today by Premier Gordon Campbell and BC Hydro chair and CEO Larry Bell. The electricity, to be generated by 14 hydro, one landfill gas and one wind energy project, will be purchased under contracts with independent power producers whose projects were bid successfully into BC Hydro's 2002/03 Green Power Generation procurement process. "This is a significant step in our plan to work with independent power producers and develop 50 per cent of our new power supplies from clean energy sources," Campbell said. (BC Hydro 2003)

Another example of BC Hydro's support for private "green" energy is contained in its description on its website of the virtues of thirteen private power projects from which it is purchasing energy:

> The green energy that BC Hydro acquires from independent power producers will help BC Hydro meet our commitment that 50 percent of new supply will be obtained from clean energy sources over the next 10 years, as well as commitments related to our Power Smart Green Power Certificates Product.

Of course, the environmental community is not homogenous, and a number of environmental groups, such as the Western Canada Wilderness Committee, have been highly critical of private hydro projects such as Ledcor's Ashlu project. Environmental advocates in communities across the province have voiced criticisms similar to ours regarding the negative impacts of many small hydro projects.

Another environmental aspect of the government's Energy Plan was highlighted by BC Hydro's acceptance of two coal-fired power plants as part of its 2006 tender call. While some were shocked at the inclusion of coal, it was always clear from the Energy Plan that this was an acceptable option. Its designation of a minimum of 50 percent of new energy from "clean" sources opened the door to coal as part of the other 50 percent.

In developing its 2006 tender call, BC Hydro faced considerable pressure from large industrial customers represented by the Joint Industry Electrical Steering Committee that wanted to ensure that the call was "open." They wanted to continue to have access to low-cost energy, and coal seemed to be one of the cheapest sources of new energy. In making the call "open," BC Hydro signaled it would accept bids from any source of energy (other than nuclear) generated within the province. The mining industry, and particularly its coal component, was also very interested in having BC Hydro purchase energy from this source because it would provide a market for coal, and also, possibly, open the door to additional coal-fired plants in the future. (Alberta already generates 70 percent of its energy from coal.)

There is much debate about the possibilities of developing "clean coal" as a suitable source of energy. Proponents of clean coal, such as Professor Mark Jaccard, argue that by using new technologies it is possible to so significantly reduce greenhouse gas emissions and overall pollution such that coal-fired generating plants can by operated in a way that is relatively benign environmentally (Jaccard 2006). This debate is particularly heated in the United States where, according to the Department of Energy's Energy Information Administration, coal is the largest single source of energy for electricity generation — as well as the largest source of toxic pollution and greenhouse gas emissions. American environmentalists are pushing to reduce reliance on coal as an energy source. The subject of "clean coal" is attracting a lot of international interest, given that China, in particular, relies heavily on coal-fired electricity generation and is increasing its use of coal at a very rapid rate as its economy expands.

However, with the exception of the limited use of coal for self-generation by a few large industrial plants to supplement wood waste, coal is not a fuel source that has been utilized in B.C. for electricity production. Its introduction would be a major break from past energy policies.

One of the two successful coal bidders is Compliance Energy Corporation. According to its website, Compliance "is a Canadian company engaged in the development of coal resources located in British Columbia." It has two thermal coal properties on Vancouver Island, as well as the Basin Coal Mine near Princeton. Its subsidiary, Compliance Power Corporation, signed a contract under the 2006 BC Hydro tender call to build a 56-MW power plant near Princeton. It will deliver 421 GWh annually to BC Hydro over a thirty-year period. The power plant will burn wood waste as well as coal.

Compliance indicates that payments from BC Hydro will increase from $40 million to $55 million annually during the term of the contract (Compliance Energy 2006). While the actual price of this energy is confidential, these numbers result in an estimated average cost of $95 per MWh. This is a very generous amount for coal, in light of both the costs of other options and the estimates provided to BC Hydro's Integrated Electricity Planning Committee in 2005, which indicated that coal was likely to be the cheapest source of new energy other than Site "C," with an estimated price range far below what BC Hydro will now pay.

The second coal contract was with the AES Wapiti Energy Corporation. BC Hydro gave it an EPA to build a 184 MW coal-and-biomass power plant producing 1,620 GWh annually. According to a company press release issued in September 2006, the $500-million plant will burn 550,000 to 600,000 tonnes of coal annually (AES 2006a). The new plant will be located approximately thirty kilometres north of Tumbler Ridge and use coal supplied by Hillsborough Resources Limited, a B.C.-based international mining company (Hillsborough Resources 2006).

AES Wapiti is the Canadian subsidiary of AES Corporation, which is traded on the New York Stock Exchange. According to a September 27, 2006, presentation by Victoria Harper, AES Corporation's Executive Vice-President and Chief Financial Officer, to a Merrill Lynch Global Power and Gas Leaders' Conference, the parent corporation has revenues of U.S.$11 billion from its global power generation and distribution activities (AES 2006b). It has energy projects in more than thirty countries around the world. AES is one of the world's largest wind-farm developers, with 600 MW currently in operation and another 2,600 MW planned in the near future. It is also a major producer of electricity from coal (AES 2006b, 2007). In its 2006 U.S. Securities and Exchange Commission filings, AES Corporation referred to a number of legal proceedings it has faced regarding allegations of price manipulation in the California energy market. The company maintains that all such allegations are unfounded and that it is innocent of any wrongdoing in these matters (AES 2006c).

Given that BC Hydro appears to be paying premium prices for this coal-based energy, and given that the question marks over how environmentally benign burning coal will be in practice, the Crown utility's decision to source such a large amount of its new energy from coal-based projects appears unwise. By initiating an "open" tender call while simultaneously restricting bids to coal-fired plants within the province, BC Hydro has succeeded in getting the worst of all worlds: high prices and negative environmental impacts. And, it has given AES, one of the world's major global energy corporations, a significant role for the first time in B.C.'s electricity system.

There is one other recent development affecting BC Hydro's environmentally questionable decision to purchase coal-generated electricity. Since the coal contracts were awarded in the summer of 2006, the government has suddenly experienced a "green" revelation. Influenced by his new relationship with California's Governor Arnold Schwarzenegger, Premier Campbell has announced that fighting global warming is now a key priority of his government. As part of this new agenda, he is committing the province to tackling greenhouse gas emissions. This new policy agenda calls into question the advisability of building conventional coal-powered plants in B.C. The government has recently imposed additional restrictions on power plants using coal. All new plants must use technology that dramatically reduces environmentally damaging emissions, presumably through sequestering the carbon back into the ground. This technology appears to be considerably more expensive than conventional coal technology.

The two firms affected were not expecting this decision. Compliance is apparently contemplating substituting wood waste for coal, a practice that it thinks (at the time of writing) may be feasible. But substituting wood waste for coal may be much more difficult for AES, given both the size of its planned generating plant and arrangements it has made to purchase coal. So, at the time of writing, it is not clear whether it will be able to meet the new provincial guidelines using sequestration technology, or whether this will undermine the economics of the project.

Given that AES Wapati has an EPA with BC Hydro, it will be interesting to see what redress, if any it will seek from the government as a result of this policy change. It may well have grounds for seeking compensation, both as a result of the EPA it has with BC Hydro and, perhaps, as a result of its NAFTA rights as an American investor. At this juncture, whether it pursues either or both options remains to be seen.

Finally, a brief discussion of how the government has handled its "Power Smart" initiatives is in order. When "Power Smart" was first developed in the early 1990s, BC Hydro was a vertically integrated single supplier of electricity for the entire province (outside a small area served by West Kootenay Power, a utility that operates in the southeast corner of the province). BC Hydro had responsibility for forecasting future energy requirements and building generating facilities to meet those requirements. Prices were based on the long-term average cost of energy, and this involved blending the costs of older and newer generation investments. Prices were not based on marginal electricity costs established by the energy market, although as we have noted elsewhere, BC Hydro did purchase some power from (and sell some power to) utilities and other parties outside the province.

"Power Smart" was intended as a conservation initiative to slow the overall growth of electrical energy use in the province, an objective that could be realized most effectively with a single supplier of electricity. In light of BC Hydro's responsibility to supply the province with energy from its own generation, "Power Smart's" demand-side management made sense if the cost of new generation investment was higher than the cost of demand-side management subsidies, because BC Hydro could avoid the major capital costs associated with new investment in generation. As a single supplier, it could "capture the benefits" of conservation initiatives. Conversely, where demand-side management savings did not exceed the cost of new generation, BC Hydro would still be able to construct new generating facilities as needed. All of this was predicated on a system in which electricity prices are based on the long-term cost of production, not short-term markets. And it could only work effectively if there was a single supplier able to capture the benefits without having to be concerned with issues such as competition from other suppliers who would like to expand the market so they could make more money.

However, the current situation is quite different, due to government policy changes designed to eliminate BC Hydro's dominant role and open the door to private energy developers who require a growing market to justify their investments. The government's requirement that all new generation come from private sources (except for minor upgrades to BC Hydro's existing facilities) means that BC Hydro will not benefit from energy conservation as a result of "Power Smart" initiatives. They will not help BC Hydro avoid or delay the capital costs of new generation investments because it will no longer be making such investments.

Thus, the rationale of the "Power Smart" program has shifted fundamentally to a different — and arguably much inferior — approach based on imputed savings determined by the difference in price between BC Hydro's Heritage Contract price and current electricity prices. But the price of BC Hydro's electricity, historically, was based on long-term average costs, not short-term energy market prices. BC Hydro's rates used to be adjusted according to the overall average of the costs of old and new generation investments. The Heritage Contract has ended the process whereby the cost of public investment in new generation was incorporated into BC Hydro's cost-based rates. The Heritage Contract effectively freezes rates for electricity from BC Hydro's public generating facilities. Because there will be no new major additions to BC Hydro's public generating facilities, there will be no new public generating costs to be incorporated into BC Hydro's cost-based Heritage rates.

It is this politically determined, artificially low Heritage price against which "Power Smart" demand-side management savings are being measured. This is doubly perverse. First, normal price adjustments based on the cost of significant new public generation investments will not be made. The result is that BC Hydro's electricity is being sold at prices lower than would be the case if it included the cost of new public generation. Second, because of this artificially low price, BC Hydro's calculation of the "savings" from its "Power Smart" program are correspondingly much more optimistic. The floor price is being set at an unreasonably low level. This is particularly the case with respect to the Heritage rate of $37 MWh, which provides little incentive for major pulp mills and mines to conserve energy. And, BC Hydro's policy of subsidizing these firms through "Power Smart" to install new energy-saving equipment means that the public is losing in two ways. It is losing revenues due to the low Heritage energy price, and it is subsidizing the introduction of new energy-saving machinery and equipment that companies would probably purchase anyway if they had to pay more for their electricity. (As a result of criticism that its industrial subsidy program is quite different from other "Power Smart" initiatives, BC Hydro now avoids the use of "Power Smart" to refer to its industrial subsidies.)

A second — and more fundamental — point is that there is an inherent contradiction between the underlying principles of B.C.'s emerging energy market (the creation of which is the objective of government policy) and conservations goals. The market functions on the basis of competing energy producers all trying to increase sales and market share. Market participants have no incentive to limit the growth of demand. The higher the demand, the more they are able to expand their operations. A halt to growth in energy consumption would mean an end to expansion and the curtailment of new profit opportunities.

In an open electricity market, nobody is responsible for — or has an interest in — curbing the growth of energy consumption. Consequently, BC Hydro's conservation efforts are now occurring in the context, not of a single supplier with overall responsibility for meeting all of B.C.'s electricity needs, but rather of a new market framework in which the expansion of demand is the key factor needed to create new investment opportunities for private energy interests. There is a basic contradiction here between trying to limit the growth of energy use and trying to maximize market opportunities for private power developers. And this is why the current "Power Smart" program is far less likely to achieve its goal of energy conservation. This is not to say that the objectives of the original "Power Smart" program should be discarded, but rather that the current policy framework acts to undermine these objectives.

When we look at the environmental outcomes of the various components of the government's energy policies, it becomes very difficult to see how they can be described as environmentally responsible. Pushing through new private projects that may not be needed in the first place, allowing the anticipated profits for private power developers to be the guiding force in determining the timing and location of new "green" energy projects, reducing environmental assessment safeguards under the guise of eliminating "red tape," undermining the basic conservation principles of "Power Smart," and introducing coal-based generation all add up to an environmentally irresponsible approach to addressing B.C.'s future energy needs. The government has managed to put a policy framework in place that is irresponsible not only from the financial perspective of ratepayers, but from any reasonable environmental perspective as well.

NOTES

1. The question of why some large hydro projects are not designated as "green" is an interesting one. Arguably, a single large project may not do as much overall damage to the environment as dozens of small projects built in sensitive eco-

systems. As Marjorie Griffin Cohen notes, large and small hydro have a similar ranking on the Pace University Center for Environmental Legal Studies-ranking of the environmental impacts of various energy sources (Cohen 2006). But, historically, provincial governments have been the major developers of large hydro, while private interests have only built smaller projects. By lobbying to see that no large hydro projects can be designated as "green," private power developers have ensured that there is a much larger market for their energy, particularly in jurisdictions that require a specified portion of "green" energy to be included in their resource mix. Effectively, they have eliminated all competition from large, publicly owned hydro generating facilities. Faced with energetic lobbying from private energy interests, provincial governments have been reluctant to challenge this approach.

2. It is worth noting that the conservation mandate of the B.C. Sustainable Energy Association is much wider than electricity. Many of its recommendations on other environmental issues are quite progressive.

Chapter Twelve

Co-opting First Nations

Along with its efforts to neutralize the concerns of environmentalists and local communities, the government has also targeted First Nations as another major interest whose potential opposition it must overcome in order to implement its private power agenda. Unlike other groups, First Nations are in a much stronger negotiating position due to extensive — and largely unresolved — land claim issues across the province. Many of the proposed new power plants, dams, transmission lines, roads, and other energy infrastructure are being developed on territories on which First Nations currently live and over which they may have land claims. Not only must the government find a way to persuade First Nations to support — or at least not oppose — such projects: it also must address the fact, noted earlier, that it has given water licences for virtually all the best small hydro sites in B.C. to its friends in the private power industry.

Of course, the fundamental question of why First Nations were not given first options on water licences — given that the province was anxious to award these to private interests rather than BC Hydro — is one the government is not anxious to see raised. If water licences were to be given out on a first-come, first-served basis, First Nations, it can be argued, should have been at the head of the queue. But only a handful of water licences have been granted to First Nations. In fact, the chances of getting a handful of water licences or a prime site for a new wind farm were far, far greater if you happened to work on Howe Street or traded stocks on the Vancouver Stock Exchange than if you — or your ancestors — actually lived near the site of a project. The government forgot to include First Nations on the invitation list for the new gold rush. But, as an afterthought, it realized that they had to somehow be included in the process: otherwise their opposition could derail the party.

To understand why First Nations are now an important factor in the politics of private power development it is useful to review their past experience with such projects. When W.A.C. Bennett decided to develop the Peace and Columbia hydro projects, First Nations' interests were largely ignored by both the provincial government and BC Hydro. There was virtually no consultation on the initial decision of whether to build these projects. Subsequently, the government provided very little compensation to First Nations for the enormous damage these projects inflicted on their communities, their way of life, and their traditional economies. First Nations were also largely excluded from the job opportunities and other economic benefits of the construction process. And, while there were efforts in following decades to address some of their legitimate grievances through training and employment opportunities and by establishing an Aboriginal Relations Department within BC Hydro itself, this hardly compensated for the earlier hardships imposed on First Nations communities. So there is a legacy of legitimate First Nations' grievances over energy development in the province.[1]

However, since the major BC Hydro dams were built, there have been many significant changes in relations between First Nations and the government, most notably as a result of obligations built into Canada's Constitution and subsequent court rulings. The courts have directed governments to consult with First Nations on proposals involving use of resources or lands that are subject to historical land claims or treaty negotiations. The province can no longer deal with First Nations in the same high-handed manner it did three or four decades ago. It must seek their cooperation.

It is not the focus of this book to review the details of key court decisions that have come down in the past two decades. But the direction given by the courts is clear. First Nations have rights, and governments at all levels must respect them. In B.C., most First Nations never signed treaties abrogating any of their rights, so the issue of reaching agreements satisfactory to all parties remains an ongoing challenge. There are 197 First Nations bands in B.C. as well as a number of tribal councils and a number of organizations that represent the collective interests of First Nations, each of which has a different approach to dealing with these issues. These include the Union of B.C. Indian Chiefs (which is not a participant in treaty negotiations), the B.C. Assembly of First Nations, and the First Nations' Summit.

From the perspective of the government and the private power industry, the main issue is to secure a stable and secure investment climate. The importance of resolving issues with First Nations has been outlined by the B.C. Treaty Commission as follows:

> Province-wide, treaties will bring certainty to land ownership and jurisdiction, a major cash injection and new investment. Total benefits from treaties, including increased investment, could be as high as \$50 billion — \$1 billion to \$2 billion each year for the next 20–25 years. A Treaty Commission-sponsored survey of businesses confirms investment will follow treaties. Of the 143 companies responding to the survey, including 118 headquartered in British Columbia, two-thirds cite unresolved land claims as an important factor in investment decisions. It is clear from this survey that the absence of treaties impacts our economy every day. One in five companies surveyed reduced their investment in B.C. due to unresolved

> land claims. That adds up to hundreds of millions of dollars of lost investment just among those companies surveyed. And those investments would have created jobs and attracted additional investment. The lost opportunities are substantial. The financial community says unresolved land claims and the resulting uncertainty scare off investors. This is especially true for the resource-based economy, which has been the backbone of small-town British Columbia.
>
> One in four companies surveyed would increase investment if a significant number of claims were settled. That, too, adds up to hundreds of millions of dollars in investment just among those companies surveyed. (B.C. Treaty Commission 2007)

The challenge posed by First Nations' rights and interests was highlighted by Donald McInnes, President of Plutonic Power, in his presentation to the Standing Committee on Finances and Government Services on October 13, 2004:

> Another area that's very scary for the IPP community and business generally in British Columbia is the First Nations situation. Currently, I know of at least six independent power producers that out of frustration, I would suggest, have signed agreements with local First Nation groups, giving them a 1 percent gross revenue royalty in order to proceed to build their projects.
>
> Now, there are not many businesses that like to give away 1 percent of the gross cash flow, but this industry is so young and new and the power project proponents are so interested in moving their businesses forward that they've been doing this on their own. I don't think this is an area that private industry should be getting into.
>
> I think communities like First Nations groups want to be treated well and have good job prospects and things like that, but the issue of revenue sharing is, I think, a government mandate. The provincial government needs to get involved in this area. I can't see many major pulp mills or mines or Microsoft, for that matter, establishing operations in British Columbia and giving the local First Nations group a 1 percent gross revenue royalty. I think some work needs to be done there. (McInnes 2004)

Setting aside the question of whether 1 percent of the hugely profitable revenue stream is excessive, the reality is that obtaining the consent of First Nations is essential if private power interests are to avoid costly — and risky — future litigation over ownership and compensation for building on contested land. Concerns of private power developers over land claims issues are illustrated in a U.S. Securities and Exchange Commission filing by Sea Breeze Power Corporation. In its third-quarter 2004 "Management Discussion and Analysis," the company notes, under the heading "Land Title":

> Risk: The Company must ensure clear title to the lands on which it proposes to operate. The Company's wind-farm development projects are on lands for which there exists asserted aboriginal title. These land claim issues presently remain unresolved.
>
> Mitigation: The Company has an in-house tracking system in place to monitor the status of Land Use Permits, Licences of Occupancy, and related applications, with the B.C. government. The Company has an obligation under the Knob Hill Environmental Assessment Certificate to consult First Nations who have land claims that overlap the Company's project sites. To that end, the Company is engaged in active and formal discussions with the Quatsino First Nation and the Tlatlasikwala First Nation and intends to continue meaningful consultations with both groups. In addition, discussions are ongoing with both First Nations to reach agreement on community benefits relating to the Company's presence on northern Vancouver Island. (Sea Breeze 2004a)

Having belatedly realized that First Nations' cooperation is essential for the smooth implementation of its private power agenda, the government has initiated a comprehensive strategy to get First Nations on board. It has directed BC Hydro, the new B.C. Transmission Corporation, and staff from various ministries involved in the approvals process to organize extensive "stakeholder" consultations designed to bring First Nations onside with the government's agenda. These stakeholder consultations enable private energy proponents to identify First Nations' concerns about specific development proposals and provide an opportunity for them to work out compensation arrangements that will facilitate First Nations' approval of projects.

One approach is to make First Nations junior partners in a power project by offering them a small stake in assets or revenue stream. Another is to provide jobs — and possibly training — during the construction phase. (However, as noted earlier, these facilities are capital-intensive and job-thin, so long-term employment possibilities are necessarily quite limited.) Some developers have also proposed funding various community facilities for First Nations as a *quid pro quo* for approval. And, in at least one case — Ledcor's Ashlu project — First Nations have been offered the prospect of ownership of a facility after a fixed period of time. (In Ledcor's case, this is forty years, although the exact terms of the offer have not been made public, so it is not clear what conditions may apply. However, the consequence has been that Squamish First Nations have been among the most active supporters of approving the project.)

One of the key strategies of the province's approach to addressing the concerns of First Nations is to facilitate consultations with prospective developers during BC Hydro's periodic tender calls to the private sector for new energy. To assist the smooth implementation of EPAs, BC Hydro has established a process that brings together investors, First Nations, suppliers, and, in some cases, community groups and other designated "stakeholders." BC Hydro describes this process as follows:

> For this Call BC Hydro plans to build on the existing practice of obtaining input on Call elements from potential bidders by expanding the dialogue and opportunity to comment to include First Nations, regulators and stakeholders. BC Hydro will seek written input from these parties as part of the design phase of the Call. BC Hydro will weigh and incorporate where appropriate the various perspectives of participants while making the ultimate decision about the Call design and characteristics.
>
> BC Hydro's objectives for First Nations and stakeholder engagement for the 2005 Call are to:
>
> - design a Call that yields a product meeting the needs of BC Hydro and its customers;
> - design a Call that attracts varied and competitive bids, while being cost effective and efficient for both BC Hydro and bidders;
> - obtain a procurement outcome that is acceptable to bidders, First Nations, regulators and stakeholders; and
> - build mutual understanding of BC Hydro, bidder, First Nations, regulator and stakeholder interests related to BC Hydro's power acquisition activities.
>
> In order to meet these objectives BC Hydro will:
>
> - provide regional opportunities for external dialogue and input before issuing the Call;
> - listen to and seek to understand potential bidders, First Nations, regulators and stakeholders interests regarding the Call, by providing timely and accessible opportunities in face-to-face meetings and through our website to provide written comment;
> - review comments and decide on changes to the proposed process, terms and evaluation for the Call; and
> - convey to potential bidders, First Nations, regulators and stakeholders how their input deepened BC Hydro's understanding

> and influenced decisions about the final Call design. (BC Hydro 2005a)

In its submission to the BCUC describing the process it followed in developing and implementing the 2006 tender call, BC Hydro provides additional details on the consultation process:

> The F2006 Call was designed through the spring and fall of 2005 and included significant First Nations and stakeholder engagement. First Nations and stakeholders were given three opportunities to provide comment on the F2006 Call: 1) draft terms and conditions in the spring of 2005; 2) the negotiation settlement process; and 3) final draft documents in the fall of 2005. (BC Hydro 2006b)

After these consultations, BC Hydro claimed it made a variety of amendments to its tender proposals and to the terms of its EPAs to enable First Nations to participate more extensively in the process. However, it appears that, in practice, few of these changes specifically addressed First Nations issues: virtually all of them dealt with requests by "stakeholders" — primarily private energy companies — to modify the proposed call for tenders in ways that would accommodate their needs, in some cases at the expense of BC Hydro. It can be argued that the purpose of the changes and, indeed, of the "stakeholder" consultations themselves — is not primarily to protect the interests of First Nations, but rather to protect the interests of investors who do not want to deal with the uncertainty of land claims or other First-Nations issues that could prejudice the construction and operation of their projects.

One major weakness of the process the government has followed is that it encourages private developers to make deals with individual bands. This can result in a very unequal negotiating table. First, the developer normally already has the water licence (or is first in line with its application), so it has the key to the future development of the site. Second, the developer has all the financial information and technical data associated with what is required to build the power plant. How much of this information it chooses to share with the First Nations band it is negotiating with is likely to vary depending on the experience and negotiating skills of the band. This asymmetry in information gives the developer a major advantage. Without some knowledge of the energy industry and the future revenues likely to flow from private power development, First Nations may end up with a much smaller share of the assets or revenue stream than they would otherwise win.

On top of this, developers will normally be knowledgeable about commercial contract law and the various contractual requirements needed to maximize the interests of their investors, and this knowledge may result in shifting risks to First Nations. It is worth remembering that many developers involved in private power projects have a history of involvement in venture-capital projects and in penny-stock promotions. Their negotiating skills are likely to be well-honed.

One common tactic is for developers to start negotiations with a commitment that all discussions will remain confidential and that the terms of draft agreements will not be shared with outside parties. They may also ask that final agreements remain confidential. This may mean that others knowledgeable about financial issues in the power industry are not in a position to provide their analyses to First Nations. And it can also result in resentment between First Nations and local communities when the latter are denied information about the terms of agreements between First Nations and private power developers.

Another issue is the extent to which rights and title end up being extinguished once First Nations enter into an agreement with a private power developer. It is generally assumed that private property is not to be included in treaty negotiations, so once a band has signed a deal — regardless of whether it subsequently realizes it was not a good one — it will still have to respect the fact that the developer now has a right to the assets and future revenue stream. The privatization of the water resource is not only a privatization from the wider public, but also from any future treaty claims.

The government's Energy Plan has precluded the development of other options in dealing with First Nations' legitimate issues. Of course, the province could negotiate a package of financial benefits with First Nations directly affected by power projects. Given that the public will end up indirectly paying whatever compensation private power developers provide to First Nations, it would be no less costly for the province to provide such compensation directly.

If BC Hydro were directly involved in developing these projects, it could incorporate a number of innovations that would ensure a larger share of their benefits accrued to First Nations. BC Hydro's construction subsidiary developed an extensive training and employment equity program which was copied — and successfully implemented — in the $1.3-billion Vancouver Island Highway Project. This project provided training and employment for local First Nations, who received approximately 9 percent of the overall jobs and payroll in an industry in which their employment rate has normally been between 1 and 2 percent (Calvert and Redlin 2003).

Public control of the assets of power projects would ensure that First Nations could play an ongoing role in monitoring power projects to ensure they were operated in a manner that maintained fish stocks and ensured that community priorities were respected. But this would have required a very different vision of the appropriate relationship between government and

First Nations, and a very different understanding of the role small hydro and wind projects should play in B.C.'s energy future.

NOTE

1. In December 2006 BC Hydro, presumably with the blessing of the province, announced that it had reached a tentative agreement to provide compensation to two First Nations directly affected by the construction of the Williston dam. It provides approximately $14 million to each First Nation and ongoing annual payouts of about $1.9 million to the Tsay Keh Dene and $1.5 million to the Kwadacha, with future adjustments for inflation. As well, BC Hydro agreed to provide a total of $11 million for heritage projects. Such compensation was long overdue.

Chapter Thirteen

Destroying BC Hydro

In previous chapters, we have examined the government's energy policies from a variety of different perspectives. We have reviewed the historical background. We have looked at some of the key players shaping B.C.'s current policies. We have analyzed the economic consequences of these policies. We have looked at their impact on communities in various parts of the province. We have discussed their negative environmental implications. And we have analyzed government efforts to get First Nations to support its privatization agenda. However, the one area we have not addressed systematically is the impact of these policies on the province's major utility: BC Hydro.

Perhaps the most significant of the government's misleading claims is that its energy policies will not undermine BC Hydro's viability. It has made this claim repeatedly to reassure the public that they will not lose the benefits of their most important — and valuable — Crown corporation. Contracting out a third of its workforce to Accenture, carving out the transmission system and deregulating its use, subsidizing the expansion of private energy developers, selling energy to major industrial customers at rates less than half what it is paying for new energy, and all the other items in the government's electricity policy agenda will not, we are told, result in any loss of the benefits the public has come to expect from BC Hydro. But, as should now be apparent, these claims are fundamentally misleading. The long-term impact of the current government's policies will be to destroy the Crown utility's historical role as a supplier of affordable energy and a driver of economic development within B.C. The privileging of private interests through the government's policy agenda will also undermine B.C.'s long-term energy security and may well lead to foreign control of the province's electricity system as well.

To understand the extent of the damage being done to BC Hydro, it is useful to review some of the reasons why it has made such an important contribution to B.C.'s economy. These benefits include the very low-cost energy it provides to its residential and commercial customers, the enormous competitive advantage of low-cost energy for major industrial customers, the annual dividends it pays to the province, the water rentals it pays for use of the public water resource, the taxes in lieu (school tax) it forwards to the government to compensate local governments for its tax-exempt status as a Crown corporation, its regional development programs, and the benefits of the jobs, expertise, and investments that it has provided for B.C. Table 23 summarizes the direct financial benefits — dividends, water rentals, and

Table 23: Contributions by BC Hydro to the Provincial Government

Fiscal Year	Taxes ($millions)	Water Rentals ($millions)	Dividends ($millions)	Total ($millions)
1994	170	216	245	631
1995	171	231	198	600
1996	169	232	115	516
1997	169	254	279	702
1998	177	238	366	781
1999	173	252	326	751
2000	172	255	343	770
2001	174	250	372	796
2002	166	224	333	723
2003	145	259	338	742
2004	147	246	73	466
2005	143	234	339	716
2006	147	272	223	642
Total	2,123	3,163	3,550	8,836

Source: BC Hydro Annual Reports

taxes — it pays to the government. Since 1994, the Crown corporation has paid more than $8.8 billion dollars to the government — and this despite the fact that it has, at the same time, provided ratepayers with energy at prices that are virtually the lowest of any utility in North America. This is quite a feat and is particularly significant when B.C.'s rugged terrain is taken into account.

And, to all this we must also add the benefits of the Columbia River Treaty, which in recent years has been providing an average of about a quarter of a billion dollars in additional revenue to the province. This is not money BC Hydro collects, but it is money that is the result of construction of BC Hydro's reservoirs and is a consequence of public ownership of these reservoirs. When this is added to the amounts in Table 23, we see that the Crown utility has been providing B.C. with about a billion dollars in financial benefits per year. To put this in perspective, the total amount received annually by the province in corporate taxes from all businesses operating in the province is, on average, only slightly more than BC Hydro's contribution. This is an enormous benefit to the people of B.C.

Another of the key benefits of the creation of BC Hydro — one often taken for granted — has been the impetus it gave to the development of energy expertise within B.C. In the years following the nationalization of the

B.C. Electric Company, the Crown utility built up a large staff of engineers, technicians, and energy policy experts who have provided the province with the capacity to keep on top of developments in the industry, both nationally and internationally. Either as a direct result of government policies (and legislative scrutiny), or indirectly as a result of information requests through the BCUC process, an enormous amount of information (which private utilities would not share to the same degree because of "commercial confidentiality") has been made widely available to the public. Ironically, private power developers have used this information to identify policy changes that the government could implement in order to transfer benefits from BC Hydro to their own bank accounts.

As well, BC Hydro has developed a provincial energy infrastructure that has also benefited the private sector. It has done so through awarding contracts to a wide variety of B.C.-based energy consultants, engineers, and construction firms, thus supporting the development of a strong, locally based group of private companies with expertise in energy development issues. The evidence of this legacy is readily found in the numerous firms that have used their contracts with BC Hydro to expand outside the province and become major players in Canada and abroad.

However, government policies have already dramatically reduced the ability of BC Hydro to maintain its own in-house expertise and to continue to support local energy businesses, because of the truncated role now assigned to the utility and because more and more of its limited functions are being out-sourced to companies such as Accenture. This is a direct result of government's policies and of directives from the BCUC, which, for example, has embarked on a program to force BC Hydro to contract out more of its technical and engineering services through competitive tendering. In the short term, this may give a boost to some local businesses. But the problem is that, with WTO, NAFTA, the Agreement on Internal Trade among the provinces and, more recently, the B.C.-Alberta Trade, Investment and Labour Mobility Agreement procurement obligations now in force, it is very difficult to keep tendered work within the province. And so contracting out increasingly results in jobs and expertise leaving the province.

Arguably, the long-term consequence of government policy changes will be to dismantle much of the Crown utility's remaining expertise, both in current hydro operations and in major areas of new technology. Its ability to provide well-researched, impartial advice to future governments on policy options will diminish over time because of the smaller number of technical staff remaining on its payroll and because it will no longer be involved directly in many areas of energy development.

If BC Hydro is to remain knowledgeable about many of the financial, technical, and environmental issues associated with small hydro, wind, solar, and geothermal projects, it must have the "hands-on" experience gained by building and operating such facilities. This experience is acquired by carrying out the research necessary to maintain a working knowledge of new technical developments in the generating plants themselves, as well as by studying the long-term environmental, social, and community impacts of such facilities. Hands-on experience is also important to an understanding of the economics of these facilities. To be an effective advocate for the province's ratepayers, BC Hydro must know the real cost of producing energy, including the potential benefits and risks of investing in various energy options.

Government policies are also resulting in lost opportunities that could have been extremely beneficial to ratepayers. By operating small hydro and wind-generating facilities while continuing to do research on other new technologies such as geothermal, solar, and tidal energy, BC Hydro would be in a much stronger position to assess which new technologies merit investment and which do not. The gains resulting from this knowledge would benefit B.C. ratepayers, rather than being captured by private interests. Another strong argument for BC Hydro to be involved in wind and small hydro development, specifically, is that it would allow it to achieve the economies of scale associated with operating a significant number of similar plants — economies that are much harder for companies with a small number of power plants to achieve.

The reverse of this is also true. As a result of the tendering process, a large number of private companies are scrambling to build similar types of generating facilities using technologies and equipment sourced from a variety of different countries around the world. This means that each private proponent has to go through its own learning curve. Lessons from one project may not be passed on to the developer of the next project if they are owned by competing firms. While it is true that a number of the major firms may be building projects in other parts of Canada, or internationally, the government's rationale for the expansion of this sector is partly to enhance the development of small, environmentally friendly businesses in B.C.

To the extent that the actual investments reflect this rationale, they will result in duplication of mistakes and the absence of a suitable learning curve for such projects within the province. Given that the public is the purchaser of the resulting energy, the costs of this duplication will be borne by B.C. customers in the form of higher prices for long-term energy supply contracts, but with no corresponding transfer of expertise to BC Hydro.

As we noted in our discussion of the challenges of integrating wind and small hydro facilities into the province's energy grid, BC Hydro is increasingly facing the challenge of how to ensure system reliability by having enough capacity to match the large amount of non-firm energy the government now directs it to purchase from private wind and small hydro developers. If, instead of being politically directed to acquire new energy that it may not need from areas of the province that may not be locations where new energy should be developed, BC Hydro were instead able to plan on a system-wide basis, it could much more easily decide how much new small hydro and wind it requires and build accordingly. While there is a strong argument that BC Hydro's storage provides it with opportunities for integrating wind and hydro energy into the system, the way it is now required to do so undermines rational economic planning in developing these energy sources. Ratepayers will bear the full costs of this wrongheaded approach.

Government policies in a number of other areas are also hurting BC Hydro's long-term viability. The government plans to close the Burrard thermal plant. We have argued that this is a short-sighted decision, because it will remove a key source of capacity in the lower Mainland. But BC Hydro's ownership and operation of Burrard also gives it an interest in — and a window on — developments in the natural-gas industry. Given how important this energy source is in North America's energy mix, and given developments in the international liquefied natural-gas industry, a strong case can be made that maintaining some expertise in this area will reap long-term benefits for BC Hydro and its ratepayers. Knowledge of energy developments other than large hydro has provided important data for public policy development and has ensured that the government has access to relevant information on issues such as environmental impacts, design and engineering issues, and, not unimportantly, the costs of alternative sources of energy.

The Energy Plan's ban on BC Hydro building new generating facilities means that policies designed to maximize provincial benefits from BC Hydro investments and procurement have been largely abandoned. Historically, one of the public policy purposes of creating BC Hydro was to use it as a vehicle for economic development. This policy was initiated by the creator of BC Hydro, W.A.C. Bennett, and was followed by successive governments to varying degrees from the early 1960s onward.

On the construction side, the utility's subsidiary, Columbia Hydro Constructors, pursued policies of local training and employment during construction of major dams and transmission lines, and it continued these policies when undertaking smaller upgrades and maintenance projects. It also strongly supported apprenticeship for trades requiring a Trades Qualification, and private firms across the province have benefited from the skills acquired by BC Hydro-trained employees who have moved on to other employers. During the 1990s, under direction from BC Hydro's Board and in line with the province's policy of providing more opportunities to members of traditionally disadvantaged groups, it expanded this mandate to provide training and job opportunities for members of designated equity groups, including First Nations, a policy approach that was very successfully transferred to the construction of the Vancouver Island Highway project, where almost a thousand workers were trained and more than 93 percent of the payroll went to local residents.

On the procurement side, BC Hydro tried to use B.C. companies as suppliers by giving them "first-buy" opportunities for small contracts. This was part of a conscious effort to use the Crown utility's purchasing power to promote small businesses in the regions and to encourage the use of B.C. materials and labour. A turbine refurbishment contract with General Electric, negotiated in the mid-1990s, in which that company committed to locate some of its other operations in B.C. as a *quid pro quo* for obtaining the contract, provides perhaps the best example of efforts to leverage additional benefits for the province from BC Hydro's purchasing. This contract reflected the government of the day's analysis that major suppliers might be willing to invest in other areas of B.C.'s economy if they were given some credit for that investment as part of their tender submission. In the case of the GE contract, the province obtained important new investments largely because it pushed bidders to think about what they could contribute to the provincial economy through other parts of their business operations not necessarily related to electricity activities. GE's bid was both the lowest and the one that offered the most in provincial economic benefits. Had the province not asked for these additional benefits through BC Hydro, they might well not have materialized. The current government has abandoned such approaches, relying instead on the market to make such decisions. Private companies have no obligation to seek out B.C. suppliers or to use B.C. contractors in the design, construction, and operation of their facilities.

Another cost to BC Hydro — and to the public — is the give-away of water licences and wind-farm tenures. As we noted earlier, companies have engaged in a speculative bonanza in which they have been acquiring effective ownership of all the best locations for future small hydro and wind-farm developments. The value of these assets is enormous, but they have been recklessly handed over to private — and often foreign — power developers for virtually nothing. As the costs of private energy from BC Hydro's 2006 tender call and the subsequently aborted Alcan contract illustrate, the public will end up facing huge rate increases down the road, as private investors cash in on the value of these assets by demanding prices far above the cost of production.

Another major consequence of the government's Energy Plan has been to saddle BC Hydro with the very substantial costs associated with the fundamental restructuring of B.C.'s electricity system to accommodate the demands of private energy developers. Aided by a compliant BCUC, whose mandate and recent decisions have defined the "public interest" far too narrowly, the province has been able to shift many of the direct costs of this restructuring onto the Crown utility.

The B.C. Transmission Corporation was not created to improve the performance of BC Hydro, but rather to appease the demands of American energy interests and Canadian private energy developers. It has been funded almost entirely by BC Hydro, which now has to pay it for the right to use the grid on the same basis as other private energy interests. Because it is still the dominant user of the grid, the charges it pays are effectively funding the operation of the system, but the benefits are almost entirely accruing to the private sector (Cohen 2002b, 2003). As well, giving private interests the right to access the grid raises other issues associated with establishing the appropriate tariff. Should we value access based on the historical cost of a system built during the 1961–1984 period? Or should we charge access fees based on what it would now cost to build the system? If the new rate charged by BC Hydro is relatively low, it allows private interests to use the grid at a highly subsided price. Just as water-rental rates do not reflect the real value of B.C.'s water resource, transmission access fees may now represent another major handout to private energy developers.

Aside from the immediate costs of creating the B.C. Transmission Corporation, the loss of control over its transmission system has enormous implications for BC Hydro's ability to manage its own generating assets in a manner that maximizes public benefits. BC Hydro now has to plan in a context in which private interests may have already purchased transmission rights that limit its ability to use the grid — and its enormously valuable storage facilities — in the most flexible and cost-effective manner.

Loss of this flexibility is not a small issue. With a series of interconnected reservoirs and transmission lines, BC Hydro can achieve significant economies of scale by managing the entire system in a unified way. The choice to use water from one reservoir or another is made on the basis of system-wide considerations, which may include market prices at the border, the level of water in each reservoir, available transmission capacity, projected demand, and so forth. Much of this flexibility is based on having full access to the grid and being able to move energy where and when it makes sense from the perspective of the overall system. Losing this flexibility by being treated as just another purchaser of transmission access in competition with private interests has major financial and operational impacts for BC Hydro. And these, in turn, have costs for ratepayers.

While BC Hydro is not allowed to benefit from investments in small hydro, wind, and other new energy technologies, it is still funding research in these areas — research whose benefits will flow to private interests. It has a whole division devoted to renewable energy research. BC Hydro is collecting data on many projects that have already received EPAs — data paid for by ratepayers that will help their private owners operate them more efficiently. We have already noted that wind-monitoring facilities put in place by BC Hydro as early as 1981 have now been turned over to private wind farm developers, along with their accumulated data. More recently, the B.C. Transmission Corporation has been funding research for wind-farm developers. Yet another subsidy to private energy developers.

And there is another cost, more difficult to calculate, but important just the same. It is the introduction of a raft of new private interests into B.C.'s electricity system — interests whose concern is not to supply affordable, reliable energy to B.C. residents, but rather to maximize returns to their investors. The government's restructuring of BC's energy system has brought literally hundreds of new energy companies, banks, investment houses, contractors, engineering firms, consultants, and many others into B.C.'s electricity system.

These companies not only have a financial stake in the system, they are also political actors, making campaign contributions to the governing political party and using their lobbying capacity to pressure the government into making even more concessions to their interests. For example, in its 2007 Energy Plan, the government has indicated that it will direct BC Hydro to provide a standing order for private power developers with projects of less than 10 MW in capacity, in addition to the periodic tender calls it will continue to announce. As a result, these companies will not even have to wait for new tender calls to arrange for EPAs with BC Hydro. And, the government has asked BC Hydro to consider subsidizing the cost of new transmission lines connecting private power projects to the main grid.

These private interests will not disappear when the current government leaves office. They will be part of a new political fabric that all future governments will have to deal with in crafting electricity policies. With their powerful connections in Washington and Ottawa, as well as within the province, they can be expected to oppose any proposed policy changes that benefit BC Hydro and the public at investors' expense. And, they can also be expected to push for additional benefits on top of those they are currently receiving from their new power plants, their lucrative EPAs, and their opportunities to become energy exporters.

Future efforts, for example, by governments to restrict private energy exports in order to reduce the need of building new power plants in B.C., or to ensure security of supply for the province, are likely to be strongly resisted by private interests. And, unlike 1961, when W.A.C. Bennett was able to nationalize the B.C. Electric Company in order to promote the broader economic objective of developing the province, future provincial governments will have to face the reality of NAFTA's onerous Chapter Eleven investor rights obligations, which will apply not only to any proposed nationalization efforts, but also to any effort by future governments to regulate private interests, if such regulation interferes with anticipated profits.

The government is also saddling BC Hydro with enormous financial obligations flowing from the costs of its new energy purchases. As we saw earlier, the 2006 tender award resulted in an estimated $15.6 billion in future commitments to private energy developers. And the government plans even more of these contracts in the future, so the Crown utility will end up paying very large amounts to private interests over the coming decades without having any assets to show for its expenditures. If a future government were to attempt to have BC Hydro build generating facilities again, it is quite possible that the existence of these obligations would be used to argue that it should not be allowed to borrow any additional funds for its own projects, given the extent of the financial commitments it has already undertaken. All of this underlines the negative repercussions of allowing future investment in our electricity system to be taken over by private interests.

Of course, there has always been another alternative: strengthening the existing public system. The government could have used BC Hydro as the key developer of new, renewable energy within the province. Yet, as we have seen, it rejected this option. It is worthwhile, in this regard, to review some of the arguments used both by the government and private power interests to justify their rejection of this public option.

One common objection to the idea that BC Hydro should build small hydro or wind-energy facilities is that the Crown corporation is too big and bureaucratic to do so. Critics — primarily from the private power industry — who stand to benefit from the absence of competition from BC Hydro argue that the public utility, with its large overheads and well-paid, unionized staff, cannot build small-scale projects in an economically efficient manner. Some of these critics may acknowledge that, on a major capital project such as a new dam or a major new transmission line, BC Hydro may be able to carry out the work in a cost-effective manner, although others take a more extreme view and claim that there is virtually nothing BC Hydro could now build that would be less costly than if undertaken by private interests.

This problem with this criticism is that it is not based on evidence. The evidence is clear: BC Hydro's track record at keeping costs in line has been good. This is reflected in both its record of maintaining low rates for customers and in the very high standard of system reliability. As noted earlier, BC Hydro's current cost of producing energy from its major hydro facilities is far, far below the current market price. And, more significantly, it is also only a tiny fraction of what it is paying private developers through its EPAs. However, ideology, not evidence, is what drives the argument of those opposing BC Hydro.

Those who oppose an expanded role for BC Hydro have another major obstacle to overcome. It is the inherent advantage that BC Hydro has to borrow capital at interest rates much lower than those available to private energy developers. A difference of several percentage points in the interest rate paid on money borrowed to build a project translates into many millions in savings. No private power developer can borrow money as cheaply as BC Hydro, which benefits from the province's AAA credit rating. This means that its cost of borrowing is significantly lower than that of private developers, even those who use their BC Hydro EPAs as collateral for their projects. Lower interest rates provide a huge cost advantage in building capital-intensive projects where subsequent operating costs are only a small fraction of the initial capital cost.

In contrast, the cost of capital for private energy projects — unless they secure a BC Hydro EPA — is generally in the "junk bond" category. Developers have to pay premium interest rates to secure the capital due to the short-term risks associated with permitting, environmental approvals, construction, and the final marketing of the energy. Indeed, some of the more speculative energy investments involve borrowing at rates as high as 20 percent annually. Thus, even projects that eventually get a BC Hydro EPA still incur significant additional financing costs. And they will normally still pay higher interest rates on money secured by an EPA with BC Hydro.

A second major obstacle that critics of an expanded role for BC Hydro have yet to overcome is the long-term benefits of public ownership of generating assets. Even if the immediate costs of building projects are roughly the same as for the private sector, when the public owns such projects they provide much lower-cost energy once their capital costs are written down. When the public owns the asset, ratepayers benefit by paying rates based on the cost of production, not on the energy market or the inflated prices embedded in EPAs. Conversely, private ownership exposes ratepayers to future price increases, especially when we consider long-term trends. Investors will continue to demand market rates for their energy — as Alcan and Cominco have clearly demonstrated — even after the capital costs of their projects are paid off and their cost of energy production is only a tiny fraction of their selling price.

Another strength of BC Hydro has been its commitment to high standards of engineering and construction. Ironically, one reason BC Hydro is frequently accused of being an expensive project developer is that it builds to such very high standards. But these high standards are precisely what make its facilities less prone to outages and other problems that negatively affect the public in other jurisdictions. Design and construction standards can increase — or reduce — the likelihood of interruptions in water flows or accidental spills that damage fish and fish habitat. Design issues may also affect the ability of projects to accommodate other public uses. And, most importantly, they are integrally connected with ensuring that the system provides secure, reliable energy for customers.

Turning to the issue of post-construction maintenance and operations, one of the challenges facing owners of individual power projects is the need to either keep key technical staff on the payroll or have access to such staff from outside providers in order to deal with major emergencies. While some larger companies may be able to benefit from economies of scale to some degree, smaller ones cannot. In contrast, with its extensive network of staff and facilities across the province, BC Hydro is well suited to providing the back-up maintenance and emergency support these projects may require in the event of equipment failures or weather damage. Its experienced and technically qualified workforce gives it the ability to respond flexibly to problems arising in the system. In serious emergencies, qualified staff can be temporarily re-assigned from other parts of its operations to address outages and other crises or to deal with new challenges that, while appearing in one locality, may be of a system-wide nature. BC Hydro has been very effective in minimizing the impact of major windstorms and other unforeseen events on its transmission system, in part because it has the flexibility to re-deploy trained staff already available in the region at short notice.

It is difficult to see how an individual small hydro proponent can maintain a similar quality of back-up service without incurring significant overheads — overheads that would only be required to deal with emergencies. Indeed, many newly built or proposed run-of-the-river projects will have only a skeleton staff of full-time people, often monitoring the site through remote technology from distant urban centres. Taking into account the need for twenty-four-hour coverage seven days a week, the challenge of having suitable back-up staff to deal with emergencies is not insignificant.

While we have discussed options for small hydro, it is worth noting that many of the same arguments apply to the development of wind-farm energy as well. Here we have a very clear example of a practical, and viable, alternative to the government's current approach. Saskatchewan chose to develop two of its three wind farm projects through SaskPower. And the third, the smallest, is a joint venture, with SaskPower being the leading partner. When it began operations, SaskPower's largest project was also the largest wind farm in Canada, evidence that it was not simply a small-scale public experiment, but rather a major expansion of publicly owned electricity generation.

The government could have directed BC Hydro to do the same, thus ensuring not only that it acquired expertise about this new technology but also that the sites themselves would be retained within the public sector for future generations. Public control would also provide B.C. with the opportunity to use wind-farm investment to stimulate B.C.-based suppliers.

Wind energy can be most effectively used when it is accompanied by storage, such as BC Hydro has in its main reservoirs. The two sources of energy are complementary, and the existence of storage makes B.C. a far more favourable jurisdiction for wind farms than many others. Instead of developing policies that would take full advantage of this opportunity for the public, the government has simply given wind-farm tenures away to private energy developers. And they can be expected to lobby vigorously for private access to public reservoirs to store their energy and inflate its value as an export commodity in American markets.

To sum up, the government's overall energy policy framework is nothing short of disastrous for B.C. It has squandered enormously valuable water and wind resources to appease the demands of private energy developers for profitable investment opportunities. It has undermined B.C.'s low-cost electricity by manufacturing an energy crisis and using it to require BC Hydro to enter into enormously expensive EPAs that should not have been offered in the first place, given that so many better options were available. Through these EPAs the government has given its friends in the private sector secure revenue streams to fund the construction of their new private power plants. And these newly enriched power developers will benefit from a generous revenue stream from B.C. ratepayers for generations to come.

The government has restructured the transmission grid to facilitate private energy exports, thus enhancing the value of new private power plants at the expense of provincial energy security. It has broken apart — and dismembered — much of BC Hydro through contracting out to Accenture, through carving out the transmission system, and through ending the Crown utility's role as the builder of B.C.'s future energy facilities. It has opened the door to foreign ownership of much of B.C.'s electricity system while guaranteeing that, in future, the system will be managed on the basis of a policy framework established south of the border. In sum, the Campbell government's legacy will be to have dismantled what is arguably Canada's most successful Crown corporation and to have squandered one of B.C.'s most important competitive advantages.

All of this underlines the urgency of adopting a new and fundamentally different approach to dealing with B.C.'s energy needs. I hope this work will make a modest contribution to this process.

APPENDIX

Ownership of Private Water Licences in B.C. (Includes Number of Licence Applications)

Company	No	Company	No	Company	No	Company	No
0717016 B.C. Ltd	1	Coats, Clyde	1	KMC Energy	14	Rennaissance Power	1
728078 B.C. Ltd	1	Cogenix Power	1	Kotowick Denise	1	Ribco Leasing	1
28165 Yukon Inc	1	Copeland Power	1	Kwoiek Creek	2	Ring Creek Power	1
3986314 Canada Inc	3	Copeland Resources	1	Lakeside Pacific Forest	1	Robertson Peter Smith	1
446026 B.C. Ltd	2	Creek Power	5	Larson Farms	1	Robro Six Holdings	3
574768 B.C. Ltd	6	Creekside Resources	2	Ledcor Power	14	Robson Valley	1
579220 B.C. Ltd	1	East Twin Creek	2	Link Power	2	Rockford Energy	1
6167047 Canada Ltd	4	Earthgen Enterprise	1	Lorenz, Norman	2	Run of River Inc	1
666921 B.C. Ltd	1	Eckert Thresa	1	Macmillan, Colin	1	Rutherford Creek	2
684996 B.C. Ltd	1	Epcor	6	Marion Creek Hydro	2	Ryan River	1
755748 B.C. Ltd	3	ESI Walden	4	May, David F	1	Second Realty Effects	7
Advanced Energy	3	Enterprise Power	1	MC Hydro Holding	3	Silversmith Power	4
Alcan	3	Executive House Power	1	Miller Creek	2	Similkameen Hydro	2
Alice Arm	10	Fear, Darcy	2	MKW'alts Energy	2	Sound Energy	1
Alpine Power	36	Flett Forestry	2	Monashee Power	2	South Sutton Creek	1
Ankenman, Jeff	2	Focus Energy	1	Moorehead Valley	6	SN Power	3
Anyox Hydro Electric	4	FortisB.C.	5	Murphy Creek Power	1	Starland Mark Andrew	1
Arrow Lakes Power	1	Friends of Pitt Lake	1	New Era Hydro	1	St James Enterprises	1

Axiom Power	6	Furry Creek	2	Northridge Canada	1	Summit Power Corp	10
Bergevin George Elie	1	Generex Hydro	1	Nortwest Cascade	11	Synex Energy	8
Boston Bar	2	Gitga'at Development Corp	1	NVI Mining	3	Taku Land Corp	3
Brilliant Expansion	2	Hanson, Daryl	1	Pacific Rim Power	1	Teck-Cominco	6
Brilliant Power	2	Highwater Power	1	Pamaweed Resources	8	Territon Hydro	1
Bugaboo Power	1	Holms Hydro	1	Pattison, George	1	TP Log Salvage	1
Burdett, Robert C	1	Hoodicoff, Ron	1	Peterson, William	1	TransCanada Energy	2
Canadian Hydro Developers	15	Hupacasath First Nation	1	Pingston Power	2	Upnit Power	1
Cascade Pacific Power	1	Hydromax Energy	38	Plutonic Hydro	21	Valhalla Power	2
Cavers, Donald	2	Innergex Inc	5	Plutonic Power	7	Valisa Energy	1
Central Coast Power	4	Interpac Resources	1	Powerhouse Developments	1	Walsh Michael	1
Cheakamus Gorge Hydro	2	Interpac Power Corp	5	Powell River Energy	5	Wanita Expansion	2
Chilliwack Power	2	Kemiss Mines	1	Princeton Energy	9	Wester Pulp	2
Clean Power Operating Trust	7	Kingston and Associates	1	Raffuse Energy	1	Western Forest Products	5
Cloudworks Energy	27	Kisei Industries Ltd	1	Raging River	3	Zeballos Lake	2
Coastal River Power	5	Kitsault Hydro	5	Regional Power Inc	6		
Coast Mountain Hydro	1	Kitsault Resort Ltd	2	Remote Structures Inc	1		
Coast Mountain Power	3	Klitsa Creek Hydro	1	Renewal Power Corp	2		

Source: Land and Water B.C. website, downloaded Nov. 2006. Table compiled by author. <http://www.lwbc.bc.ca/03water/licencing/application/index.html>

REFERENCES

Adams, Tom. 2006. "Review of Wind Power Results in Ontario: May to October 2006." Toronto: Energy Probe. November 15.

AES Corporation. 2006a. "AES Subsidiary Signs 30-Year Agreement to Provide Electricity in British Columbia." September 7 press release. Arlington, Va.

_____. 2006b. Presentation to Merrill Lynch Global Power and Gas Leaders' Conference by Victoria Harper, Executive Vice-President and Chief Financial Officer. September 27.

_____. 2006c. U.S. Securities and Exchange Commission 2006 Third Quarter 10Q filing.

_____. 2007. "2006 Financial Review and 2007 Outlook." May 25.

Alcan. 2001. "Position Paper on Energy Policy for British Columbia." Submitted to the B.C. Energy Policy Task Force. November 1.

Bear Mountain Wind Limited Partnership. 2006. August 28 press release. Calgary.

Bernstein, M. H. 1955. *Regulating Business by Independent Commission.* Princeton: Princeton University Press.

Berris, Catherine. 2003. "Cascade Heritage Power Project Recreation and Tourism Assessment." Prepared for International Powerhouse Energy Corp. Vancouver.

B.C. Citizens for Public Power. 2002. "Pulling the Plug: How the Liberals' Plan to Dismantle BC Hydro Threatens Taxpayers, Businesses, Communities and Jobs." Vancouver.

BC Hydro. 2000–2006. "Annual Reports." Available at <http://www.bchydro.com> accessed July 2007.

_____. 2000. "Inventory of Undeveloped Opportunities at Potential Micro Hydro Sites in British Columbia." Vancouver: Sigma Engineering. Available at <www.bchydro.com/rx_files/environment/environment1837.pdf> accessed July 2007.

_____. 2001. Green Energy Division. "Green Energy Study for British Columbia, Phase 1: Vancouver Island."

_____. 2002a. "Green Energy Study for British Columbia, Phase 2: Mainland, Small Hydro." Vancouer: Sigma Engineering. Available at <www.bchydro.com/rx_files/environment/environment3931.pdf> accessed July 2007.

_____. 2002b. Green Energy Division. "Green Energy Study for British Columbia: Phase II: Mainland."

_____. 2002/03. Green IPPs: 2002/02 Green Power Generation. Available on BC Hydro website <http://www.bchydro.com/info/ipp/ipp958.html>, accessed June 2007.

_____. 2003. August 26 press release.

_____. 2004a. "Resource Expenditure and Acquisition Plan."

_____. 2004b. "Revenue Requirements Application, 2004/05 and 2005/06."

_____. 2004c. "Vancouver Island Small Hydro Project Update (Mears Creek)."

_____. 2005a. "Resource Expenditure and Acquisition Plan." Submission to B.C. Utilities Commission. August 18.

_____. 2005b. "Open Call for Power." December 8.

_____. 2005c. Presentation to the 2004–05 Integrated Electricity Planning Committee. March 30.

_____. 2006a. "Integrated Electricity Plan and Long Term Acquisition Plan." March 29. Available at <http://www.bchydro.com/rx_files/info/info43514.pdf> accessed July 2007.

_____. 2006b. "Report on the F2006 Call for Tender Process." Submitted to the B.C. Utilities Commission. August 31. Available at <www.bchydro.com/rx_files/info/info48009.pdf> accessed July 2007.

_____. 2006c. "Integrated Electricity Plan." Revisions Submitted to B.C. Utilities Commission. April 19. Available at <www.bchydro.com/info/epi/epi8970.html> accessed July 2007.

_____. 2006d. "Annual Report." Available at <www.bchydro.com/info/reports/reports853.html> accessed July 2007.

_____. 2006e. "Resource Expenditure and Acquisition Plan."

_____. 2006f. Letter by Joanna Sofield, Chief Regulatory Officer, BC Hydro, to Robert Pellatt of the B.C. Utilities Commission re: "Project Number 3698446 and 3698419." November 17.

_____. 2006g. Letter by Joanna Sofield, Chief Regulatory Officer, BC Hydro to Robert Pellatt of the B.C. Utilities Commission re: "Alcan LTEPA Plus." December 5.

BC Hydro Power Pioneers. 1998. *Gaslights to Gigawatts: A Human History of BC Hydro and Its Predecessors.* Vancouver: Hurricane Press.

B.C. Sustainable Energy Association. 2005. "Sustainable Energy Policies for British Columbia." Victoria. April 5.

British Columbia Transmission Corporation. 2005. "Service Plan Update for Fiscal Years 2005/06–2007/08." Vancouver.

B.C. Treaty Commission (BCTC). 2007. "There are Compelling Economic Reasons: Treaties are Good for the Economy." May 28. Available at <http://www.bctreaty.net/files/economic-ed1.php> accessed July 2007.

B.C. Utilities Commission (BCUC). 1995. "The British Columbia Electricity Market Review." Vancouver.

_____. 2003. "Annual Service Plan Report, 2002–03."

_____. 2004. "Certificates of Public Convenience and Necessity: CPCN Application Guidelines."

_____. 2005. Letter to the B.C. Sustainable Energy Association. May 5. Available at <http://bcsea.org> accessed November 26, 2006.

_____. 2006. Letter from B.C. Utilities Commission Secretary Robert J. Pellatt to Joanna Sofield of BC Hydro. December 29.

_____. 2007. "Order No. E-1-07." January 18.

Bisetty, Krisendra. 2006. *Business in Vancouver.* Issue 852, February 21–27.

Caldicott, Arthur. 2007. "Rivers of Riches." *Watershed Sentinel.* January-February.

California Public Utilities Commission. 2007. "Application of Pacific Gas and Electric Company for Recovery of Generation Feasibility Study Costs Associated with the Evaluation of Wind-Generated and Other Renewable Electric Power in British Columbia." Decision 07-03-013. March 1.

Calvert, John. 2006a. "Private Power Developers and the B.C. Government's Water Licence Give-Away." *B.C. Commentary*. Fall. Vancouver: Canadian Centre for Policy Alternatives.

_____. 2006b. "BC Hydro's Amazingly Bad Deal for Taxpayers: We Give Big Firms $15 Billion: We Get Higher Prices, No Assets, No Guarantee of Supply." *The Tyee*. Oct. 30.

_____. 2007a. "Sticker Shock: The Impending Cost of BC Hydro's Shift to Private Power Developers." Vancouver: Canadian Centre for Policy Alternatives.

_____. 2007b "B.C.'s Billion Dollar Wind Give Away: We're Heavily Subsidizing Private Power Developers — Will Californians Profit Big?" *The Tyee*. May 14.

Calvert, John, and Blair Redlin. 2003. "Achieving Public Policy Objectives Through Collective Agreements: The Project Agreement Model for Public Construction in British Columbia's Transportation Sector." *Just Labour.* Volume 2: Spring.

Campbell, Gordon. 2000. "Address to the Canadian Institute of Energy." November 29. Available at <http://www.bcliberals.com/news/speeches/speech11290001.html>.

Carrol, Rory. 2005. "Go home, Teck says, as union demands talks." *American Metal Market.* July 22.

Cascade Heritage Power Park Project Committee. 1999. "Draft Project Report Specifications for the Powerhouse Energy Corp. Cascade Heritage Power Park Project." November 2.

Cohen, Marjorie Griffin. 2001. "From Public Good to Private Exploitation: GATS and the Restructuring of Canadian Electrical Utilities." *Canadian-American Public Policy.* Number 48, December. The Canadian-American Centre, University of Maine. Available at <http://www.questia.com/googleScholar.qst;jsessionid=GN5T3L6gSbpd5TnNQYnjCcWPc1nMTsxdvsylTbv0Ntpx2Y9WptJp!-1190871732?docId=5002436360> accessed July 2007.

_____. 2002a. "Electricity Deregulation, Privatization and Continental Integration: GATS and the Restructuring of Canadian Electrical Utilities." Ottawa: Canadian Centre for Policy Alternatives.

_____. 2002b. "The Political Economy of Electricity Competition: The Case of BC Hydro." Vancouver: Canadian Centre for Policy Alternatives.

_____. 2003. "High Tension: BC Hydro's Deep Integration with the U.S. through RTO West." Vancouver: B.C. Citizens for Public Power. Available at <http://www.citizensforpublicpower.ca/articles/mt/archives/2003/03/high_tension_bc.html> accessed July 2007.

_____. 2006. "Electricity Restructuring's Dirty Secret: The Environment." In Josée Johnston, Michael Gismondi and James Goodman (eds.), *Nature's Revenge: Reclaiming Sustainability in an Age of Corporate Globalization*. Peterborough: Broadview Press.

Compliance Energy Corporation. 2006. "Compliance Signs Energy Purchase Agreement with BC Hydro." July 27 and September 5 press releases. Vancouver.

Coyle, Eugene P. 2000. "Price Discrimination, Electronic Redlining, and Price Fixing in Deregulated Electric Power." Report prepared for the American Public Power

Association.
Curtis, Malcolm. 2001. Untitled article, page B1, *Victoria Times Colonist.* October 10.
District of Kitimat. 2002. "Interim Report Analysis of Alcan's Business Objectives, Consequences on Public Benefits in British Columbia." July 28.
_____. 2005. "Half Sized Smelter to be Announced." Leaflet.
Elections B.C. 2001–2005. "Annual Financial Reports." Available at <http://www.elections.bc.ca/fin/finance.html> accessed July 2007.
E.ON. 2006a. "Data and Facts Relating to Wind Power in Germany." Supplement to the "E.ON Netz Wind Report." Bayreuth, Germany.
_____. 2006b "Corporate Social Responsibility 2005: Successful Business — Responsible Choices." Dusseldorf. Germany.
Fisher, Carl. 2006. Letter from B.C. Ministry of Finance re: "Freedom of Information Request: Public Accounts Note on Contractual Obligations," to the Canadian Union of Public Employees. October 2. (Letter is addressed to Keith Richards of the Canadian Union of Public Employees, but Fisher got the last name wrong. It should have been Keith Reynolds.)
Girard, Richard. 2005. "Can Alcan Claim To Be the Best? Its Corporate and Social Responsibility in Question: A Profile of Canadian Aluminum Giant Alcan." Ottawa: Polaris Institute.
Government of B.C. 1949. *Industrial Development Act.* c. 31, s. 1.
_____. 1950. "Agreement Between the Government of British Columbia and Aluminium Company of Canada." December 29.
_____. 2001. "Strategic Considerations for a New British Columbia Energy Policy, Interim Report of the Task Force on Energy Policy." Victoria: November 30.
_____. 2002. "Strategic Considerations for a New British Columbia Energy Policy: Final Report of the Task Force on Energy Policy." Victoria: March 15.
_____. 2003. *Significant Projects Streamlining Act,* S.B.C. 2003, c. 100 (Bill 75).
_____. 2004. Project Information Centre. Untitled Document on Holberg Wind Farm Application. Originally produced July 10, 2003. Updated Jan 8, 2004. Available at <http://www.eao.gov.bc.ca/epic/output/html/deploy/epic_document_228_16161.html> accessed May 20, 2007.
_____. 2005a. "Land Use Operational Policy: Wind Power Projects." File 12705-01.Victoria. October 21.
_____. 2005b. Ministry of Energy, Mines, and Petroleum Resources. Minister Richard Neufeld. October 14 press release.
_____. 2007a. Ministry of Environment Water Stewardship Division. "Annual rentals payable for the following water licence purposes by sector."
_____. 2007b. Ministry of Finance. "Budget and Fiscal Plan 2007/08–2009/10."
Grant, Tavia. 2006. "Power Play for Alcan's South African Smelter." *Globe and Mail* Nov. 24.
Greenpeace. 2002. "Wind Energy Study in British Columbia." Montréal: Helimax Energy Inc.
Hall, David, and Sam Weinstein. 2001. "The California Electricity Crisis — Overview and International Lessons." London: University of Greenwich.
Hall, Trafford. 2007. "A Cautionary Tale: Private Control of Public Resources." PowerPoint presentation to community forum, "Shaping the System for

Sustainable Energy." January 17.

Hassan, Gerrard. 2005. "Assessment of the Energy Potential and Estimated Costs of Wind Energy in British Columbia." Report for BC Hydro, May 25.

Heflick, David. 2004. Letter on behalf of Citizens for a Bi-National Review of the Dam re: "Cascade Power Plant Proposal," to Garth Thoroughgood, Project Coordinator, B.C. Environmental Assessment Office. February 16.

Heywood, Guy. 2006. "Independent Power Production: Benefits to Local Communities." Draft discussion paper prepared by Renaissance Power Corporation. Available at <http://www.renaissancepower.ca/downloads/Benefits_To_Local_Communities.pdf> accessed July 2007.

Hillsborough Resources Ltd. 2006. July 27 press release.

Hornung, Robert. 2006. Canadian Wind Energy Association letter to Minister Neufeld and BC Hydro CEO Larry Bell. August 4.

Howe, Bruce, and Frank Klassen. 1996. *The Case of BC Hydro: A Blueprint for Privatization.* Vancouver: The Fraser Institute.

Independent Power Producers Association of B.C. 2001. "B.C. Electricity Market Reform: Policy Recommendations." Submitted on November 1 to the B.C. Energy Policy Development Task Force. Available at <http://www.vcn.bc.ca/edrs/pdf/IPABCELE.PDF> accessed July 2007.

Jaccard, Mark. 1998 "Reforming B.C.'s Electricity Market: A Way Forward for British Columbia." Final Report of the Task Force on Electricity Market Reform. January.

_____. 2006. *Sustainable Fossil Fuels.* Cambridge, U.K.: Cambridge University Press.

Katabatic Power. 2006. "AAER Announces CDN$35 Million Wind Turbine Sale — Richmond-Based Katabatic Power to Use Turbines at B.C. Wind Farm." November 22 press release. Available at <http://www.aaersystems.com/files/AAER/apress_release_Katabatic.pdf> accessed July 2007.

_____. 2007. "Company Overview." Available at <http://www.katabaticpower.com> accessed March 22, 2007.

Kennedy, Robert F. Jr. 2005. "An Ill Wind Off Cape Cod." *New York Times.* December 16.

Kettle River Review Committee. 2004. Letter to Provincial Environmental Assessment Officer Derek Griffin re: "Potential Effects of the Cascade Heritage Power Project on the Allocation of Water in the Kettle River Basin." October 15.

Knittel, Christopher. 2006. "The Adoption of State Electricity Regulation: The Role of Interest Groups." *Journal of Industrial Economics.* Volume 54.

Kunin, Roslyn and Associates Inc. 2002. "Analysis of Alcan's Business Objectives: Consequences on Public Benefits in British Columbia." Prepared for the District of Kitimat. July 28. Available at <http://www.dontsellusout.com/03report/pdf/report.pdf> accessed July 2007.

_____. 2003. "An Economic Study of the Use of Hydro Power in Kitimat for Aluminium Production as Opposed to Export." Vancouver. Available at <http://www.dontsellusout.com/03report/pdf/study.pdf> accessed July 2007.

Larsen, S. 2003. "Promoting aboriginal territoriality through interethnic alliances: The case of the Cheslatta T'en in northern British Columbia." *Human Organization.* Volume 62, Issue 1.

Lavoie, Judith. 2004. *Victoria Times Colonist.* November 2.

MacDonald, Donald S. 1996. "A Framework for Completion." Report of the Advisory Committee on Competition in Ontario's Electricity System, Prepared for the Ontario Minister of Environment and Energy. Toronto.

Mair, Rafe. 2005. "How We Got Screwed on the Terasen Deal." *The Tyee.* August 15.

Makinen, Timo. 2004. "A Review of the Costs and Benefits of the Proposed Cascade Heritage Power Project." Prepared for Powerhouse Energy Corporation. December 22.

Marowits, Ross. 2007. "Alcan and Ma'aden Plan $7B Mine-to-Metal JV in Saudi Arabia." Canadian Press. April 30.

Mattison, James S. 2006. Comptroller of Water Rights, Land and Water B.C. Letter dated January 11. File No. 43285-30/General.

McInnes, Donald. 2004. "Presentation to the Government of B.C.. Select Standing Committee on Finance and Government Services." *Hansard.* October 13.

McLaren, Richard. 2006a. Submission to B.C. Utilities Commission, BC Hydro Section 71 Filing (Exhibit C17-2). December 6–8.

_____. 2006b. "Argument of Richard McLaren. Private Citizen, Kitimat re: BC Hydro Section 71 Filing: LTEPA with Alcan." B.C. Utilities Commission Order G-142-06/Project No. 3698446. December 18.

_____. 2007. Speech to Kitimat town hall meeting. February 7.

McLean, Bethany, and Peter Elkind. 2003. *The Smartest Guys in the Room: The Amazing Rise and Scandalous Fall of Enron.* New York: Penguin Books.

McPherson, Sherri. 1999. Letter to Derek Griffin, Project Assessment Director, Environmental Assessment Office. August 6.

Metcalf, Malcolm. 2003. "Submission to the B.C. Utilities Commission on the Heritage Contract for BC Hydro's Existing Generation Resources, Stepped Rates and Transmission Access." Vancouver: B.C. Citizens' for Public Power.

NaiKun Wind Developers. 2007. <http://www.naikun.ca/the_project/index.php> accessed July 2007.

Neufeld, Richard. 2006. Minister of Energy, Mines, and Petroleum Resources letter to John Turner, Chair, Squamish-Lillooet Regional District. September 29.

New York Times. 2004. "Alcan Pays Powerex $110 Million to Settle Claim." December 30.

North Columbian Monthly. 2000. "No Dam Good" May.

Nuttall-Smith, Chris. 2001. "Don't count on rate freeze for too long, new Hydro boss says." *Vancouver Sun.* September 5. Available at <http://www.sqwalk.com/NuttallSmith_VancouverSun_20010905_LarryBell2.htm> accessed July 2007.

O'Malley, Kathy. 2007. Interview with author. February 27.

Peltzman, S. 1976. "Toward a More General Theory of Regulation." *Journal of Law and Economics*. Volume 19. August.

Plutonic Power. 2006. "Plutonic Power Grants GE Right to Provide CAN$500 Million for Hydroelectric Project in British Columbia." August 30 press release.

Pollution Probe/Pembina Institute. 2006. "Maximizing Energy Efficiency and Renewable Energy in British Columbia." Vancouver.

Powerhouse Energy Corporation. 1999. "Cascade Heritage Power Park Project

Approval Certificate Application, Volume 1 Application."

Prince Rupert Daily News. 2006a. "Mount Hays Wind Farm Plan Key Issue Tonight." March 1.

_____. 2006b "Wind Firm Airs Its Vision for Mt. Hays." June 8.

Public Citizen. 2001. "Blind Faith: How Deregulation and Enron's Influence Over Government Looted Billions from Americans." Washington.

_____. 2002. "The Public Utility Holding Company Act and the Protection of Energy Consumers: An Examination of the Corporate Records of the Top Companies Pushing for PUHCA Repeal." Washington.

_____. 2003. "PUHCA for Dummies: An Electricity Blackout and Energy Bill Primer." Washington.

Pynn, Larry. 2006. "Alternatives at what cost? Scientists raise alarm about Chetwynd project's risk to birds." *Vancouver Sun*. September 27.

Redlin, Blair. 2002. "Pulling the Plug: How the Liberals' Plan to Dismantle BC Hydro Threatens Taxpayers, Businesses, Communities and Jobs." Vancouver: B.C. Citizens for Public Power.

Reimer, Greg. 2005. Letter to Mr. Paul Edgington, Administrator, Squamish-Lillooet Regional District. November 28.

Richardson, Lisa 2004. "A Green Threat to B.C.'s Rivers?" *The Tyee.* August 30.

Robinson, Allan. 2005. "Wind power costly, Canaccord finds." *Globe and Mail.* July 18.

Sea Breeze Power Corporation. 2004a. "Management Discussion and Analysis: Third Quarter." Vancouver. November. (U.S. Securities and Exchange Commission filing.)

_____. 2004b. U.S. Securities and Exchange Commission filing. (Form 20-FR.)

_____. 2005. "Management Discussion and Analysis: Third Quarter." Vancouver. September 30. (U.S. Securities and Exchange Commission filing EX-99.5 6 exhibit5.htm EX-99.5.)

_____. 2006a. "Management Discussion and Analysis: Third Quarter." November 28.

_____. 2006b. U.S. Securities and Exchange Commission Form 8K (signed June 30 by Paul B. Manso, President and CEO).

_____. 2007. "Consolidated Financial Statements December 31, 2005 and 2006 (Stated In Canadian Dollars)." Vancouver. April 23, 2007.

Sea to Sky Land Resource Management Plan. 2004. *Final Report.* October 18.

Shaffer, Marvin. 2004. "Review of BC Hydro's Industrial Power Smart Expenditures." A study prepared for B.C. Old Age Pensioners Association's submission to the B.C. Utilities Commission. April 20.

_____. 2006. "Direct Evidence of Marvin Shaffer." B.C. Utilities Commission hearings on LTEPA plus. November 30.

Smith, Charlie. 2005. "May I take your order, please?" *Georgia Straight.* August 25.

Smith, Stuart. 2005a. "Weighing In on the Independent Power Debate: Part One." *Whistler Question.* January 27.

_____. 2005b. "Kayakers Thank SLRD for Ashlu Decision." *Whistler Question.* Letter to the editor, January 21.

Squamish-Lillooet Regional District (SLRD). 2003. "Independent Power Project Development in the SLRD." April 28. Available at <www.slrd.bc.ca/files/

%7BA64AC3D7-AE72-4F8BA946-B653DFEF70CD%7DIPP_Policy_Final.pdf> accessed July 2006.

_____. 2005. "Re: Provincial Government Response to SLRD Request for a Moratorium on IPP Approvals." November 18.

_____. 2006a. Regular Agenda January 30. Pages 38–65. (Contains a January 19 letter to Squamish-Lillooet Regional District from Steve Olmstead regarding Ashlu rezoning application.)

_____. 2006b. "Independent Power Production Bill 30 – 2006 Miscellaneous Statutes Amendment Act (No. 2), 2006." May 2 press release.

Stothert Engineering Ltd. 2003. "Small Hydro Generation Building Block Profile." Victoria: B.C. Ministry of Sustainable Resource Management.

Supreme Court of B.C. 2007. "District of Kitimat and Wozney v. Minister of Energy and Mines et al." Vancouver.

Swainson, Alexander. 1979. *Conflict over the Columbia: The Canadian Background to an Historic Treaty*. Montreal: McGill-Queen's University Press.

Tampier, Martin. 2004. "Building the Renewable Energy Market in North America." Presentation on behalf of the Clean Air Renewable Energy Coalition to the NAFTA Commission on Environmental Co-operation. October 28–29, 2004.

Thomas, Steve. 2001. "The Wholesale Electricity Market in Britain: 1990–2001." London: University of Greenwich.

Thompson, Kim. 2006. "SLRD Agrees to Fight Bill 30." *Whistler Question*. May 26.

Tieleman, Bill. 1983. "The Political Economy of Nationalization: Social Credit and the Take Over of the B.C. Electric Company." Master of Arts Thesis, Faculty of Graduate Studies, University of British Columbia.

_____. 2006. "Big bucks for Hydro ad campaign: FOI request reveals BC Hydro spent $2 million on self-promoting ad campaign." *Vancouver 24 Hours*. December 18.

U.S. Federal Energy Regulatory Commission. 1997a. "Promoting Wholesale Competition Through Open Access Non-Discriminatory Transmission Services by Public Utilities and Recovery of Stranded Costs by Public Utilities and Transmitting Utilities." (Docket Nos. RM95-8-001 and RM94-7-002. Order No. 888-A.)

_____. 1997b. "Promoting Wholesale Competition Through Open Access Non-discriminatory Transmission Services by Public Utilities and Recovery of Stranded Costs by Public Utilities and Transmitting Utilities." (Docket Nos. RM95-8-004 and RM94-7-005. Order No. 888-B.)

_____. 1999. "Regional Transmission Organizations." (Docket No. RM99-2-000; Order No. 2000.)

_____. 2002. "Initial Report on Company-Specific Separate Proceedings and Generic Revaluations: Published Natural Gas Price Data; and Enron Trading Strategies Fact-Finding Investigation of Potential Manipulation of Electric and Natural Gas Prices." (Docket No. PA02-000.)

_____. 2005. "Preventing Undue Discrimination and Preference in Transmission Services." (Docket Nos. RM05-25-000 and RM05-17-000.)

_____. 2006. "Remedying Undue Discrimination through Open Access Transmission Service and Standard Electricity Market Design." (Docket No. RM01-12-000.)

Vancouver Sun. 2005. "Alcan Plans Smelter." July 14.

Warkentin, Grant. 2005. "B.C. Not Yet Ready For Wind Power." *Campbell River Mirror*. July 29.

West Coast Environmental Law Association. 2003. Bill 75 (2003) *Significant Projects Streamlining Act.* Vancouver. November 11.

Whitewater Kayaking Association of British Columbia. 2006. "Ashlu Power Project Threat." Available at <http://www.whitewater.org/RIAC/efforts/ashlu.htm> accessed July 2007.

Windpower Weekly. 2007. "Grappling with an overheated market." May.

Yakabuski, Konrad. 2006. *Globe and Mail Report on Business Magazine.* December.

Yarnell, Patrick. 2001. "Socioeconomic Assessment of the Proposed Cascade Heritage Power Park at Cascade Canyon: Local Economic Impacts and Tourism and Recreation Impacts." Prepared for the Kettle River Review Committee. Vancouver. September 21.

———. 2005. "Tourism and Socioeconomic Impacts of Power Generation at Cascade Canyon; Review of Related Reports." Prepared for the Kettle River Review Committee, Christina Lake, B.C. Vancouver. July 11.

INDEX